THE
CHANGING RHYTHM

STUDIES IN ARABIC LITERATURE

SUPPLEMENTS TO THE JOURNAL OF ARABIC LITERATURE

EDITED BY

M. M. BADAWI, University of Oxford
P. CACHIA, University of Edinburgh
M. C. LYONS, University of Cambridge
J. N. MATTOCK, University of Glasgow

VOLUME II

LEIDEN
E. J. BRILL
1973

THE CHANGING RHYTHM

A STUDY OF NAJĪB MAḤFŪẒ'S NOVELS

BY

SASSON SOMEKH

LEIDEN
E. J. BRILL
1973

ISBN 90 04 03587 7

PRINTED IN BELGIUM

To Terrie

CONTENTS

Preface IX

I. The Emergence of the Egyptian Novel, 1914-45 . . . 1

II. The Making of a Novelist 35

III. Egypt, Old and New 60
A. The Historical Novels 60
B. The "Social" Novels 65
General 65
Characters 70
Structure 88
Language and Dialogue 94
C. A Cairene Oedipus : *al-Sarāb* 100

IV. The Changing Rhythm 106
The Trilogy—General 106
Characters 113
Other Characters 122
Structure 127
Language and Dialogue 133

V. The Sad Millenarian 137
Awlād Ḥāratinā — General 137
Characters 142
Structure 146
Language and Dialogue 151

VI. Into the Labyrinth 156
The Short Novels — General 156
Characters 160
Structure 181
Language and Dialogue 187

Postscript 191

Appendix I. Editions and Dates 199
Appendix II. Plot Outlines of Maḥfūẓ's Novels 201

PREFACE

This book is an attempt to introduce the reader to the works of one of Egypt's greatest modern authors. It deals with all of his novels published before 1967. His short stories, which are of no less importance to modern Arabic literature, are mentioned only whenever they are relevant to Maḥfūẓ's work as a novelist, notably in Ch. II. I hope to examine these stories elsewhere.

To show the novelist's work in its true perspective, Ch. I has been devoted to a brief survey of the formative stages of the modern Egyptian novel until about 1945, when Maḥfūẓ's Cairence novels began to appear. Ch. II is a preliminary biographical sketch of the author, based on the scanty material available outside Egypt, with some references to scenes in his novels that seem to be drawn from his own experience.

The four final chapters (Chs. III-VI) analyze his novels in their chronological order. A general description of the themes and atmosphere of a novel or a group of novels is followed in each case by short comments on characterization, structure and language.

Because of the large number of novels under consideration, I have given their plot outlines in Appendix II (pp. 201-228). The purpose of these outlines is to recall the actions and main characters of these books. I am aware that they are not neutral statements of fact : my interpretation of a work is bound to permeate my resumé of its plot.

Maḥfūẓ's works are often referred to in abbreviated form (IN CAPITALS); the list of these abbreviations can be found in Bibliography A (pp. 229-230). Footnote reference to works by other authors give the author's name, and, whenever necessary, a brief title. The full titles are listed in Bibliography B (pp. 231-234). Articles dealing with specific novels by Maḥfūẓ are grouped under the titles of these novels in Bibliography C (pp. 235-236).

* * *

The first version of this work was written at Brasenose College, Oxford, between the years 1966-1968. It was made possible thanks to generous scholarships granted by the British Council and the University of Tel-Aviv. The latter has also made a substantial contribution towards the publication of this book. I would like to extend my gratitude to them.

I am greatly indebted to Dr. Mustafa Badawi, lecturer in modern Arabic literature at the University of Oxford, who supervised my work, and without whose encouragement and help this book would never have been written. I am also grateful to the kindness of Dr. Pierre Cachia, of the University of Edinburgh, who read the entire manuscript, offering many useful suggestions, most of which were introduced herein.

A great number of other friends and colleagues extended their help at different stages, and I find it essential here to thank Prof. A.F.L. Beeston, Mr. and Mrs. V. Daykin, Mr. N.S. Doniach, Mr. A. Hourani, Dr. D. Hopwood, Mr. D. Hawke, Dr. J. Kraemer, Mrs. M. Meltzer, Dr. Z. Rubin, Dr. D. Semah, and the late Dr. S.M. Stern.

Tel-Aviv University, S. Somekh.
September, 1972.

CHAPTER ONE

THE EMERGENCE OF THE EGYPTIAN NOVEL[1]

1914-1945

The history of the novel in Egypt is a relatively short one. Indeed one need hardly go back much further than fifty years in one's search for this genre in modern Egyptian literature. To be precise, it was born as an articulate literary form in 1914, with the appearance of the first edition of Muḥammad Ḥusayn Haykal's novel *Zaynab*.

Admittedly, story-tellers were at all times active in Egypt, and there is a variety of both oral and written traditions of narrative prose. To mention a few examples : the later layers of the Arabian Nights have been proved to have been composed in Egypt, presumably in the Mamluk period; the popular romances (*sīra* : pl. *siyar*) such as those of ʿAntara, Banū Hilāl, al-Ẓāhir Baybars, products of the sub-literary folklore, related and enriched by the *shāʿirs* (popular romance reciters) throughout the middle ages.

Another source of narrative prose, which was available at all times to the literate Egyptians, is the story sections of the classical Arabic literature, e.g., *al-Faraj baʿd al-shidda*, *Kitāb al-bukhalā'*, the *Maqāmāt* literature, etc.[2]

As we shall presently see, western fiction has been known to the Egyptian public (through translation and, of course, through the acquisition of European languages) as early as the nineteenth century, and these novels became so popular as to give rise to countless emulations by local writers.

Nevertheless *Zaynab* is the first novel to portray realistic settings

[1] This chapter owes much to some recent works on the novel published in Egypt, notably Badr's study *Taṭawwur al-riwāya*, and also to such helpful discussions as that of al-Rāʿī's *Dirāsāt*, and of Ḥaqqī's short but acute remarks on several novels and novelists in his *Fajr*. The unpublished theses of Dr. El Sakkout and Dr. El Hazmi were also consulted by courtesy of the librarians of Cambridge and London Universities respectively. (For full titles see Bibliography B).

[2] The question of how much fiction there is in classical Arabic literature has been in the last decades subject to discussions and counter-discussions *ad-nauseam*. Of the more recent treatments of the question, mention can be made of Maḥmūd Taymūr's *Muḥāḍarāt*, 1958.

and characters; to possess a reasonably coherent plot, motivation and causation.

Written by a young law school graduate[1] who was at the time in France pursuing a course of higher studies, the novel was embarked upon, as the author tells us,[2] out of a poignant longing for his native land, for the Egyptian countryside. Haykal also relates that his longing coincided with an admiration for French literature, acquired during his stay in France. He was thus motivated to try and write a short story which would convey his memories of home. The short story which he had planned swelled, in the process of writing, into an eighty thousand word novel. "*Zaynab* then," concludes the author, "is the product of longing for the homeland at large, portrayed by a Paris dweller who, though homesick for Egypt, was full of admiration for Paris and French literature."[3]

We see then that an ambition to emulate French fiction plays a clear role in generating *Zaynab.*[4] Nevertheless it would be wrong to consider only the European influences in the emergence of a genre which is essentially western. It would be more useful to stress influences of the Egyptian modernists such as Qāsim Amīn and Aḥmad Luṭfī al-Sayyid, both of whom Haykal revered and regarded as masters. Amīn's campaign for the emancipation of the Oriental woman[5] is clearly reflected throughout the novel. The fate of the Egyptian woman and its impact on the fate of Egyptian society as a whole is in fact the essence of *Zaynab*'s plot.[6] Luṭfī al-Sayyid's call for the

---

1 He was later to become one of the most prominent writers of modern Egypt, and also a very influential statesman and journalist. Born in 1888 and died in 1956. See Ḍayf, pp. 270-77; Badr. pp. 317-33; Ḥaqqī, *Fajr*, pp. 38-53.

2 *Zaynab*, second edition (Maṭbaʿat al-jadīd), Cairo [1929], introd., p. 5.

3 *Ibid.*, p. 7.

4 The French influence is evident to any reader of this novel who is familiar with eighteenth and nineteenth century Romantic fiction, e.g., Rousseau, Alexandre Dumas *fils*, Victor Hugo—both in the general vein of writing and in the treatment of love, nature, and life as a whole. Of special French flavour is the hero's confession to the Ṣūfī shaykh (*Zaynab*, pp. 230-3), a scene which has been treated by many critics (*inter alia* Ḥaqqī, *Fajr*, p. 50; al-Rāʿī, p. 32) and said to be of Catholic, not Muslim, flavour. On the French influence see also Gibb, *Studies*, pp. 292-3; Muḥammad Ghunaymī Hilāl, "al Mu'aththirāt al-gharbiyya fil-riwāya al-ʿArabiyya," *al-Ādāb* (Beirut), March 1963, pp. 17-25.

5 See Hourani, pp. 164-9.

6 Amīn's name is mentioned in the course of the novel (p. 225) when one of his maxims is quoted. Ḥāmid's discursive letter to his father (pp. 236-50) is a queer blend of the Spencerian natural philosophy (which has also a clear impact on Amīn's book

creation of an Egyptian personality[1] is also discernible in the novel, not only in the occasional mention of the Pharaonic roots of Egyptian country life,[2] nor in the fact that the author published the first edition under the pseudonym "Peasant-Egyptian" (*miṣrī-fallāḥ*[3]); but above all in the direct line of influence of the "master of the generation" ("*Ustadh al-jīl*" as al-Sayyid is called by many Egyptian intellectuals) in his passion for the Egyptian countryside. "In spite of its poverty and squalor," to quote A. Hourani,[4] "[al-Sayyid] knows the beauty of village life : he evokes the sights and sounds of the cotton fields, paints in bright colours the virtues and happiness of the good peasant, and exhorts the younger generation to respond to the beauty of Nature ..." *Zaynab's* sub-title, "Countryside Scenes and Manners" (*manāẓir wa-akhlāq rīfiyya*), adequately describes the dominant colour of the novel : passionate attachment to the land and its dweller. It is, in fact, loaded with lengthy, though often breathtaking, descriptions of nature and people.

It is false to conclude, however, that *Zaynab* is a "cause novel" tailored to suit a preconceived theory. It is the very fact that this is a non-didactic work of fiction that possibly entitles Haykal's attempt, notwithstanding its shortcomings, to be called the first Arabic novel. A real, sparkling picture of life is embodied in the pages of this book.

It is a hard undertaking to try to summarize the story. The book is full of deviations and burdened with lengthy discourses on love, nature, social conditions, philosophy. But the main difficulty lies

---

Taḥrīr al-mra'a, [1901]), and some fragments of Rousseau's and Tolstoy's social ideas; all these, coupled with rather naïve reflections on marital and sexual problems of the young Egyptian male.

[1] Hourani, pp. 170-81.

[2] E.g., p. 25. It is to be added, however, that Haykal is far from the idealizing attitude to the life of the Egyptian *fallaḥ* which we encounter in Tawfīq al-Ḥakīm's *'Awdat al-rūḥ* (1933).

[3] Haykal remarks in his introduction to *Zaynab*'s second edition (1929) (which appeared under his full name), that in 1914 he used a pen name because he was aware of the fact that publishing a work of fiction was apt to jeopardize his career as a lawyer. This, truly enough, might be regarded as sufficient reason, since the genteel public loathed story tellers, and an apologetic note was customary in introductions to many novels (the novel is, in most cases, justified by its author as having some educational or other moral). But cf. Ḥaqqī, *Fajr*, p. 43, who attributes Haykal's reluctance to disclose his name to the fact that the novel deals openly with *love*.

[4] *Arabic Thought*, p. 177.

in the fact that the plot pivots around too many central characters, and possesses at least two poles of action.

The first pole is that of Zaynab, a poor, beautiful and sensitive country girl who is employed in picking cotton during the harvest. She is in love with Ibrāhīm, the poor work-supervisor who returns her love, but she is forced to marry Ḥasan, Ibrāhīm's well-to-do friend, who was able to pay her *mahr* to her father. Ḥasan proves to be an attentive and loving husband, and Zaynab tries to forget her old attachment and to be faithful to her husband, but to no avail. Her love for Ibrāhīm smoulders, and when he is made to join the army (again because of his inability to pay for exemption), Zaynab is tortured by her passion for him. She soon falls ill of tuberculosis, dying while pronouncing Ibrāhīm's name and asking for the handkerchief that he left behind to be buried with her.

The second pole is that of Ḥāmid, son of a rich land-owner and a student in Cairo. While spending his vacations in the village he flirts with Zaynab and other village girls. Yet his heart belongs to ʿAzīza, a relative, with whom he cannot freely communicate, being inhibited by their class dignity and traditions. ʿAzīza returns his love and even writes clandestine letters to him, but is unable to refuse a marriage arranged by her parents. Having lost ʿAzīza forever, Ḥāmid now turns to Zaynab, but she discourages him, pleading fidelity to her husband.[1] The frustrations of two successive loves make Ḥāmid realize the inhumanity of the prevailing social norms, and after much soul-searching he decides to desert his family, work for his living and search for a "genuine love." He, in fact, sinks into a nebulous existence, the exact nature of which is undisclosed.

In the novel, to quote Sir Hamilton Gibb,[2] "trifling episodes, without significance for the story, are often introduced simply, it would seem, as a peg on which to hang another interlude, and here and there sentences, overloaded with trivial photographic detail, lose shape and substance." In fact, the reader has to work hard to make sense of the events and to establish their chronological order, especially as far as Ḥāmid's story is concerned. The author himself seems to have felt this confusion and in the last part of the book gives us a résumé of Ḥāmid's ups-and-downs by making him deliver a confession

[1] The affair Ḥāmid-Zaynab looks affected and incoherent. In fact it constitutes a third pole of the plot devised (possibly in the course of writing) to join together the two distinct and concurrent stories of Zaynab-Ibrāhīm and that of Ḥāmid-ʿAzīza.

[2] *Studies*, p. 293.

to a Ṣūfī shaykh[1] and later write a lengthy letter to his father.[2] Admittedly these two recordings of the events clarify the story, but they also emphasize the feeling that the events were originally narrated in an insufficiently clear manner.

The characterization is not even. Ḥāmid who is, to a certain extent, a reflection of young Haykal,[3] is fully developed, but as has just been remarked, the motivation of his actions is supplied *a posteriori*, not in the course of events. Zaynab, on the other hand, behaves and reacts in a plausible manner, yet it is still necessary for the reader to fill too many gaps in her personality and psychological make-up. As for 'Azīza, she remains out of our reach, and the only hints to her character are supplied by her letters to Ḥāmid.

Whatever defects we discern in *Zaynab*, it is undoubtedly a dramatic breakthrough in modern Egyptian literature. It takes an interest in real people and endeavours to portray their inner lives and not only their acts and adventures. It is ambitious enough to attempt to develop genuine dramatic situations. It also sets an example in a matter of immense importance for writers of Arabic fiction, namely: the language of the dialogue. Haykal's characters often speak their real language, i.e., the Egyptian rural dialect (though modified), and not the literary language.[4]

It must be emphasized at this point that though Haykal's story has been regarded as the first Egyptian novel, it is by no means the first encounter of the Egyptian reading public with this literary form. The first decades of the twentieth century, as well as the last ones of the nineteenth, witnessed a great abundance of novels, many translated and some composed in Arabic.

Thousands of stories were translated from French and English.[5] The translators were mainly Syrian-Lebanese immigrants who settled in Egypt after 1860,[6] bringing with them a considerable

---

[1] *Zaynab*, pp. 230-3.

[2] *Ibid.*, pp. 236-50.

[3] See, e.g., Dr. Haykal's admission to this fact in Ṣidqī, *Ṣuwar ḥayya*, pp. 96-9.

[4] There is only one scene (pp. 117-25), where classical Arabic is fully employed in the dialogue, and this is the only scene that takes place outside the village. Here Ḥāmid discusses with four of his Cairene friends issues such as marriage, westernization, etc.

[5] See Najm, *al-Qiṣṣa*, pp. 13-21 : Pérès, in *Annales*, 1937, pp. 266-337.

[6] But a well known Egyptian educationalist and reformer, Rifā'a Rāfi' al-Ṭahṭāwī (1801-1873), published in 1867 an Arabic paraphrase of the seventeenth century tale by Fénelon, *Les Aventures de Télémaque* under the rhyming title of *Mawāqi' al-aflāk*

knowledge of European languages (chiefly French), and a strong taste for western fiction. A number of periodicals specializing in translated fiction were established.[1] The general newspapers, which began to flourish in this period, also took to serializing novels in order to attract the less educated readers. These stories were, as can be expected, of a poor quality, dealing mainly with adventure, mystery, and naïve amorous affairs. The Arabic versions were, by and large, inadequate both as to accuracy of translation and to correctness of the Arabic language.[2]

Needless to say, this deluge of cheap fiction could by no means serve to inculcate in its readers a better appreciation of literature, nor did it favourably represent the European novel. The majority of translations were taken from works of writers like Michel Zévaco, Maurice Leblanc, Ponson du Terrail, and even lesser thriller writers.[3] Yet a few well known novelists (e.g., Scott, Hugo, Dumas, and even Dickens and Tolstoy) were occasionally translated, often in condensed form.

The translated novels were soon imitated by many of the immigrants and later by indigenous writers. These local novels had hardly any literary value, originality, imagination, or local reality. They were badly written imitations, overburdened with incredible adventures and implausible characters and settings. Moreover, many of the plots were plagiarized from western writers with only the names of places and people Arabized. The dominant theme in these novels is an adventure of two young lovers facing intrigues and wicked plotters; an adventure which in most cases ends with the victory of love and the defeat of villainy. The plots are crowded with concatenations of strange events and with hosts of stock characters, none of whom is vividly characterized.[4]

A few of the newcomers, however, used the art of fiction to more

---

fī waqā'i' Tilīmāk. His disciple Muḥ. 'Uthmān Jalāl, an active translator, translated Bernardin de Saint-Pierre's novel *Paul et Virginie* (in 1289/1872) in a similar manner.

[1] See list in Najm, *al-Qiṣṣa*, pp. 6-12.

[2] See Badr, pp. 122-36; Shawkat, pp. 64-7.

[3] Often the name of the author was dropped and the title altered; in many cases the translator would claim a novel for himself. See Badr, pp. 133-5. For list of novels translated from the French, see Pérès, *Annales*, 1937, pp. 290-311.

[4] For a select list of these novels see Badr, pp. 411-21; Pérès, *Annales*, 1937. Dr. Badr (on pp. 141-68) discusses the plots and characters of many such novels; see also Najm's book, *al-Qiṣṣa*, for plot-outlines of some forty novels by Lebanese and Egyptian-Lebanese writers.

useful ends; namely, in writing history, or in disseminating knowledge or moral values through the guise of novels. The most important among these is undoubtedly Jurjī Zaydān (1861-1914), a journalist born in Beirut, who settled in Egypt and, between the years 1891-1914, published twenty-three novels, each of which formed a part of an ambitious undertaking to cover the whole of Islamic history in a popular narrative. Zaydān was a well-read person, versed in European and Oriental languages, and possessing a considerable knowledge in many fields of arts and sciences.[1] Thus the historical periods depicted in these volumes are scrupulously studied and accurately described. But his main achievement lies in the fact that his novels make enjoyable reading. The historical facts are related by means of a sound plot and, in contrast to most novels written at the time, in a straightforward style. How readable they are can be illustrated by the fact that among all the works of fiction written before World War I, Zaydān's historical novels are the only ones that continue to be popular : new editions of his books are supplied to book stalls of the entire Arab world to this day.

Yet Zaydān's enterprise, vast and interesting as it is, can hardly be thought of as a major contribution in the emergence of the Egyptian novel. In the first place, his books are not novels in the proper sense. They were meant to be anything but *fiction*. Their sole message is to *teach* history.[2] The story is to him a superfluous factor designed only to tempt the reader to follow an otherwise dry discourse. Nothing can be farther removed from Zaydān's concept of the historical novel than a story using the past to reflect contemporary realities, or of history serving as a convenient background for dramatic action. His interest lies in actual historical events as emerging from the prime historical sources. Zaydān knows only too well that his works do not resemble European historical novels. He clearly contrasts his method with that of some western novelists whose "primary objective is to write a novel, introducing historical facts for the sole purpose of giving the story a guise of reality, [a practice] which causes [them] to relate the historical events in a lax manner, thus misleading their readers."[3]

---

[1] Besides his novels, he wrote many copious works on the history of Arabic literature, Arabic civilization, world history, linguistics, biography, and general education. Many of these, especially on the first two subjects, are still useful today.

[2] See Zaydān's introduction to his novel *al-Ḥajjāj bin Yūsuf al-T͟haqafī*.

[3] Introduction to *al-Ḥajjāj*.

This attitude of Zaydān's meant not only relegating the plot and characters to a secondary position, but also a complete indifference to the aesthetic aspects of his works. All his characters are "flat", lacking in depth and motivation. His plots are so similar in structure that on reading a few of his novels one acquires a "key" to virtually all the others—the only distinctive factor being the difference in historical settings and names. He has little recourse to dialogue, which is so formalized that it reveals little of the character of the speaker. The actions are arbitrary and haphazard. In brief, while the factual portions of these novels are highly informative, that which is fiction is feeble. *Qua* novels, they share, with the popular novels of their period the appallingly low level of originality.

Another Egyptian of Lebanese origin who attempted to write fiction is the well known secularist, Faraḥ Anṭūn[1] (1874-1922). He wrote a few novels, two of which are clearly didactical in nature, and the third historical, though bearing philosophical undertones. Like Zaydān, Anṭūn shows no great interest in the story as such, but in contrast, his novels lack the element of suspense and brisk action. Very often they lose the thin layer of fiction, becoming outright moralizing tracts. Anṭūn's novels are now long forgotten; they have left no evident imprints on the shaping of modern Arabic literature. Neither did Anṭūn's brother-in-law, the prolific journalist Nīqūlā Ḥaddād[2] (1872-1954) make any clearer impact although he published, between the years 1903-1950, more than thirty novels with both historical and contemporary settings. Ya'qūb Ṣarrūf[3] a scientifically-minded journalist (1851-1927) also dabbled in fiction. His novels (e.g., *Fatāt Miṣr*, 1904; *Amīr Lubnān*, 1907; *Fatāt al-Fayyūm*, 1908), though better known to the reading public, are of an even more journalistic nature, introducing a variety of facts and episodes that usually come under the heading of "general education'.

Indigenous Egyptian writers were very reluctant to follow the Lebanese example. The poor quality and "suspect" moral value of many of these novels (which were in most cases the only novels of which they knew), made them regard the whole genre as frivolous if not harmful and sinister. The more serious writers turned to the

---

[1] On whom see Hourani, pp. 253-9; for outlines of his novels see Najm, *al-Qiṣṣa*, pp. 80-6; 187-90; Badr, pp. 83-7.

[2] Najm, *al-Qiṣṣa*, pp. 87-106; for list of his novels see Najm's index in *al-Abḥāth*, Beirut, 1963.

[3] Najm, *al-Qiṣṣa*, pp. 107-113.

traditional field of Arabic literature—poetry. It was here that they made their most impressive contribution by gradually relieving the *qaṣīda* of a great deal of its late medieval artificiality.

An effort to employ an originally Arabic form of story-telling, the *maqāma*, was made by a few Egyptian writers of classical training, presumably to counter the mounting wave of popular novels. The most ambitious[1] of these attempts was *Ḥadīth ʿĪsā bin Hishām* by Muḥammad al-Muwayliḥī (1858-1930), which was published in book form in 1907.[2] It consists of some forty episodes, most of which occur in late nineteenth century Cairo.[3] In his dream, the narrator meets a Pasha who is raised from his grave fifty years after his death. The new realities (mostly of pseudo-western nature) which have meanwhile developed in Egypt shatter the Pasha and bring him into unpleasant conflicts not only with the people, but also with the judicial system and other unfamiliar institutions and norms of life. While the Pasha, accompanied by the narrator, moves from place to place, and from calamity to calamity, we are given a wide and colourful picture of Cairo which by now hardly bears any resemblance to that described some seventy years earlier by Edward Lane in his memorable survey of that city.

Ḥadīth is essentially a critique of modern life and its author has been successful in the choice of framework, since in viewing the new realities through the Pasha's eyes, we are given an excellent perspective. The "frame story," incredible though it is, also serves to give some coherence to the otherwise unrelated episodes.

The episodes in themselves are humorously described, and many of the people whom the Pasha meets are playfully caricaturized. The style is lively and, contrary to the established magniloquent tradition of the post-Hamadhānī *maqāma*, al-Muwayliḥī shows no great interest in displaying his command of the language. He frequently drops the rhyme altogether.

---

[1] An earlier attempt, though of outright didactic nature and of no lively action, is *ʿAlam al-Dīn* (four vols., Alexandria, 1299/1882), by the prominent educationalist ʿAlī Mubārak. Ḍayf, *al-Adab* etc., pp. 236-7, finds a direct influence of this work on al-Muwayliḥī's *Ḥadīth*.

[2] On *Ḥadith* see H. Pérès, "Les origines d'un roman célèbre de la litterature arabe moderne," *Bullettin d'études orientales*, X (1944) 101-118; Roger Allen, "*Hadith 'Isa Ibn Hisham* by Muhammad Al Muwaylihī : A Reconsideration," *Journal of Arabic Literature*, Vol. I (1970), pp. 88-108.

[3] In the fourth edition (1930) several chapters were added that take place in Paris.

Al-Muwayliḥī's work was favourably received. At least four editions of *Ḥadīth* were published in the author's lifetime. It was also imitated by several of Egypt's men of letters among whom we find the well-known poet Ḥāfiẓ Ibrāhīm in his *Layālī Saṭīḥ* (1907/8).[1] None of the imitations, however, is comparable to *Ḥadīth* as far as freshness of vision and plasticity of style are concerned.

But can *Ḥadīth* be spoken of as part and parcel of the Egyptian *novel*? Can it be regarded as a threshold to modern fiction, or still more, as a first Egyptian novel? Certain Egyptian literary critics today tend to regard it as such.[2] Some of them have even compared it to[3] (or contrasted it with)[4] *Don Quixote*. But surely *Ḥadīth* is nothing more than a collection of sketches and journalistic *feuilletons* brought together under a unifying narrative design. It has no plot in the accepted sense of the word. Neither of the two persons who appear throughout the book (namely, the Pasha and 'Īsā, the narrator) is a protagonist. True, the Pasha is of major importance in the early anecdotes, but later he is no more than a passive observer and commentator.[5] The irony that arises from Quixote's conflict with a reality different from that imagined, is missing in *Ḥadīth*. It is reduced to a comparison between two historical periods and the humorous situations rising from the Pasha's misunderstandings. (Very often these misunderstandings are of a semantic nature, i.e.: they

---

[1] See Mandūr, *Qaḍāya jadīda*, pp. 48-58; Gibb, *Studies*, p. 290; Badr, pp. 78-83.

[2] See, e.g., al-Rā'ī, pp. 7-22; Badr. pp. 66-77; Shukrī, *Thawrat al-fikr*, p. 183. The fact that Prof. Gibb has attached a considerable importance to *Ḥadīth* (in his article on the Egyptian novel in BSOS VII, pp. 1-22, reprinted in *Studies*, pp. 286-303; 314-19) seems to have helped establish its reputation as a precursor in the field of the Arabic novel. Gibb, however, was still hoping for an original form of the Egyptian novel to emerge, a form combining "technical competence and Egyptian inspiration" (see *Studies*, pp. 291, 303). But while these expectations were logically permissible in the early thirties, when only a handful of Egyptian novels of quality existed, they can hardly be justified today when the bulk of Arabic fiction shows no evidence of having learnt much from either *Ḥadīth* or classical Arabic literature.

[3] al-Rā'ī, pp. 11-13.

[4] Shawkat, p. 23.

[5] Thus al-Rā'ī's assertion (*Dirāsāt*, p. 21) that the Pasha *changes* in the course of the book is irrelevant, since the change (from irritable-morose-indifferent to benign-lively-curious) takes place only when the Pasha is no more the centre of our interest, and when the social sketches take place independently from his predicament. The "change" is, in fact, essentially a pretext for the author to bring in more social scenes as the Pasha becomes more and more interested in probing the new society. Artistically this change is arbitrary and not conditioned by the course of events.

are caused by the Pasha's misinterpreting some words and expressions which were current in his day, but which have meanwhile acquired some new significance, e.g., *jarīda, shahāda*).

Ḥadīth then can hardly be said to have had an accelerating role in the history of the Egyptian novel. Its main importance lies in the fact that it pointed to the raw material from which Egyptian fiction must be drawn if it is to become of any artistic value. It grappled with the Egyptian reality and portrayed backgrounds, human types, and situations which were to be employed by novelists of the thirties and forties.[1]

* * *

To sum up; fiction remained, throughout the nineteenth century, beyond the borders of literature proper. Those who wrote did not take it seriously. They had no ambition to produce artistic works which would convey deep human passions and depict true human types. For the most part they viewed fiction as light entertainment produced mainly for commercial ends. In other cases fiction was regarded as a convenient guise under which history or general education could be imparted to the semi-educated public. Thus, while long lists of "original" novels of the late nineteenth and early twentieth century can be cited, no single work can be correctly described as an *Egyptian novel.*

To the reading public, these novels could not have engendered a respect either for the genre or for its Arabic practitioners. Nor did they contribute much which would enlighten, deepen the human understanding, or widen the horizons of the reader. The opposite may be true; the readers were more likely to learn to think and feel in a dilettantish manner [2].

With the spread of general education, the reading public became more discriminating. More people began to read European fiction in the original, and this led them to demand Arabic novels different from those in circulation. In 1908, the first modern Egyptian University was established, and this, coupled with efforts made by intellectuals to adopt western thought and methods, to rid their

[1] E.g., the inadequacy of an imported judicial system, a theme which is to be developed by Tawfīq al-Ḥakīm in *Yawmiyyāt nā'ib fil-aryāf* (1937); the naïve villager dazzled by Cairo; and above all : the major theme of the Oriental man's encounter with the western ethos, which is to become the backbone of many important Arabic novels.

[2] *Zaynab*, second edition, p. 23.

people of medieval practices and superstitions and to create an "Egyptian identity", undoubtedly gave further impetus to the rise of the real Egyptian novel.

Neat as the arrangement of historical facts may seem, the novel did not proceed in a mechanical conformity with these facts, and *Zaynab* was not followed by a flood of realistic novels. In fact, for the next fifteen years no major contribution can be pinpointed. The world of fiction looked much the same in the post-war years as in the preceding decades. True, between the years 1914-1930, one can easily find at least sixty titles of locally written novels.[1] Furthermore, a quick look at such a list would indicate that more and more indigenous writers (as opposed to those of Lebanese origin) were writing fiction. Nevertheless, the general level of these novels is no higher than that of works discussed earlier. If anything it is worse, since those Egyptian writers were less versed in European languages. They are thus less likely to have had direct access to world literature, and in writing popular novels, were, in fact, secondhand imitators.

However, more young Egyptian intellectuals became genuinely interested in the art of fiction, and many of them wrote realistic short stories. A group of modern-minded writers was founded sometime in the early twenties which was named half seriously 'The Modern School."[2] This group professed a deep interest in European fiction (notably in the Russian giants—Dostoyevsky, Tolstoy, Chekhov, Turgenev; but also in English and French nineteenth century fiction). On establishing a magazine of their own,[3] they considered at first confining it to translated stories "because of the superiority of foreign works of genius in fiction which renders it futile—if not stupid—to compete with them."[4] Later, and after much heated argument, they changed their minds and decided to encourage originally written stories in order to help create a new literature. This group, many of whose members were to become leading men of letters in Egypt (e.g., Maḥmūd Taymūr, Yaḥyā Ḥaqqī, Ḥusayn Fawzī, Ṭāhir Lāshīn),

[1] See list in Badr, pp. 415-19.

[2] See Ḥusayn Fawzī's article in *al-Ahrām* (Cairo), April 30, 1965, where the inauguration of this group is located after the death of Muḥ. Taymūr (1892-1921); see also Ḥaqqī, *Fajr*, pp. 74-82; Dawwāra, *'Ashrat udabā'*, pp. 52-3 (interview with Maḥmūd Taymūr).

[3] Named *al-Fajr—ṣaḥīfat al-hadm wal-binā'* ('The Dawn—journal of destruction and construction'). The paper was short-lived. See Ḥaqqī, *Fajr*, p. 80.

[4] Ḥaqqī, *Fajr*, p. 79.

gave vital impetus to the development of the short story (chiefly under the influence of Chekhov and de Maupassant). It can also be said to have vitalized the art of fiction as a whole, for two or three of its members were later to write some of the best *nouvelles* in the Arabic language.

The appearance of *al-Ayyām* by Ṭāhā Ḥusayn[1] (1929) can also be regarded as furthering interest in fiction. The work, as is well known, is by no means a novel; it is a series of poignant pictures describing the wretched boyhood of the blind genius and invoking several family scenes of his village. Though written in the third person narrative, its auto-biographical nature is evident. Furthermore it has no vital movement, no impressive structure and is sparse in dialogue. Nevertheless its contribution to Arabic fiction is indisputable. Its intelligent penetration into the inner self of the boy again underlined the necessity for characterization. Its equally intelligent and highly dramatic sketches (e.g., Chapter 18) portrayed at a low pitch and conveyed in a highly elaborate and idiosyncratic style, rendered it more than mere biography. *Al-Ayyām* thus becomes inseparable from the history of the novel in Egypt. Its impact, both in style and subject matter, on modern Arabic literature is enormous.

* * *

A new stir in the relatively shallow water of the novel in the twenties was again caused by Dr. Haykal towards the end of the decade. In 1929 a second edition of *Zaynab* was published, this time under his real name.[2] At about the same date his journal *al-Siyāsa al-usbū'iyya*, as well as other newspapers, opened their pages to a heated

---

[1] The book was serialized earlier (Dec., 1926 - July, 1927) in *al-Hilāl*. On Ṭāhā Ḥusayn, "the doyen of Arabic literature" (b. 1889) see Pierre Cachia's Ṭaha Ḥusayn, London, 1956. An English translation of *al-Ayyam* by E.H. Paxton was published (London, 1932) under the title *An Egyptian Childhood.*

[2] Dr. Ismā'īl Adham (Adham-Nājī 1945, p. 36, f. 2) maintians that it was the second edition which made an impact on Arabic fiction since this edition had the advantage of its author being the now important personality. But Gibb (*Studies*, p. 294), suggests a different order of emphasis. "Its republication in 1929," he writes, "was the result of a public demand, stimulated by several factors, amongst which may be included the strengthening of that national self-consciousness which it already foreshadowed, the literary eminence attained by the now confessed author, and the adaptation of the book as the subject of the first cinematograph film produced in Egypt."

discussion on the future of the Arabic novel.[1] Questions as to how dependent the Arabic novel should be on the literary heritage and on European models, how far Egyptian reality (notably the position of women and the Islamic attitude towards love relations in general) allows the rise of a genuine fiction, were exhaustively discussed. As a result, a number of leading literary figures found themselves facing an urgent need to give encouragement to, if not actually cultivate, the novel. Many of them accepted the challenge. Thus throughout the fourth decade, we were to witness the phenomenon of important poets, critics and playwrights, joining the ranks of novelists.

Their contribution, in fact, amounts to a new stage in the history of the novel, and throughout the thirties their novels came forth to establish the first coherent tradition of Arabic fiction. The main representative novels of this period are, chronologically :

1931 — *Ibrāhīm al-Kātib*	by Ibrāhīm al-Māzinī
1933 — *'Awdat al-rūḥ*	by Tawfīq al-Ḥakīm
1934 — *Ḥawwā' bilā Ādam*	by Ṭāhir Lāshīn
1934 — *Du'ā' al-karawān*	by Ṭāhā Ḥusayn
1938 — *Sāra*	by 'Abbās Maḥmūd al-'Aqqād
1939 — *Nidā' al-Majhūl*	by Maḥmūd Taymūr

Each of these novels constituted a landmark in Egyptian fiction and left an unmistakable imprint on Arabic literature as a whole. They forged the main modes of the local novel and their example was to be imitated and elaborated upon by younger writers.

It is well beyond the scope of this survey to discuss these works in detail. Many have received ample attention both from Arab and European writers. A short appraisal is nevertheless necessary not only to illustrate this critical stage, but also to understand further developments.

* * *

When Ibrāhīm 'Abd al-Qādir al-Māzinī (1889-1949) published his first novel *Ibrāhīm al-Kātib* ('Ibrahim the Writer') in 1931, he had already made his mark as a man of letters : poet, critic, translator and journalist. He had published many short stories and sketches

---

[1] An extensive account of this discussion is given by Gibb, (*Studies*, pp. 295-98), who summarizes the opinions of Haykal, 'Inān and Zakī Mubārak.

which evinced an unmistakably personal style and point of view, the main feature of which was a mild cynicism combined with intellectual perspicacity. His language is lucid and rich, drawn largely from the early prose of classical Arabic, but cast in a modern mould.

The above mentioned controversy as to the nature and mode of Arabic fiction, in which most Egyptian literary figures participated, could not have failed to compel al-Māzinī to take sides. His contribution, however, took the shape of a novel. But while in his introduction to the novel he goes out of his way to assert that the love theme is by no means indispensable to the art of fiction, and that it is untrue that a novel has to be shaped like the European models —the contents of his novel flies in the face of his own "terms of reference". *Ibrāhīm al-Kātib* is in fact a *tour de force* designed to prove that a writer of al-Māzinī's standing can squeeze a variety of love situations out of the Egyptian reality of the twenties.

The protagonist of this novel is a fastidious intellectual of twenty-eight (who shares many qualities with his creator). In the space of a few months he is lucky enough to have three love affairs, each taking place in a different setting and introducing a different type of woman.

The first (chronologically, but not in order of narration) concerns a short love affair with a nurse, Mary, a young Lebanese widow whom Ibrāhīm (a widower himself) comes to know when undergoing an operation. This successful affair is, however, brought to a sudden end (for reasons not sufficiently clear), and Ibrāhīm retires to a country estate belonging to his relatives. There he very soon indulges in the second affair—this time with a young cousin, S̲h̲ūs̲h̲ū, who loves him with all the naïveté of a teenager. Ibrāhīm returns her love and the happy couple enjoy a few weeks of spiritual elevation, which again comes to an abrupt end : Ibrāhīm asks for S̲h̲ūs̲h̲ū's hand, is rejected, and angrily leaves the scene.

Ibrāhīm's next adventure occurs in Luxor, in the south of Egypt, where he meets Laylā, a modern woman of twenty-six, who also falls madly in love with him, tends him during his illness and becomes pregnant. Ibrāhīm's happiness is once more terminated when the altruistic Laylā comes across S̲h̲ūs̲h̲ū's passionate letters to him. She makes Ibrāhīm shun her by falsely insinuating that she has an impure past, and that she does not really care for him. She undergoes an abortion and disappears from Ibrāhīm's life. The latter resumes his relations with Mary for a while, but again jilts her to retreat to his self-centered meditations.

The story suffers from the artificiality of the settings and the implausibility of the characters. The actions of Ibrāhīm and the other characters are often inadequately motivated. Moreover, the three episodes of the plot do not form an integrally related whole.[1] It is interspersed by unnecessary erudite observations on human nature, history, etc. Nevertheless the novel makes entertaining reading and demonstrates the author's command not only of language and style, but also of swiftness in narration.

The character of Ibrāhīm dominates the whole book yet many sides of his world remain in the dark. There is a blatant contradiction between his portrait as a wise, intelligent, benevolent man on the one hand, and his feebleness, selfishness and obliviousness to many facts of life on the other. Certainly these two contradictory groups of qualities can form two sides of the same coin, provided that they are balanced parts of an intricately developed portrait; but al-Māzinī seems to be too interested in the superficial manifestations of his hero's abilities to care to explain his weaknesses. These weaknesses appear more as unsuccessful excuses used (by the author and by his hero alike) to justify the rapid shifts of the love scenes.

The women who love Ibrāhīm are still more uneven. They are, on the whole, no more than puppets whom Ibrāhīm manipulates with ease. They are unconvincing because they are often too European in their behaviour and too intellectual in their reactions and words. Even Shūshū, who is the most convincing of the three, is too much of a philosopher to be accepted without reservations.[2] On the other hand, she does not show any real will-power or distinct personality.

Laylā is still less true-to-life. She behaves in an absolutely European manner—stays in a remote hotel alone, flirts in public and even practices sexual freedom. This takes place, it is to be remembered, in Egypt in the twenties.

The most successful of al-Māzinī's characters are the subsidiary ones, e.g., Najiyya (Shūshū's elder sister), her husband Shaykh 'Alī, the housemaid Fāṭima, etc. They are flat characters, lively and highly humorous.

[1] The rather amusing introduction which endeavours to explain the defects as resulting from the hectic history of the writing and printing of this novel can hardly be accepted as sufficient excuse.

[2] Even though we are told that she is a graduate of a French school in Alexandria, we cannot expect from a teen-aged girl such intellectual ability as we witness in the novel. Ibrāhīm, on entering her bedroom (sic !), finds at her bedside—among other books—works of Spinoza, Freud, Tolstoy and Shaw.

In general, *Ibrāhīm al-Kātib* is a novel with a great deal of romanticizing. At the same time it offers many interesting portrayals of Egyptian reality and in the context of the Egyptian novel, it constitutes a contribution of considerable originality.[1]

The dialogue is written in modified *fuṣḥā*,[2] but in a few cases —especially when the minor characters are concerned—dialect is used. The *fuṣḥā* of the dialogue is flexible and functional, and very rarely sounds bookish.

***

If al-Māzinī wanted to prove that a genuine Egyptian love story was possible, Tawfīq al-Ḥakīm[3] (b. 1898) in his novel *'Awdat al-rūḥ* ('The Soul Returned') which appeared in 1933, undertook a much more ambitious task. His novel goes beyond the naïve telling of the story to impose on the realistic layer an all-embracing symbolic significance.

Al-Ḥakīm, the most important figure in modern Arabic playwriting, is, like Haykal, a French-orientated writer. He too spent a few years in Paris as a postgraduate law student and wrote a first version of his novel in France (presumably in French),[4] basing the story on semi-autobiographical elements. Here too we are given a picture of the Egyptian countryside and of the *fallāḥ*'s life.

The main plot, however, takes place in Cairo. In a tiny flat in the old city we meet a young schoolboy, Muḥsin, son of a wealthy landowner. He lives with his three uncles, also of country stock, now working or studying in Cairo, and with a spinster aunt. Saniyya, daughter of a retired doctor living next door, manages to attract not only the young Muḥsin, but also two of his uncles as well as their servant. They all fall in love with her, and in so doing a feeling of self-consciousness overcomes them, resulting in a weakening of their group solidarity. The aunt, in turn, in her desperate search for a husband, spares no means (including witchcraft, which consumes

---

[1] It would be unjust to exaggerate the influence of such novels as Artzybashev's *Sanin* on this story (see Gibb, *Studies*, pp. 302-3; Fu'ād, *Adab al-Māzinī*, pp. 258-63). Scenes which have some affinity with *Sanin* constitute a negligible part of the novel, while the greatest part of the novel is of a clearly Egyptian background, including some admirable local portraits and scenes.

[2] See also the novel's introduction, pp. 8-9.

[3] See Adham-Nājī (Edham-Nagi), *Tawfīq al-Ḥakīm*, Cairo, 1945.

[4] *Ibid.*, p. 92; Ḍayf, p. 289.

the best part of the family income) to attract a rich bachelor who lives nearby. The whole complex game of courting and scheming comes to a heartbreaking end when the adorable Saniyya becomes engaged : her fiancé, to make matters worse, being none other than the rich neighbour. Before long, however, the 1919 revolution erupts, and the soul is returned not only to the nation as a whole, but also to the miniature nation living in their compact flat (the *sha'b*, as they humorously called themselves). They take an active part in the demonstrations and as a result are all—excluding the aunt—thrust into jail, united and undaunted.

The plot is constructed in highly symmetrical patterns. The symbolism runs throughout the story (the *sha'b*, which is crammed into the little flat, stands for the Egyptian nation) and is brought out by quotations from the *Book of the Dead* of ancient Egyptian mythology. Yet al-Ḥakīm's preoccupation with symmetry, far from serving his aesthetic ends, renders many parts of the novel preposterously artificial. Many recurring themes in the plot, which are conditioned by the superimposed symbolic symmetry, have damaging effects on the plausibility of the realistic layer. The book, for instance, begins and ends with a nearly identical scene, namely : that of the whole *sha'b* lying in a narrow room and visited by an astonished doctor (the first time being in their flat; the second, in the prison hospital; the doctor is the same in both cases). These two scenes are presumably contrived to symbolize an oppressed and poor nation, united in the face of adversity.

Above all, the symbolic loftiness renders trifling the otherwise enjoyable mundane occurrences of the novel. "There is a lack of balance," remarks Yaḥyā Ḥaqqī, "between the inner and outer aspects. The inner facet is grandiose; for instance : the title, the quotations [from the *Book of the Dead*] ... while the outer facet is nothing but childish incidents, highly affected."[1]

Symmetrical as it is in intent, *'Awdat al-rūḥ* suffers from many digressions which are neither functional nor integral. For instance, a good part of the novel takes place in the village house of Muḥsin's father, and all that happens there has hardly any bearing on the story of the *sha'b*. Furthermore many scenes are foreign to the mainstream of the plot (such as the long-drawn-out debate between the French archaeologist and the English irrigation engineer [Vol. II,

---

[1] Ḥaqqī, *Fajr*, p. 133.

Chapter 6]; Muḥsin's philosophical musings on the eternal qualities of the Egyptians [Vol. II, Chapter 5, *et passim*]; Muḥsin's recollection of his joining in a singer's chorus in his early boyhood [Vol. I, Chapter 9]; Saniyya's father recalling his Sudanese adventures [Vol. I, Chapter 17]; and others).

Nevertheless, it remains to be emphasized that the vitality of the "outer layer" is unprecedented in Egyptian fiction. Al-Ḥakīm's novel is rich in humour, crowded with interesting characters who are warm, full-of-life and real Egyptians.

Perhaps al-Ḥakīm's most impressive achievement is that his characters *speak* for themselves. Their vitality is conveyed, not by extensive background analysis, but by their own words and deeds. The dialogue of this novel—which is given in vigorous vernacular—is probably among the best in Egyptian fiction, an achievement hardly surprising for those who are familiar with the author's dialogue in his plays.

***

The short novel by Maḥmūd Ṭāhir Lā<u>sh</u>īn, *Ḥawwā' bilā Ādam* ('Eve without Adam') made little impression on the general public when it appeared in 1934,[1] and for many years to come it was seldom mentioned by Egyptian critics.[2] Its aesthetic merits and profundity of vision, however, are by no means inferior to those of the best Arabic novels written in the thirties. The author[3] (1894-1954) was an active member of "The Modern School."[4] In his novel, as in his short stories[5] an individual voice can be heard. Every sentence reflects a conscious striving after original expression and a continuous search for an artistic solution to the situations described.

The plot of *Ḥawwā'* is simple—one might almost say too simple : *Ḥawwā'*, a teacher of thirty-two, lives with her kind but superstitious grandmother in a humble house that she has acquired as a result

1 The novel was originally serialized in *al-Hilāl* in 1933.

2 It is mainly thanks to Yaḥyā Ḥaqqī (*Fajr*, [1960]) and to Dr. Badr (*Taṭawwur*, 1963) that this talented writer was re-appraised. The latter author discussed *Ḥawwā'* in much detail (*Taṭawwur*, pp. 260-77).

3 On whom see Ḥaqqī, *Fajr*, pp. 83-100; <u>Kh</u>idr, *al-Qiṣṣa*, pp. 203ff.

4 See *supra*, pp. 12-13.

5 To be found in his collection, *Su<u>kh</u>riyyat al-nāy* 1926(?) *Yuḥkā anna* 1928(?); *al-Niqāb al-ṭā'ir* 1935(?). In the last mentioned collection the author informs us of a forthcoming novel of his named *Sirr al-muntaḥir*, of which I could find no mention in the available indexes.

of hard toil. Thanks to her social activities she finds herself in the house of an aristocratic family where, after school hours, she tutors the daughter. There she meets Ramzī, the Pasha's son, who is ten years her junior. Ḥawwā' falls in love with him and imagines that she finds some encouragement from him. A vague dream that she nourishes for a while is painfully shattered when Ramzī gets engaged to a young and rich heiress. As the wedding date draws nearer, Ḥawwā' is dejected and ill, and in a weak moment, she allows herself to be treated by her grandmother's witch-doctor. When she realises what she has done she becomes disgusted with herself and commits suicide on the eve of the wedding.

The style of the novel is rapid and vibrant. The dialogue is crisp and functional. The characterization co-ordinates both "outer" and "inner" techniques resulting in economical and well-focused writing. Thus this short novel (less than twenty thousand words) gives an adequate representation of an interesting gallery of Cairene types, ranging from the humorous to the sad, from the boorish to the genuinely intelligent, from the destitute to the rich. The most striking quality of this novel is, however, its clear coherence of both plot and character. Humorous characters and events, for instance, are not introduced merely to entertain; they have a manifest bearing on Ḥawwā's life. They bring out her social milieu and serve as a contrast to her image. While Ḥawwā' is dreaming of love, the illiterate servant Najiyya, is having a more successful love affair with the local butcher. While Ḥawwā' toils to enlighten people, her own home is full of superstition. Lāshīn's relish in exotic characters is skilfully woven into the fabric of the plot. His social criticism, sharp and pungent though it is, is not made in a declamatory manner, and above all, he does not exlude factors such as Ḥawwā's weird temperament, which leads to her theatrical suicide.

***

Ṭāhā Ḥusayn's first imaginative novel[1] *Du'ā' al-karawān* ('The

[1] Ṭāhā Ḥusayn also wrote in this period two sequels to *al-Ayyām* (*al-Ayyām II*, 1939, but also *Adīb*, 1935), some short stories, and three volumes of narrative episodes from early Islamic history (*'Alā hāmish al-Sīra*, 1933-43). His other novels of the thirties and early forties include one whose protagonists are exclusively French (*al-Ḥubb al-ḍā'i'*, serialized in 1937-8) and an imaginary story (*Aḥlām Shahrazād*, 1943), which constitutes (under the guise of "sequel" to Arabian Nights) a vigorous critique of current politics. In 1944 he published another novel on contemporary social scenes,

Plover's Call') written in 1934[1] can also be included in the category of literature of social criticism. Yet its author's inclinations makes the novel at once didactic and lyrical.

A woman of Bedouin origin, together with her two daughters, is forced to leave her village following the disgrace of her husband, which led to his assassination. The three women settle in a provincial town and become domestic servants. The elder daughter is seduced by her master, a young unmarried engineer. No sooner does the mother discover what has happened than she takes both her daughters and leaves the "sinister town". The mother's brother soon appears, and in the dark of night kills his pregnant niece in cold blood and buries her in the desert. The younger sister, Āmina, who witnesses the murder, is aghast and runs away from her mother who, she feels, is as guilty as her uncle. She goes back to her good-hearted employers (where she had learned to read and write together with the master's daughter). She is determined to take revenge on her sister's seducer, and when she hears that her master's daughter is about to marry this same engineer, she prevents the marriage by disclosing her sister's story. She then manages to join the engineer's household as a servant, Her new master, unaware of her being the sister of his former servant, finds her attractive but unattainable. Gradually a strained and complicated relationship develops between them, with Āmina's strong will dominating the scene. The master is now infatuated with her and his personality changes. Āmina becomes the sole object of his desires. The girl, on her part, suddenly discovers that she is in love with him, and ultimately accepts her penitent master's offer of marriage.

The plot is not sufficiently clear cut, nor are the characters always vivid. Yet this novel brings into Arabic fiction a new note of lyricism. The plover's call which is evoked by Āmina throughout the novel gives it not only rhythm and shape, but also an unsophisticated

---

Shajarat al-bu's, of which a further mention will be made in this chapter. For plot outlines and analysis of most of these novels see Cachia, pp. 192-204, 240-8.

[1] The date "September 1934" is explicitly inscribed in the last page of the novel (p. 160 of al-Ma'ārif edition of 1960); while Najm in his index (*al-Abḥath*, Beirut, 1963) dates the novel as late as 1941 which is confirmed by Anawati-Kuentz, *Bibliographie*, Cairo, 1948, p. 124; and by the reviews in *al-Risāla* for Jan. 26, 1942 (by al-'Aqqād); and *al-Thaqāfa* for Feb. 24, 1942, (by Dhuhnī). A French translation of the novel under the title *L'appel du Karaouan* was published in 1963 in Beirut (translator : Raymond Francis).

symbolism. This symbolism is not artifically imposed, but is generated spontaneously from Āmina's tormented soul.

Most remarkable is the fact that lyricism is employed here to portray people of the lower walks of life : servants, women matchmakers, villagers, and Bedouins. Most of the novels discussed above tackled the intellectual character, while the others (notably servants and villagers) were employed very often as comic figures. They were often ridiculous (e.g., the negro servant in *Ibrāhīm al-Kātib*, the servant Mabrūk in *'Awdat al-rūḥ*). Ṭāhā Ḥusayn, in contrast, chooses a housemaid to be the hero of his lyrical novel. Āmina is portrayed with love and insight (especially her transformation from an avenger to a lover). As has often been remarked,[1] she shows too much intelligence, and her reactions and poetic reflections can hardly be conceived of as coming from a servant of Bedouin stock. Yet it would be unfair to demand meticulous realism from a story which is basically lyrical.

* * *

In the wide range of writing produced by 'Abbās Maḥmūd al-'Aqqād (1889-1964) his only novel *Sāra* (1938) stands out as a curiosity of literature. His attitude to fiction had always been unfavourable. To him it was inferior to other literary genres, notably to poetry.

That he should undertake a novel at all is amazing enough; the result is an oddity. It is written in an astonishing manner and given an unconventional structure.

The story is, on the face of it, nothing more than a psychological study of a man who suspects his beloved of infidelity, but is unable to take a decisive step. His love for her is intense, but the evidence of her unfaithfulness is no less agonizing. While the hero is tormented by indecision, we are provided with "background information". This information is arranged in separate chapters bearing such titles as "Who is she?", "How did he come to know her?", "Why did he love her?", "Why did he suspect her?". These ostensibly preplanned essays, however, depict an interesting portrait of the beloved, Sāra. Her natural intelligence coupled with effervescent youth and femininity are depicted with relish and thoroughness. Many of the situations described attest a mastery of narration.

Thus in spite of its rigorous structure and style, *Sāra* deeply im-

---

1 For example Mandūr, *Fil-mīzān al-jadīd*, p. 53, and cf. al-Rā'ī's reply to this argument (*Dirāsāt*, pp. 140ff.).

presses the reader with the freshness of its story. The author's rationalizing general scheme is often defied by the flow of life.

***

Maḥmūd Taymūr's short novel *Nidā' al-majhūl* ('The Call of the Unknown') first published in 1939, is a more successful attempt of its author when compared to his earlier short novels.[1] It takes place in the mountains of Lebanon where Miss Evans, a mystically-inclined Englishwoman, is trying to recover from a sad love affair by losing herself in the mysteries of the East. Accompanied by two local people and the narrator, she sets out to explore a secluded and deserted mountain palace, around which many weird legends have arisen. After a rough and dangerous journey, they arrive at the castle, and much to their surprise, they find the heir to the palace who has been living there in complete isolation for many years (he fled there after killing his beloved on the day she was to marry another man). He is injured by the exploring party when he tries to resist them, becomes delirious, and mistakes Miss Evans for his dead love. He recuperates thanks to the good care of the Englishwoman and becomes attached to her. Miss Evans, in turn, seems to have become enchanted by this unhappy prince. The company finally leaves the palace and the prince, and two days later they wake up to find that Miss Evans is missing. She has furtively gone back to the mysterious palace.

In spite of its somewhat naïve plot, Taymūr's novel is by no means a superficial adventure story. It is an interesting study of his characters (some of whom are very humorous); its Lebanese setting is admirably recreated, and the mystery and suspense are introduced in an unobtrusive manner.[2]

***

1940-1945 : The writing of fiction by prominent men of letters in the thirties was, it is true, sporadic and infrequent. To many of

[1] Namely *Rajab afandī* (1928) and *al-Aṭlāl* (1934), on which see Badr, pp. 233-60. Maḥmūd Taymūr (b. 1894) is a prolific author who is considered a central figure in the field of the Arabic short story. He has also written a number of longer novels such as *Salwā fī mahabb al-rīḥ* (1948).

[2] This novel of Taymūr's has been translated into English by Hume Horan (Mahmoud Teymour, *The Call of the Unknown*, Beirut [Khayat's] 1964).

them it was simply one of the various aspects of literary and public activity. Yet it signifies a change on the part of authors and readers alike. Fiction writing was no longer regarded as an inferior literary activity as compared, for instance, with poetry.

Certainly the successive generations of the modern school- (and later, University-) graduates have by now become the main audience for literature, while the proportion of women readers has risen constantly. The number of those who could now read European fiction in the original had risen sharply. But it is only in the forties and fifties that the local breed of intellectuals are to become not only the readers, but also the main *writers* of fiction.

The first year of the fifth decade supplies us with an excellent illustration of the emerging generation of writers. In 1941, the Ministry of Education initiated a novel-writing competition. The response was overwhelming; no fewer than 66 entries were received, fifteen of which were found to be worth consideration by the referees. The judging committee, which was nominated by the Arabic Language Academy (and comprising some of the main figures of Egyptian literature), eventually decided not to grant a first prize, but instead to name the five best novels. Amazingly enough the first three novels named were by three unknown University graduates who were later to emerge as leading novelists.[1]

Many of these young writers had been writing short stories which they published in literary magazines (such as *al-Risāla*, *al-T̲h̲aqāfa* and *al-Riwāya*) and in popular journals. But very rarely did they publish novels. The resort to short story writing was, it seems, not necessarily due to the authors' preference of this form in particular. It is more likely that it was imposed upon them by the lack of publishers interested in original novels (still less in works of young novelists). On the other hand, one must remember the obvious eagerness of literary magazine editors to print short stories, articles and poems. In fact we know of many novelists (including Najīb Maḥfūẓ), who for years were looking in vain for means of publishing their novels.

The year 1943 witnessed a dramatic breakthrough in the field of novel-publishing. A young writer, ʿAbd al-Ḥamīd Jūda al-Saḥḥār, initiated a publishing body which was mainly interested in publishing

---

[1] They are : (a) ʿĀdil Kāmil (his novel being *Malik min s̲h̲uʿāʿ*); (b) ʿAlī Aḥmad Bākat̲h̲īr (*Wā Islāmāh*); (c) Najīb Maḥfūẓ (*Kifāḥ Ṭība*). For details see *Majallat majmaʿ Fu'ād al-awwal lil-lug̲h̲a al-ʿArabiyya*, V (1948), pp. 209-13.

works of young writers of the "University Generation,"[1] chiefly in the field of fiction. This body, which functioned for many years, introduced many talented novelists to the public, among whom were Maḥfūẓ, Kāmil, and Bākathīr, who were now able to publish, among other things, their above-mentioned novels. In the same year (1943) a well-established publishing firm in Cairo, Dār al-ma'ārif, inaugurated a monthly series of books (edited by Ṭāhā Ḥusayn, al-'Aqqād and others) in pocket-book format, under the name *Iqra'* ('Read!'). The series included a variety of titles, not necessarily fiction, but including many novels (the first number, in fact, was the short novel *Aḥlām Shahrazād* by Ṭāhā Ḥusayn). This series, however, can hardly be said to have encouraged young novelists; the novels which it offered were by well-established writers of the earlier generation such as al-Māzinī, al-Jārim, Abū Ḥadīd and Yaḥyā Ḥaqqī.

This sudden and unprecedented activity in the publication of serious fiction, in which old and new writers alike participated, was preceded by a long period of anticipation on the part of the writers. Many of the novels published in the years 1943-1945, were in fact written several years earlier and were now handed over to the publishers because of their sudden interest in novels. On the other hand, it can be said that this interest itself motivated some experienced writers to return to fiction and others to start writing novels. Many examples can be cited. For instance, between 1931, when *Ibrāhīm al-Kātib* came out, and 1943, al-Māzinī published no novels at all. However in the years 1943-1944 he produced no fewer than four. 'Alī al-Jārim (1881-1949), a poet of the old generation, embarked in the forties upon historical fiction and his first four novels appeared in this period. Yaḥyā Ḥaqqī (b. 1905), a critic and short story writer of "The Modern School" published in 1943 his first *nouvelle, Qindīl umm Hāshim.* Tawfīq al-Hakīm, who since publishing *'Awdat al-rūḥ* in 1933 had written no novels in the strict sense of the word,[2] now published *al-Ribāṭ al-muqaddas* (1944). Lastly Muḥammad Farīd Abū Ḥadīd, who in 1926 published a novel *Ibnat al-Mamlūk* (dealing

---

[1] The name of this body was "Lajnat al-nashr lil-jāmi'iyyīn;" the printer and publisher being Maktabat Miṣr.

[2] He has however published in 1937 his *Yawmiyyāt nā'ib fil-aryāf* (a most touching account of village life in diary form), and in 1938 *'Uṣfūr min al-sharq* (a semi-biographical account of his Paris years). Both of these works—and especially *Yawmiyyāt*—are regarded by many critics as novels proper. An English translation of this work appeared in London in 1947 under the title *The Maze of Justice* (trans. A.S. Eban)

with the period of Muḥammad ʿAlī), suddenly returned to the scene to become a prolific novelist.

Scanning a list of the novels appearing in this period, one's notice is instantly attracted by the fact that a great number of these stories deal with historical topics. In the competition mentioned above, the fifteen works that passed the first test included *at least* five historical novels (of which four drew on the history of Pharaonic Egypt and one on Islamic history). Furthermore, of the five novels which were named by the committee, the first three were historical. At least five of the novelists who emerged in those years were predominantly historical novelists (Abū Ḥadīd, al-Jārim, al-Saḥḥār, Bākathīr and al-ʿIryān). Others (like Maḥfūẓ and Kāmil) started by writing historical novels, but later turned to contemporary subjects.

It is intriguing to inquire into the actual motives that inspired the sudden and rather ephemeral wave of historical novels. Many critics have maintained that the clue lies in the rise of nationalistic feeling.[1] This is undoubtedly true in general, since most of the historical novels of the forties reflected patriotic emotions, and unlike Zaydān's novels, were not designed to be detached accounts of different historical periods. But why, one might ask, did they emerge in the early forties and not, for instance, around the year 1919, in the midthirties, or early fifties—all of which were periods of extreme nationalistic feeling. It seems likely that the global war, then at its peak, had something to do with the rising of patriotic tendencies among the intellectuals. Yet one would be on safer ground if one were to consider the fact that most of those novelists actually belong to the first generation of Egyptian writers who had their training exclusively in Egyptian Universities, and thus developed a genuine interest in Egyptian history (Pharaonic and Islamic alike) and Arabic history in general.

The novel depicting ancient Egyptian history is a rather late reflection of an interest that appealed to many Egyptian nationalists, especially in the first quarter of the present century.[2] The list of those who were inflamed by the glorious Egyptian past included many Muslim intellectuals of western training, such as Amīn, Al-Sayyid (and even such an early writer as Rifāʿa Rāfiʿ al-Ṭahṭāwī).[3] They

[1] E.g., Badr, p. 398; El-Hazmī's dissertation Pt. III, Ch. I.

[2] In the field of creative literature, we can find much evidence of this preoccupation in the works of Shawqī, Haykal, al-Ḥakīm and others.

[3] See Hourani, pp. 70, 79f.

incorporated their reverence for the great past in the framework of their aspirations towards Egyptian national independence. This trend culminated in the establishment of a faculty of Egyptology in the Egyptian University in the early twenties. Its most ardent exponent in the twenties was Dr. Haykal, who devoted many pages of his newspaper *al-Siyāsa* (and especially its weekly supplement) to Pharaonic literature, art, and history.[1] This enthusiasm, however, subsided around the year 1930, and it was replaced by a wave of interest in Islamic-Arabic history.[2] The fancy of many non-Azharite intellectuals was taken—throughout the thirties and forties—by the great patriarchs of Islam, Islamic thinking, and Islamic literature, and, with the establishment of the Arab League in 1945, the allegiance to Arab nationalism took precedence over other national allegiances.

Between these two poles—Pharaonic and Arab-Islamic—a third, less obtrusive trend was making some advances, namely the Egyptian-Islamic. The most important spokesman of this trend in that period was the Arabic scholar Amīn al-Khūlī, who made many converts among his students at the University. In a way, this was a new and more refined version of the earlier Egyptianism—i.e., the Pharaonic, which was distasteful to many Muslim Egyptians. It underlined the uniqueness of Egyptian life and culture, which, though Arabized with the advent of Islam, nevertheless retained its individual character and mentality. In the field of literary history, al-Khūlī and his circle laid special emphasis on the study of Egyptian-Islamic literature (e.g., Ibn al-Fāriḍ) as distinct from Arabic literature of other Arab regions. Similarly in the field of history, they found in the separate development of Islamic Egypt their main concern. To al-Khūlī

> he who denies the Egyptian quality of Egypt is belied by its pyramids and other radiant illustrations of its past; he who denies the Arabic quality of Egypt is belied by its [Arabic] language, and his mistake is heralded by its minarets. Egypt is a totality of all these. They are all components of its milieu, its personality, its individuality.[3]

The historical novels of the early forties reflected all three trends in viewing the national past. The Pharaonic subject, although, as

[1] Some of his articles on the subject can be found (with some alterations) in his books *Fī awqāt al-farāgh* (1926), *Tarājim Miṣriyya wa gharbiyya* (1929), *Thawrat al-adab* (1933).

[2] See e.g., Haykal's introduction to his book *Fī manzil al-waḥy* (first published 1937), third ed., Cairo 1958 (?), p. 24ff.

[3] *Fil-adab al-Miṣrī* (1943), p. 134.

we have seen, found its way into many novels, was never specialized to any degree. None of the authors studied Pharaonic history systematically. Their main sources of information were the more or less popular histories of the period, some of which were translated into Arabic. Furthermore, among the few serious writers who attempted this subject, only Maḥfūẓ treated ancient history as a mirror of the present political scene, and as a symbol for national aspiration.[1]

A different attitude to history is exemplified by 'Ādil Kāmil's novel *Malik min shu'ā'* (1945) whose protagonist is Akhenaten. Its main theme, however, is not a national, but a spiritual struggle. Moreover, in the course of the story, Akhenaten, the benevolent and musing king, preaches peace and non-violence even at the expense of Egyptian national independence. It is only because of the machinations of a vindictive high priest, who incites the people to murder their king, that Egypt is able to fight off the invading tribes.

The author's interest does not lie in the first place in national rights and wrongs, but in the spiritual salvation of humanity. His hero sees the light, and becomes intent on replacing the existing religion, with its inhumane, corrupt priesthood, by a new monotheistic (or rather, monistic) religion, a religion of love and peace. He is unsuccessful, however, and is betrayed by all his friends, save his wife Nefertiti. The novel is, in general, pessimistic and gloomy. The wicked are powerful, the good—solitary and helpless, and the people—nothing but an ignorant mob. This work is now, for some reason, forgotten (possibly because of its "defeatist" content) but in the history of Egyptian fiction it marks an attempt to defy the accepted attitude to a literary genre, namely that a historical novel should serve either an edifying or patriotic end. Kāmil—here and elsewhere—follows an individualistic and less frequented path.[2]

Another Pharaonic story worth mentioning is the short novel *Sinūḥī* (1943) by Muḥammad 'Awaḍ Muḥammad. The author, a geographer by profession, retells in his own fashion the story of the well-known courtier of old, Sinuhe, and does so with much wit and charm. However, there is too little movement and characterization to make it a novel in the true sense. It is, rather, a brief account of life and manners in the ancient Egyptian court.

---

[1] Maḥfūẓ's three historical novels will be discussed in Ch. III of this book.

[2] A literary biography of Kāmil can be found in Ṣabrī Ḥāfiẓ's article in *al-Majalla* (Cairo), June, 1966, pp. 85ff. A second novel of the same author will be discussed later in this chapter.

The most competent representative of the Arabic trend is undoubtedly Muḥammad Farīd Abū Ḥadīd (1893-) who, throughout his literary career, strove after "an unadulterated Arabic inspiration".[1] It is significant that the plots of the great majority of his novels take place not in Egypt, but in the cradle of Islam, the Arabian desert or its vicinity.[2] Abū Ḥadīd's style, however, is not a declamatory one, and his zeal for the Islamic subject is by no means detrimental to his art. His plots are, as a rule, not based on breathtaking adventures of super-human people. On the contrary, here we find a genuine interest in the internal development of the characters and a happy balance between the historical and fictional elements. In some cases the movement of the plot is too slow and the suspense is weak. But by and large, his books make enjoyable reading. His language is rich but not stilted, and its rather idyllic rhythm is in pace with the general mood and milieu of his stories.

Of a lesser artistic merit are the novels of ʿAlī Aḥmad Bākat͟hīr (1910-69), a prolific author who came to Egypt from Ḥaḍramaut in southern Arabia. His attitude to his subject-matter is strongly partisan, and the black and white dichotomy runs throughout his novels. Furthermore, the historical analogy to the present is often too transparent. His novel *al-T͟hāʾir al-aḥmar* (1945), for instance, deals with the struggle between the Islamic state and the Carmathian rebels (ninth century A.D.) and the reader is left in no doubt that the author's sympathies lie with the former. Ḥamdān, a youth who has joined the quasi-communistic sect as a protest against the injustices of the ruling classes, finds his new friends no less wicked and immoral. The novel winds up, however, with Ḥamdān's penitence and return to the bosom of normative Islam, but also with the Islamic state itself correcting its defects, and the rebel state crumbling. There is an undisguised reference throughout the novel to the clash between the Muslim Brothers and the Left in Egypt in the nineteen-forties and a fervent belief in the future of a purified Islam. Admittedly, references to the present scene, and even a partisan attitude, are legitimate in the realm of historical novels, but in the case of Bākat͟hīr,

---

1 See the introduction to his novel *Zinūbyā* (drawn from S͟hawkat, p. 86).

2 E.g. : *Zinūbyā* (1941), *al Malik al-ḍillīl* (1944), *al-Muhalhil sayyid Rabīʿa* (1944). Even his first novel, *Ibnat al-Mamlūk* (1926), though its plot occurs in Egypt, has as its main hero an Arabian from the Peninsula.

they are often to the detriment of plausible characterisation, well-contrived conflicts, and natural dialogue.[1]

The third trend—that which concerns itself with Egypt in the Islamic period—has not found a major writer to represent it. Its most persistent explorer is undoubtedly Muḥammad Sa'id al-'Iryān, whose novel *Qaṭr al-Nadā* (1945) inaugurated a series of stories dealing with Egypt in the Fatimid and Mamluk periods (the best known of which being *'Alā bāb Zuwayla*, 1947, describing the last years of the Mamluk period). Other novelists who took a special interest in this period in the history of Egypt are 'Alī al-Jārim,[2] and Ibrāhīm Jalāl.[3]

As we turn to the novels depicting the contemporary scene, we discern a tendency towards portraying the urban population, and it is in this sphere that some interesting new voices are making themselves heard. The authors of the older generation were also creative in the period in question, but the works which they contributed to this movement are, as a rule, neither of a better quality than the earlier ones, nor are they of a special historical significance.

Al-Māzinī's four new novels[4] continue the themes and style familiar to the reader of *Ibrāhīm al-Kātib*, but, (with the exception, possibly, of *'Awd 'alā bad'*) lack the novelty of the earlier book. Al-Ḥakīm in his novel *al-Ribāṭ al-muqaddas* (1944), tackles such topics as marital infidelity and physical-versus-artistic truth, but his treatment of the Egyptian reality is burdened with artificial situations and far-fetched characters. Often the reader is under the impression that the author is trifling with the subject of sex in a cheap manner, in an effort to appeal to the less serious reader (notably to the increasing number of women readers in the Arabic East). Finally Ṭāhā Ḥusayn's novels of the forties[5] make as enjoyable reading as any of his works, but they contain no dramatic innovations. His novel *Shajarat al-bu's*

---

[1] Other Islamic novels by Bākathīr which appeared in this period are *Sallāma al-qass* (1944), *Wā-Islāmāh!* (1945).

[2] His novels dealing with Egypt in the Islamic period are *Sayyidat al-quṣūr* (1944) and *Ghādat Rashīd* (1945). Al-Jārim, however, wrote a few other novellas portraying the lives of classical poets from Arabia and Andalusia, but they are more in the nature of popular biographies than novels proper.

[3] *al-Mu'izz li-Dīn-Allāh* (1944), *al-Amīr Ḥaydar* (1945).

[4] *Ibrāhīm al-thānī, 'Awd 'alā bad', Mīdū wa-shurakāh* (all 1943), *Thalathat rijāl wa-imrā'a* (1944).

[5] For a list of these see *supra*, p. 20, fn. 1.

(1944) however, introduces to Arabic fiction "the novel of generations"[1] and acquaints us with interesting scenes of the Ṣūfī circles in the provinces.

Of the newcomers, the most important name is undoubtedly that of Maḥfūẓ, who has now become engaged in depicting the Cairene scene. Two other writers, less prolific than Maḥfūẓ, are to be mentioned here for the originality and freshness of their contributions, although one, 'Ādil Kāmil later ceased to write, while the other, Yaḥyā Ḥaqqī, never became a major novelist.

'Ādil Kāmil, whose name was mentioned in connection with the historical novel, is no less of an individualist in treating modern Egypt than in characterizing Akhenaten. His novel *Millīm al-akbar* (1944), presents us with a strange mixture of rogues and salon-rebels, idealists and scoundrels, beggars and artists. Its setting is Cairo of the thirties and forties. It has two main characters. The one, Khālid, is a son of a rich and wicked Pasha, who was sent to England to study law. On his return, he not only refuses to work, but, even less palatable to his father, he becomes a convinced socialist and tries to recruit his father to the cause of social justice. He soon becomes frustrated, hates his "inferior" society and engages in a legal feud with his father. The other hero, Millīm, is an ignorant but charming carpenter's apprentice who lands in jail on false charges brought against him by Khālid's brother and father. On leaving prison, he joins a company of anarchists-cum-communists who have found a sanctuary in a derelict Mamluk mansion (*qal'a*) in Cairo. He soon becomes the hub of the group (being the only genuine "proletarian" member). Later Khālid finds his way to Millīm's group and is reluc tantly accepted as a member. In order to prove his worthiness of belonging to the group, he attempts a "grass-root revolutionary activity" through preaching socialism to a café crowd. But his audience ridicules him and his experiment lands him in the jail where Millīm was an inmate earlier. At this point he capitulates to his father and lives thereafter as his well-fed captive. At the same time the father sends the police to the *qal'a* and thus the happy commune comes to an end. Millīm, however, marries a European member of

[1] A practice which was to gain a greater prominence with the publication, in the mid-fifties, of Maḥfūẓ's Trilogy. Maḥfūẓ tells us, with his usual modesty, that his Trilogy owes much to this work of Ṭāhā Ḥusayn (see *al-Majalla* 73 [Jan. 1963], p. 28), but such a statement should be taken with a pinch of salt. A French translation of this novel appeared in 1964 under the title *L'Arbre de la misère* (Paris, trans. G. Wiet).

the group and the couple live in happiness and wealth (for Millīm makes a fortune by trading with the British army).

The story is told at a quick pace, allowing no time for adequate psychological penetration. Furthermore, there is much naïveté in the presentation of good and wickedness in accordance with class origin. The patterns and technical devices are sometimes crude (especially the continual presentation of Millīm as a proletarian foil to Khālid). Nevertheless the novel has much charm about it. It betrays an ability to create some amazingly live situations and to use an idiosyncratic language. The novel, together with its massive introduction (in which Kāmil is out to destroy all the "sacred cows" of *'Arabiyya*), constitutes an attempt to break with the conventional modes of writing. Its language is possibly the most sardonic ever used in Arabic fiction.

Of a different style altogether is Ḥaqqī's short novel *Qindīl umm Hāshim* (1944). The tone of this story is lyrical and the stress is on the spiritual rather than on the material aspects of life. It is concerned with one of the most crucial issues facing the East in general, and its intelligentsia in particular, namely : the confrontation with the sophisticated West, and the struggle between material civilization, on the one hand, and the age-hallowed oriental values on the other. Ismā'īl, the protagonist, is a Cairene of humble origin whose father, through much hardship, sends him to England to study medicine. There he acquires a liking for western ways of life, falls in love with an English girl, and, on graduating as an eye-specialist, returns to Egypt. On arriving home, he finds himself disgusted with his people. He resents their primitive manners and is impatient with their filth, ignorance and superstition. His cousin, Fāṭima, an orphan who has always been regarded as Ismā'īl's future wife, suffers from an eye ailment. When he discovers that she is being treated with some "holy oil" from the mosque's lamp, he becomes furious, breaks the oil-lamp and insists on treating her with his modern methods. His treatment, however, fails and the girl loses her sight, Ismā'īl goes through a severe mental crisis, at the end of which he returns to the way of life he had forsaken, marries Fāṭima (who has been cured of her blindness as a result of renewed efforts), and spends the rest of his life among the simple masses.

The story, brief and unpretentious as it is, is rightly regarded by many critics as an aesthetic achievement. It is written by a very able artist who knows how to use his language, at once laconic and poetic, how to employ poetic symbols (e.g., the mosque lamp), and leitmotifs (the prostitute in the mosque). His scenes are lively and so are his characters, and all this is carried out in quick, sharp touches. The author's attitude to his theme, naïve though it might seem at first sight, is loaded with irony, and the ambiguity of his tone is not hard to detect. Furthermore, in referring symbolically to the fate of a nation through the story of a realistically portrayed character, he does so with much more subtlety than any earlier Egyptian author.[1]

Besides resorting to history, then, the novel of the period of World War II shows a growing interest in the urban scene[2] and in the fate of the intellectual. The language and techniques are acquiring maturity, and in general the quality, not merely the quantity, of the work is encouraging.

The year 1945 has been chosen as the closing date for this survey chiefly because it coincides with the appearance of the first of Maḥfūẓ's novels on contemporary themes. Furthermore the rise of new generations of writers (in Egypt as in other Arab countries), many of whom are prolific, renders the field too wide to be dealt with adequately here and, one might add, less relevant as a background to the subject of this book.

This is the proper place, however, to remind ourselves of a question often asked in the early days of the Egyptian novel : could there be a special form of the Egyptian novel, for instance, in the nature of an elaborated *maqāma?* The generally accepted view today is that the modern Arabic novel has taken the line of the western novel and that its defects do not necessarily stem from adopting western styles. On the contrary, they are due to inferior technical competence as compared with that of western authors, or, as some would say, because the Arabic novelist is less steeped in the tradition of novel writing. A well-known Egyptian poet and critic of the younger generation, Ṣalāḥ 'Abd al-Ṣabūr, goes further by asserting that Arabic fiction was luckier than poetry in that it has no local tradition to follow. For whereas poetry was a prisoner of revered conventions, fiction could break through unimpeded, and freely emulate the western masterpieces.[3]

---

[1] Cf. M.M. Badawi, "The Lamp of Umm Hashim : The Egyptian Intellectual Between East and West," *Journal of Arabic Literature*, Vol. I (1970), pp. 145-161.

[2] It is only in 1953, with the appearance of *al-Arḍ* by 'Abd al-Raḥmān al-S͟harqāwī that the Egyptian *fallaḥ* really comes back to the novel.

[3] 'Abd al-Ṣabūr, *Ḥattā*, p. 228.

On the other hand, there still exist some Egyptian writers who have not given up hope for the rise of an original form of fiction altogether. As late as 1960 Professor 'Abd al-Ḥamīd Yūnus, for one, assures us that a revival and reactivation of local folklore would generate a fiction in the "spirit of the people", and that the local writers, if they followed his precepts, would not need to import foreign forms.[1]

It is beyond doubt, however, that the novel has already developed some distinct traits springing from national character and rhythm, and that there is an Egyptian novel in the same sense that there are, for example, Brazilian or Japanese novels. We shall have the opportunity of coming across such traits when probing the works of one of the most important novelists of modern Egypt, Najīb Maḥfūẓ.

---

[1] Yūnus, p. 117.

CHAPTER TWO

THE MAKING OF A NOVELIST

Two roads diverge in a wood, and I—
I took the one less travelled by,
And that has made all the difference.

Robert Frost, "The Road Not Taken"

Although he has been in the centre of Egyptian literary life for more than a decade, not much is known about Maḥfūẓ's biography. He is, in general, reticent and introverted. He avoids personal publicity and shuns the literary limelight. Many journalists have tried, from time to time, to peep into the more intimate aspects of his life; but Maḥfūẓ has politely evaded such enquiries lest they become, as he once said, "a silly topic in journals and radio programmes." However, a few interviews published in the last decade give us a picture of highlights of his life, readings, studies. The following biographical sketch is based mainly on such interviews.[1]

His novels and short stories naturally incorporate many scenes and characters drawn from his own experience, but they are not much use to a biographer at this stage. Even in his most "autobiographical" work, namely, his Trilogy, the facts and characters are composed, as we shall see later, as much from fictitious as genuine components. Until the author's letters, papers, etc. are made available to the public, his stories will furnish us with no more than background

[1] The interviews used are those of ʿAbd al-Tawwāb ʿAbd al-Ḥayy, in *ʿAṣīr Ḥayātī*, pp. 126-34; Jāḏhibiyya Ṣidqī in *Ṣuwar ḥayya*, pp. 117-26; Farūq shūsha in *al-Ādāb* (Beirut), June 1960, pp. 18-21; Rajab al-Bannā in *al-Adab* (Cairo), July 1960, pp. 233-7; Jamāl Sarḥān in *al-Majalla* (Cairo), Jan. 1963, p. 28; Fu'ād Dawwāra in his book *ʿAshrat udabā'*, pp. 266-92 [interview originally published in *al-Kātib* (Cairo) Jan. 1963]; Ghālī Shukrī in *Ḥiwār* (Beirut), Mar.-Apr. 1963, pp. 65-74; Jamāl Badrān in *al-Kitāb al-ʿArabī* (Cairo), Dec. 1964, pp. 32-5; ʿA. al-Sharīf in *al-Ādāb* (Beirut), Mar. 1967, pp. 26-9. S. Karīm in *al-Fikr al-muʿāsir* (Cairo), Sept. 1968, pp. 76-80.

Also of use was Philip Stewart's unpublished thesis on AWL, (1963), in which the author's interviews with Mr. Maḥfūẓ are recorded on pp. 2-7.

A few biographical details can also be found in Shukrī's book *al-Muntamī*, passim; Khiḍr's book *al-Wāqiʿiyya*, pp. 181-87; Tawfīq Ḥannā's article "al-Taṭawwur al-adabī li-Najīb Maḥfūẓ" in *al-Adab* (Cairo), Apr. 1959, pp. 73-5; Trevor Le Gassick, "A Malaise in Cairo - Three Contemporary Egyptian Authors," *M.E. Journal*, vol. 21 (1967), No. 3, pp. 145-56.

material, and, of course, with a general idea of his philosophy or attitudes to life.

Najīb Maḥfūẓ ʿAbd al-ʿAzīz[1] was born on the eleventh of December 1911 in al-Jamāliyya, an old quarter of Muʿizzite Cairo. His father was a minor civil servant.[2] His family consisted—besides his parents and himself—of four sisters and two brothers, all much older than himself. When he was six, his family moved to a new house in al-ʿAbbāsiyya, a modern quarter in the north-east of Cairo.[3] In his boyhood he was afflicted, apparently for a short period, by a kind of epilepsy which kept him at home for some time.[4] He nevertheless finished his primary schooling as early as 1925.[5]

His remarks about his boyhood leave us with the impression that it was a fairly happy one. His father—unlike Kamāl's father in the Trilogy—was not unduly strict and the boy, Najīb, was given a considerable amount of freedom. He enjoyed playing ball in the street, listening to records played on their old-fashioned gramophone,[6] and roaming about the old quarters of the city with his friends on Fridays and school holidays.[7] He was the youngest son and was especially attached to his mother. He lived with her throughout his youth and manhood (all his brothers and sisters having married and left the house), and her influence on him, especially in childhood and boyhood, must have been immense.[8] He was less than fifteen years old when a schoolmate of his left school to become a shop-owner in old Cairo. Maḥfūẓ and a group of his friends took to frequenting the shop and learned to spend their free time sitting in an old-fashioned café, drinking black tea or smoking the *narghile*.[9] It is at this point in his life that he developed a liking for the life of the old, picturesque quarters of Cairo, the setting of such novels as *Zuqāq al-Midaqq* and

---

1 Mahfuz's full—and less known—name appeared in his early works, but he later adopted a shorter name, omitting ʿAbd al-ʿAzīz.

2 Stewart, p. 2; cf. the fathers in the novels KHAN, BID.

3 Jomier, MIDEO IV, p. 30; Khiḍr, p. 181.

4 Shukrī, *al-Muntamī*, p. 26; cf. TAR, p. 70; on Maḥfūẓ's school days see ʿAbd al-Ḥayy, pp. 128-9.

5 T. Ḥanna in *al-Adab* (Cairo) Apr. 1959, p. 73.

6 He mentions as his favourite singers at this period such names as Sayyid Darwish, Salāmā Hijāzī, Munīra al-Mahdiyya, see Ṣidqī, p. 122.

7 Ṣidqī, p. 122; Khiḍr, p. 181.

8 In many of his novels we encounter a close attachment between mother and son. See TR-I-II, BID, KHAN, SAR.

9 Ḥanna, *op. cit.*, p. 74; Ṣidqī, p. 123.

Khān al-Khalīlī. While very young he became an ardent reader of detective novels and a compulsive cinema-goer.

His first attempts at writing were in imitation of the detective stories of Ḥāfiẓ Najīb, which were popular at the time. Another object for his imitation was al-Manfalūṭī, whose romantic stories and episodes were read by virtually every literate teen-ager, and whose emotional, often mawkish, style was often "borrowed" for the purpose of their class compositions. He also made a few attempts at writing traditional poetry, but soon dropped the rhyme and meter and tried his hand at free verse, apparently in the Mahjarite fashion. When he read Ṭāhā Ḥusayn's autobiographical novel *al-Ayyām*, he promptly responded by writing his own story in the same manner, giving it the title *al-Aʿwām*.[1] None of these juvenilia ever appeared in print.

His secondary school does not seem to have enhanced his literary education. He mentions no inspiring teachers; and although classical Arabic literature was taught there, the manner of presenting it in most Arabic schools was far from imaginative. The old poems were to be memorized and whatever prose was read, was dealt with in the traditional, uncritical manner. Neither did his school offer him a reasonable command of a foreign language such as English or French; thus his reading at this stage was confined to works written in, or translated into, Arabic.

Before finishing his secondary schooling he became acquainted with the works of modern Egyptian authors who were striving to introduce new ideas and methods into Arabic literature. The name of Ṭāhā Ḥusayn was mentioned above. This author was, in the late twenties, a symbol of revolt against conservatism in Arabic studies. His book, *Fil-shiʿr al-jāhilī*, which was published in 1926, was a bold challenge to the accepted norms and did not fail to arouse a hysterical reaction in Azharite circles.[2] On the other hand, it fired the imagination of a whole generation of young Egyptians by showing them the way to free themselves from medieval modes of thinking.

Maḥfūẓ was among those who were to be deeply impressed by *Fil-shiʿr al-jāhilī*. He mentions this work as the book that had the greatest influence on his intellectual development, and adds that, having read it in his youth, he always remained under its impact,

---

[1] Dawwāra, pp. 276-7.

[2] See Adams, pp. 253-9; Gibb, *Studies*, pp. 278-9; 312; Cachia, p. 60.

whether consciously or not.[1] To him the book is "an intellectual revolution which elevates reason, giving it priority above tradition."[2] Furthermore, this book, together with other works of Ṭāhā Ḥusayn on classical literature, brought home to Maḥfūẓ the deep values of Arabic literature and made him read anew the poetry of al-Ma'arrī,[3] al-Mutanabbī, Ibn al-Rūmī, and others. The philosophical poetry of al-Ma'arrī inspired him to write a "philosophic treatise" formulating his "philosophy of life, cosmos, and the Creator."[4]

Another writer whose works influenced Maḥfūẓ in these years was Salāma Mūsā. "From Salāma Mūsā" he says,[5] "I have learned to believe in science, socialism and tolerance." Salāma Mūsā could be held responsible for even more than that. Many of his major beliefs and interests were to become those of Maḥfūẓ as well. To mention a few : the extreme interest in the work of Darwin, Freud, Marx, Kant, and the writings of Tolstoy, Ibsen, Wells and Shaw; the preoccupation with Pharaonic Egypt. Maḥfūẓ was later to meet Salāma Mūsā and write for this magazine *al-Majalla al-jadīda*. (Their first meeting, is, to all intents and purposes, recorded by Maḥfūẓ in *al-Sukkariyya*, Chapter 13).[6]

Al-'Aqqād is also regarded by Maḥfūẓ as a source of inspiration. He acknowledges having acquired through him several values such as the glorification of the literary art and freedom of thought. Al-'Aqqād's enquiries into Arabic poetry helped Maḥfūẓ to develop a better understanding of it.[7]

Other writers to whom Maḥfūẓ pays homage are al-Ḥakīm, al-Māzinī, Ḥaqqī, and Taymūr. He sums up the over-all effect of the modern Egyptian writers on him as "emancipation from the traditional manner of thinking and from traditional taste".[8]

In the field of natural sciences (e.g. biology), he was able to read some of the more or less popular books, mostly those written or translated by the scientifically minded writers Ṣarrūf, Maẓhar, and Mūsā.[9]

---

1 Interview with al-Bannā. (*al-Adab*, July 1960) p. 236.

2 *Ibid.*

3 Ṭāhā Ḥusayn's first doctorate, submitted to the Egyptian University, was on al-Ma'arrī. It was published in 1915.

4 Dawwāra, p. 278.

5 Interview with Sarḥān (*al-Majalla*, Jan. 1963), p. 28.

6 See Shukrī, *al-Muntamī*, p. 41.

7 Dawwāra, p. 276; interview with Sarḥān (*al-Majalla*, Jan. 1963), p. 28.

8 *Ibid.*, p. 268.

9 *Ibid.*, p. 273.

When he was about eighteen, he was overcome by a severe religious crisis.[1] In *Qaṣr al-Shawq*, the second volume of the Trilogy, we witness Kamāl undergoing such a crisis at approximately the same age. Having been brought up in a strictly religious home, Kamāl is bewildered when he learns at school that some of the pious beliefs which he has inherited from his parents (mainly his mother) are purely superstitions. When he finds out, for example, that the so-called tomb of al-Ḥusayn, not far from their house, is "nothing more than a symbol," and that in fact the martyr's head is not buried there, he is so shocked that he bursts into tears.[2] His profound belief, however, withstood such upheavals, but was gradually reduced to the belief in God and Islam. Then came a blow which shook this belief and eventually transformed him into an atheist. On reading about *The Origin of Species* and on comparing Darwin's theories to the story of creation, as related in the Qur'ān, he finds it impossible to go on accepting the tenets of religion for "the Qur'ān must be entirely correct, or else it will not be the Qur'ān [i.e., God's Book] at all."[3]

We must assume that this part in the Trilogy represents to a large extent what happened to Maḥfūẓ himself, since he admitted on many occasions that Kamāl's crisis is his own.[4] It should be added that although he became a non-believer for a while, he never turned into an active atheist.

At about the same time—i.e., during his late secondary school years—he fell in love. On this matter Maḥfūẓ is particularly reticent, and it would be unwise to surmise how far 'Ā'ida Shaddād, the aristocratic girl we meet in the Trilogy, represents his first attachment. All that we know is that the real girl—like 'Ā'ida—lived in al-'Abbāsiyya, and that Maḥfūẓ was unable to marry her.[5] He was to remain a bachelor for many years.

Maḥfūẓ took an early interest in politics. He was born, it is to be remembered, eight years before the 1919 revolution, and throughout his boyhood and early manhood, Egypt was in political turmoil.

---

[1] Stewart, pp. 2-3.

[2] TR-II, p. 79.

[3] TR-II, p. 370.

[4] E.g., interview with Shūsha (*al-Ādāb*, [Beirut] June, 1960), p. 19; Stewart, p. 3, fn. 1.

[5] For more details (though inconclusive), see Ṣidqī, p. 123 : Khiḍr, pp. 185-6; Shukrī, *al-Muntamī*, p. 42.

It was unthinkable that an Egyptian boy of the middle-classes should not participate in the political struggle, and, for that matter, not sympathize with the Wafd.[1] Sa'd Zaghlūl was his ideal, and the day on which the old leader died (27 August, 1927) is recalled by Maḥfūẓ as one of the saddest days of his life.[2] On the whole, however, he stayed aloof from political entanglements.

In 1930 Maḥfūẓ finished his secondary schooling and entered the University of Cairo to study philosophy.[3] The University was a hive of political activity and all major political, religious, and social trends found followers among the students. The opening chapters of *al-Qāhira al-jadīda* offers us a reasonably vivid picture of the life and aspirations of these students. Admittedly none of the protagonists of this novel is a self-portrait, but the description of the intellectual development of the student 'Alī Ṭāhā (who, like Maḥfūẓ, was reading philosophy) impresses one as possibly reflecting some of Maḥfūẓ's adventures in the realms of philosophy.

'Alī Ṭāhā's religious belief was profoundly shaken at the inception of his University course. He soon found solace by reading Hegel, Ostwald and Mach, and accepting the materialistic interpretation of life and nature. A religious friend of his argued that materialistic philosophy was all too simple, but it did not offer a convincing explanation to *one* question (namely the metaphysical question). But 'Alī Ṭāhā would not bother with such a trifling matter. He was worried, nonetheless, by a different kind of problem : that of ethics. In the past, his morals were based on religion; what would now be their point of departure? For a while he wondered whether he should follow al-Ma'arrī's ascetic way of life; but surely that was no solution for a handsome and sociable man like himself? Finally he found his salvation through Auguste Comte. This philosopher brought him the message of a new God—Society, and a new religion—Science... At this point he could flatter himself by paraphrasing a line of al-Ma'arrī's poetry : "In the past I was a virtuous person by having religion without intellect (*'aql*); now I am a righteous person with intellect and without superstition".[4] Subsequently he became pre-

---

[1] Shukrī (*al-Muntamī*, p. 35) asserts that Maḥfūẓ joined the Wafd party as early as 1925, i.e., when he was less than fourteen years old; see also 'Abd al-Ḥayy, p. 129.

[2] See interview al-Bannā (*al-Adab* [Cairo] July, 1960), p. 236; Ṣidqī, p. 118; cf. TR-II, pp. 463-4.

[3] Shukrī, *al-Muntamī*, p. 30.

[4] QAH, p. 23 : كنت فاضلا بدين وبغير عقل ، وانا اليوم فاضل بعقل وبلا خرافة .

occupied with social reform, dreamed of a heaven-on-earth, and finally agitated for socialism of a militant brand. Thus "his spiritual journey which started in Mecca, finished in Moscow."[1]

Maḥfūẓ himself never became a militant Marxist. Nevertheless his attachment to socialism began as early as his freshman year. His very first article, published in October, 1930, suggests that the socialism would triumph over all other doctrines.[2] Maḥfūẓ's socialism, however, was much milder than that of 'Alī Ṭāhā, and there is no evidence that he ever believed in a socialism of a nature more militant than that of Salāma Mūsā, namely a Fabian-Utopian one.[3] Later he was to formulate a yet more individual, highly spiritual type of socialism.

While still an undergraduate, he started publishing articles on philosophical topics, mainly in *al-Majalla al-jadīda* and *al-Ma'rifa*.[4] It seems that the material for these articles was derived from the books that he read in his University courses. They were concerned with popularizing—in a rather uncommitted manner—some major trends in philosophy, psychology, sociology (e.g., on Pragmatism; the idea of God; psychology in ancient and modern times). The urge to publish goes back a few years, for he had already sent some of his early stories and articles to newspaper editors, but none of these was accepted.[5] Nevertheless he was often successful in having his name printed in newspapers by writing letters to columnists in the popular magazines, supporting or opposing their views. Often, Maḥfūẓ tells us, his name, when mentioned, was followed by some harsh words on the part of the columnists whom he had deliberately antagonised.[6] Salāma Mūsā, however, was the first editor to encourage him by publishing his articles.

---

1 QAH. p. 23: وانتهى المطاف بروحه — التى بدأت رحلتها من مكة — الى موسكو!

2 See Shukrī, *al-Muntamī*, p. 18.

3 It is remarkable that the names of Marx, Engels, Lenin, etc. are not mentioned among the thinkers who ushered 'Alī Ṭāhā into socialism; but that omission can be due to the author's wishing to be on the safe side, and not risk mentioning such awesome names (the novel, it is to be remembered, was first published in 1945 or 1946).

4 I have not been able to obtain the relevant numbers of these periodicals, and my information about Maḥfūẓ's articles in it is derived mainly from Shukrī, *al-Muntamī*, pp. 11, 46, 50-1.

5 Dawwāra, p. 278.

6 *Ibid.*, p. 279.

Maḥfūẓ also translated a book about ancient Egypt which was published in 1932.[1] In 1934 he graduated from the University, apparently with distinction, for he was accepted as a post-graduate student and set out to write an M.A. thesis on "Aesthetics" under Shaykh Muṣṭafā 'Abd al-Rāziq.[2] He also obtained a secretarial post in the University administration where he worked until 1938.[3] The choice of subject for his planned thesis indicated his natural bent towards everything artistic. He had earlier (during his third year in University) tried his hand at learning to play an Oriental string instrument, the *qānūn*,[4] assuming that by acquiring practical knowledge in music, he would have a more profound understanding of aesthetics. At the end of a year's training he discovered that, to use his own sardonic words, "there is no connection between learning to play the *qānūn* and aesthetics."[5] His main motivation for choosing the subject lies, however, in the fact his literary ambitions had never deserted him, and he thought of aesthetics as a field which linked together philosophy and literature.

In point of fact he was, on graduating, going through a tormenting experience, that of conflicting allegiances. His craving for a creative role in literature was poignant enough to mar his academic successes. The more advanced and specialized he became in his studies, the farther he was being torn from the realm of literature, and there came a point where he found himself, to use his own words, "plagued by a fearful struggle between literature and philosophy, a struggle which cannot be conceived of by anyone who has not experienced

---

1 "As the philosophy courses were mainly in French and English he was forced to work very hard. At his brother's suggestion he improved his English by translating into Arabic *Miṣr al-qadīma*." (Stewart, p. 3). This is a short, popular introductory guide written by James Baikie and originally published in the series "Peeps at Many Lands" under the title *Ancient Egypt* (London, 1912). I have not been able to see a copy of the Arabic translation, but see Faṭima Mūsā's article in *al-Kātib*, May 1968, pp. 72-4.

2 Dawwāra, p. 281.

3 'Abd al-Ḥayy, p. 132.

4 For a description of this instrument, see Lane, pp. 366-8. The choice of this "old fashioned" Oriental instrument as a means of studying such a sophisticated" Western" subject as aesthetics is significant. It is in keeping with Maḥfūẓ's well-known passion for everything which smacks of genuine local tradition.

5 Dawwāra, pp. 272-3. This short lived musical bout was not altogether a waste of time. Maḥfūẓ made good use of his knowledge of the elements of Arabic music in many of his novels, notably the Trilogy (e.g. TR-I, pp. 114-5).

it ... I had to make up my mind or else lose my senses."[1] Before long he cast his lot with literature and abandoned his graduate studies.[2]

Of the different genres of literature, he chose fiction. It has already been mentioned that he had tried his hand at writing short stories in his early youth. During his summer vacations from University, he continued to give outlet to his literary urges by writing stories, but found the journals and periodicals less interested in them than in his articles. Nevertheless he now settled on becoming a storyteller. It is remarkable that with his initial philosophical training he did not think of trying, for instance, literary criticism. Neither did he make further effort in the field of poetry (which is the "natural" starting point for so many Arab intellectuals). His single-mindedness and stubbornness against all odds are all the more impressive when one remembers that fiction had been regarded by certain sections of society as an inferior genre. And, as we have seen in the previous chapter, those influential writers who, in the thirties, wrote novels, did so only intermittently (with the exception of Taymūr). Maḥfūẓ's infatuation with fiction must have had its roots deep in his nature, an innate compulsion to tell a story.[3] His acquaintance with philosophy, psychology, and sociology, far from suppressing his passion for imaginative literature, has—it seems—made him aware of the versatility of the art of fiction.

A polemic article written by him in 1945 gives us a valuable clue as to what kind of theory of fiction he had formulated. Refuting al-ʿAqqād's strictures against the art of fiction, Maḥfūẓ maintains that artistic fiction (*al-qiṣṣa al-fanniyya*) means much more than a story; it embodies many human values such as "characterization and psychology; lyricism and humour; philosophical themes and social concepts."[4] Furthermore Maḥfūẓ regards the *qiṣṣa*[5] as the poetry of the modern age, "an age of science, industry, and facts which necessitate a new art, an art which is—as far as possible—a

---

[1] ʿAbd al-Ḥayy, p. 131.

[2] Dawwāra, p. 281.

[3] In TR-I the boy Kamāl is portrayed not only as obsessively fond of stories that he heard at home and school, but also as one inclined to—and capable of—inventing some astonishing stories, especially to impress his mother (see, e.g., TR-I, Chapters 9-10). Cf. Khiḍr, pp. 182-3.

[4] *al-Risāla*-(Cairo), vol. 13 (No. 635), pp. 952-4. The title of Maḥfūẓ's article is "al-Qiṣṣa ʿind al-ʿAqqād."

[5] This term means fiction in general, but it sometimes denotes (as is likely in this context) the novel (as opposed to *uqṣūṣa*, 'short story').

synthesis between modern man's passion for facts and his age-long attraction for imagination."[1]

This statement, written some years after his choice was made, is clearly intended to glorify fiction in "positivist" terms, but can also serve as an explanation of Maḥfūẓ's preference. He seems to have had developed a certain disillusionment with philosophy (i.e., speculative philosophy) and a great admiration "for science, technology, and facts". In the same article he argues that while in the past philosophy had concentrated on generalities, science had now shifted the interest to the details. But since Maḥfūẓ, is by training and inclination an artist, not a scientist, he dropped philosophy and took up the literary genre which is at once "detailed" and "modern".

Maḥfūẓ felt at this juncture that, in order to become a fully-fledged writer he had to know more about literature. He discovered that his knowledge of fiction was meagre and haphazard. What he now needed—as a prospective novelist—was to broaden his acquaintance with the history of fiction, and, above all, with its great masters. He was now in a better position to do so, partly because of his improved knowledge of English, a language offering an access to the many masterpieces which were not translated into Arabic, and partly thanks to his general ability, acquired through reading and personal maturity, to comprehend and enjoy the more complex novels.

He looked for a systematic guide and found it in Drinkwater's *The Outline of Literature.*[2] This book, Maḥfūẓ tells us, gave him a comprehensive outlook on world literature. Drinkwater discusses the literary scene according to period and not as literatures of different nations. "Thus," says Maḥfūẓ, "I found myself viewing world literature as an entirety, and not as works of different nations."[3]

In reading the masterpieces, Maḥfūẓ preferred to begin with the modern age (i.e., the late nineteenth and early twentieth century). He never concentrated on one author or school, but chose one or two works of each author, ostensibly the most "representative" ones.

---

[1] *Op. cit.*, p. 954: اما هذا العصر — عصر العلم والصناعة والحقائق ، فيحتاج حتما لفن جديد ، يوفق على قدر الطاقة بين شغف الانسان الحديث بالحقائق وحنانه القديم الى الخيال ... فالقصة على هذا الرأي هي شعر الدنيا الحديثة.

[2] Dawwāra, p. 265; Stewart, p. 11.

[3] *Ibid.*, pp. 269-70.

His readings at this period included, we are told,[1] such voluminous and demanding masterpieces as Joyce's *Ulysses*,[2] Proust's *À la recherche du temps perdu* (in its English translation). Other authors which Maḥfūẓ tells us he read during this formative stage are Tolstoy, Dostoyevsky, Turgenev, Chekhov, Anatole France, Flaubert, Malraux, Mauriac (later—Sartre, Camus, and others); Wells, Galsworthy, Shaw, Huxley, Lawrence; Mann, Goethe (and later—Kafka); Hemingway, Faulkner, Dos Passos, O'Neill (and later—Tennessee Williams, Arthur Miller); Ibsen, and Strindberg.

Among the novelists he lists as his favourites are Tolstoy, Dostoyevsky, Chekhov, Proust, Mann, Kafka and Joyce. Among the playwrights he names O'Neill, Shaw, Ibsen, Strindberg. Whilst these lists represent a variety of schools and tastes, it is to be remembered that not all of them were tackled at this formative period. Indeed the list included many a name that he could not have found in Drinkwater's book.[3] It would appear that the works which impressed him the most in the late thirties were mainly those of English and French writers, and, more precisely, such naturalistic and realistic novelists as Galsworthy, Bennett, Wells, and Huxley. (He also developed a liking for the plays of Ibsen, Shaw and Chekhov.)[4]

Having read the later masters of the realistic novel, he could not read, we are told, Dickens, since he represented an earlier stage of development.[5] Similarly having read Flaubert and Stendhal he could not read Balzac "the very creator of realism" whose copious descriptions Maḥfūẓ disliked.[6] Zola, surprisingly enough, is not regarded by Maḥfūẓ as one whose works have influenced his writing though, we are told, he read many of his novels.[7]

---

[1] For fuller lists of his reading and preferences in world literature, see Dawwāra, pp. 269-71; 272-5; interview with Shukrī, (*Ḥiwār*, Mar.-Apr. 1963), p. 70; Stewart, pp. 8-11. See also ʿAwaḍ, *Maqālāt* (1963), p. 373.

[2] He had also read Stuart Gilbert's interpretative work *James Joyce's Ulysses : a Study* (London, 1930; rev. ed. 1952).

[3] The 1930 edition of Drinkwater's *Guide* makes no mention of Joyce, Lawrence, Dos Passos, Mann, Kafka. Only the 1940 edition, edited and extended by H. Pollock and C. Naire introduces the works of these writers.

[4] Prose summaries of such plays were made by Maḥfūẓ and published around the year 1934, mainly in *al-Maʿrifa* (see *Rūz al-Yūsuf*, 1 April 1968, pp. 34-5).

[5] Dawwāra, p. 270.

[6] *Ibid.*

[7] Interview with Shūsha (al-Ādāb, June 1960, p. 20).

The short stories which he wrote at this period[1] (i.e., the nineteen-thirties) do not show much impact of the European Literature mentioned above. Far from reflecting such authors as Proust, Joyce, or Mann, they are more akin to the styles of Maupassant and, to a certain extent, Chekhov, or rather to that of their Egyptian disciples such as Taymūr and Ḥaqqī. In the twenty-eight stories collected in *Hams al-junūn*[2] we witness many characteristic features which are reminiscent of Taymūr's stories such as the fondness for psychologically disturbed men, and the attraction to the life of odd people, especially from the Cairene back streets.

It is beyond the scope of this work to discuss Maḥfūẓ's short stories. They are mentioned here because they represent a phase in his literary career. Furthermore some of the major themes and topics which we shall encounter in his novels are found in a rudimentary form in these early short stories. We shall, for instance, encounter the Pharaonic subject in three of these stories, but their "historicism" is marginal, and the historical framework is no more than a disguise under which is hidden a philosophical or social idea. In fact, one of the "Pharaonic" stories ("Yaqẓat al-mūmiyā'," pp. 82 ff.) can be regarded as the most blatant piece of social protest that Maḥfūẓ ever wrote (the same story, incidentally, also indicates the author's vision of the modern Egyptians as sons of the Pharaonic Egyptians in a fashion which calls to mind some of al-Ḥakīm's historical analogies in *'Awdāt al-rūḥ*).

Another theme which often occurs in these stories is that of the

---

[1] Maḥfūẓ tells us (Dawwāra, p. 279) that he had written—in this stage of his career—some eighty stories which he published, plus fifty which he destroyed. These stories were published mainly in al-Zayyāt's magazine *al-Riwāya* (where his first short story, "Thaman al-zawja" appeared, see Khiḍr, *al-Wāqi'iyya*, p. 187), but also in *al-Majalla al-jadīda*, *Majallatī*, and later in *al-Thaqāfa* and *al-Risāla*.

[2] The colophons give the date of the first publication of this book as 1938. If this is the case, some of the stories which appear in the recent editions could not have been included originally, and they must have been added in subsequent editions. In my copy (n.d.—presumably the 1963 printing) one story ("Badhlat al-asīr" pp. 156ff.) tells of incidents which relate to World War II. More surprising is the fact that at least two of the stories (including the title story) were published in *al-Risāla* in 1945 (see *al-Risāla*, vol. 13, pp. 178-80, 423-4 and 449-50). The first reference to HAMS which I could trace is in 1949, when it was published by *Lajnat al-nashr lil-jāmi'iyyīn* and reviewed by Gh.Ṭ. Farmān (see *al-Adīb*, Beirut, May 1949, pp. 49-50). There is no hint in that review or in any other that that was not the first edition of the HAMS; and see Appendix I.

formidable triangle—*time-change-death*.[1] This theme, which is later to constitute the backbone of the Trilogy and other novels, is manifest in many stories. The topic of sex—or rather the sexual behaviour and misbehaviour of men and women—also has prominence.[2]

Above all, the social theme is dominant in most of these stories. Maḥfūẓ's interest in the impoverished classes of Cairo is of a less detached and a more militant nature than that of Taymūr. The suffering of these people is portrayed with much passion and bitterness. On the other hand, the rich are, in most cases, portrayed unfavourably. They are, to judge by these stories, a set of immoral, indecent, and wicked people who are but a heavy burden on the Egyptian nation. None of Maḥfūẓ's wealthy heroes is, moreover, a round character. More often than not they are mere caricatures. Significantly, whenever there is, in a story, a confrontation between rich and poor, the point of view is always that of the poor.[3]

The year 1939 signifies a change for Maḥfūẓ both in employment and in literary career. In that year he joined the civil service as an official in the ministry of Waqfs, where he was to work for some fifteen years. It is this ministry, which is in charge of Islamic affairs, and Maḥfūẓ's work there must have made him conversant with many aspects of Muslim life and institutions. Furthermore in many of his novels[4] we are to meet the minor civil servant, and certain episodes in these novels actually take place in governmental departments. The new post, however, meant more working hours, a fact which resulted in a reduction in both literary output and reading.[5]

More important : in 1939, his first novel *'Abath al-aqdār* was published. This work, which inaugurated his series of historical novels, was published by Salāma Mūsā who, after rejecting three earlier attempts of Maḥfūẓ, decided that this story was worth publishing

---

[1] E.g. the stories, "Iṣlāḥ al-qubūr" (HAMS pp. 252ff.); Ḥayāt muharrij" (pp. 272ff.); "Ṣawṭ min al-'ālam al-ākhar" (pp. 304ff.).

[2] E.g., the stories "Thaman al-sa'āda" (pp. 192ff.); "Nakth al-umūma" (pp. 214ff.); "'Abath aristuqrāṭī" (pp. 282ff.).

[3] E.g., the stories "al-Thaman" (pp. 208ff.); "Muftaraq al-ṭuruq" (pp. 244ff.); "Filfil" (pp. 300ff.).

[4] KHAN (Aḥmad), SAR (Kāmil), THAR (Anīs) and others.

[5] See Maḥfūẓ's article "Tafarrugh al-udabā' "published in *al-Adab* (Cairo) Feb. 1959, pp. 662-5.

in full in a special number of *Majalla-al-jadīda.*[1] His other two Pharaonic novels were apparently written shortly after that date, but were not as lucky, for they had to wait for al-Saḥḥār to establish his publishing *Lajna*[2] and save them from oblivion. *Rādūbīs* was published in July, 1943 and *Kifāḥ Ṭība* in August, 1944. The latter novel was earlier submitted to the contest declared by the Fu'ād I Academy and was ranked third, winning Maḥfūẓ a prize of forty pounds.[3]

The events of World War II in Egypt and in the World deeply affected Maḥfūẓ's attitudes to life. His outlook became more pessimistic and the works which he produced during these years are among his most fatalistic and gloomy. The social polarization in Egyptian society; the decline of political parties; the raids on Cairo; the danger of a Nazi invasion (and still worse, the sympathy for the Nazis among many Egyptians, who thought of Hitler as a redeemer from the British yoke)[4] — all of these filled him with horror and dismay. He did not, however, turn into a political activist. Rather, he retreated into himself and refrained from taking the crucial step which makes a socially aware intellectual a revolutionary one. His friendship with 'Ādil Kāmil, which reached its peak in these years, was unable to save Maḥfūẓ from his melancholy. If anything it aggravated it, since Kāmil, as his works indicate, is no less of a pessimist and introvert. Kāmil's works, furthermore, reveal a sardonic nature and a marked bent towards spiritual anarchism. The two, together with Aḥmad Zakī Makhlūf, used to spend their evenings together discussing life and literature.[5] These discussions, Maḥfūẓ tells us, were laden with all embracing pessimism. They used to call the lawn area by the Jalā' Bridge, where they frequently sat, "the ominous circle" (al-dā'ira al-mash'ūma).[6] They had many doubts as to the value and usefulness of their literary endeavours and often wondered if they would not be more beneficial to their countrymen if they would do "something positive" instead of dabbling in useless emotions and ideas.[7]

---

1 Dawwāra, pp. 276, 279; interview with al-Sharīf (al-Ādāb [Beirut], Mar. 1967), p. 27; 'Abd al-Ḥayy, p. 131.

2 See *supra*, pp. 24-5.

3 This is not an unimpressive sum. The monthly salary of a great many civil servants at the time averaged ten to fifteen pounds.

4 Such views are reflected in KHAN, Chapters 6, 8, 12; TR-III, Chapters 28, 43.

5 Dawwāra, p. 289.

6 *Ibid.*, p. 290.

7 *Ibid.*, p. 289.

Kāmil and Maḥfūẓ were of the same generation (Maḥfūẓ being four years older.) They were both dedicated to fiction and both shared the same socialistic views of the Salāma Mūsā brand. The two were interested in Pharaonic history and unlike their friends Bākathīr or al-Saḥḥār were unattentive to the Arabic or Islamic past. They both wrote Pharaonic novels, but later shifted to the contemporary scene. Their successes in the novel contest of 1943 (to which each submitted a historical novel) must have heartened them, and prompted them to try their luck again, when a second contest was announced (1943 ?). Maḥfūẓ submitted his novel *al-Sarāb* and Kāmil his *Millīm al-akbar*. But a bitter disappointment was awaiting them this time. Their novels were rejected. Furthermore they were summoned to the Academy's bureau and reproached, apparently for "lax morals"[1] (and possibly for their 'untidy' language).[2] The secretary asked them to revise their novels and re-submit them. The two young writers were grossly offended at being treated in such a contemptuous manner. They decided to publish their novels, together with introductions in which they would explain their views of the art of fiction. Kāmil's novel-cum-introduction appeared in November 1944, while Maḥfūẓ's book was detained, for one reason or another, until 1948. Maḥfūẓ's promised introduction to the novel was never published.

Kāmil stopped writing, and published nothing after *Millīm al-akbar*. Maḥfūẓ however, was more persistent, and continued writing with unabated zeal. He refused to give in to despair, he tells us, because he never expected anything in return. He worked on, not in the hope of catching anyone's attention, bearing in mind that he might pass unnoticed, possibly forever.[3]

He has now deserted the field of historical fiction (he had originally planned to write thirty or forty novels, portraying the "entire" historical scene in a manner similar to that of Sir Walter Scott)[4] and shifted his interest completely to the contemporary scene. In 1945, he published the first of the series of his Cairo novels, *Khān al-Khalīlī*.

---

[1] Dawwāra, p. 289; Kāmil's *Millīm* (introd.) pp. 7 (fn. 1), 104, 128. Both novels have some facets which might have looked distasteful to squeamish Academicians. Maḥfūẓ's story deals with the sexual imbalance of a spoilt young man, while Kāmil's book is populated with a host of eccentrics and vagabonds.

[2] Kāmil's massive introduction to his novel is essentially a reply to the demand for a more formal Arabic.

[3] Dawwāra, p. 280.

[4] *Ibid*, p. 283; interview with Shukrī, (*Ḥiwār*, Mar.-Apr. 1963), p. 67.

In the following two years he came out with two more novels, *al-Qāhira al-jadīda*, and *Zuqāq al-Midaqq*.[1]

These three novels were received quite favourably in Egypt by a few reviewers of some standing. Sayyid Quṭb, then a rising critic and Koranic scholar, whose interest in Maḥfūẓ began with *Kifāḥ Ṭība*,[2] was now so impressed by the first two Cairo novels of Maḥfūẓ that he described them as the "starting point of Modern Arabic fiction,"[3] and rebuked Egyptian literary critics for not taking sufficient notice of their author. He compared Maḥfūẓ's work in the field of fiction to that of al-Ḥakīm in drama, and expressed dismay that while the dramatist was lucky enough to be adopted and promoted from the outset by Ṭāhā Ḥusayn, nothing of the sort happened to the novelist.[4]

Another admirer was Anwar al-Ma'addāwī, a respected journalist and critic, who was especially impressed by the Cairene novels, and described one of them, *Bidāya wa-nihāya*, as "a perfect work of art."[5]

No less encouraging was the welcome given to them by readers and critics in other Arab countries, especially in Lebanon and Iraq. These works received, says Maḥfūẓ, five times as many reviews in other Arab countries as in Egypt itself.[6] In general, however, they did not arouse enthusiasm and the literary world was not to acclaim them as milestones in Arabic fiction for a dozen years. The next two novels to be published, *al-Sarāb* and *Bidāya wa-nihāya* (1949, 1951 respectively)[7] did not change the situation and, if anything, they attracted even less attention than their predecessors.

Between the years 1951-56, Maḥfūẓ published no new works. His readers must have felt that he had stopped writing. The truth, however, is that in 1952 he finished writing his lengthiest and by far his most important work, namely the Trilogy. this 300.000 word novel was

---

[1] For the publishing dates of these novels - see Appendix I.

[2] *al-Risāla*, Oct. 2, 1944, pp. 889-92.

[3] *Ibid.*, Dec. 30, 1946 (rev. of QAH), p. 1140.

[4] *Ibid.*

[5] *al-Risāla*, July 2, 1951, p. 257. Maḥfūẓ often mentions with gratitude and reverence the names of Quṭb and Ma'addāwī—now both dead—thanks to whom he, to use his own words, "came out from darkness into light." He is all the more touched by their encouraging comments because neither of them knew Maḥfūẓ personally when writing their articles. See Dawwāra, p. 280; interview with Shukrī (*Ḥiwār*, Mar.-Apr. 1963) p. 70; interview with Sarḥan (*al-Majalla*, Jan. 1963), p. 28.

[6] Dawwāra, p. 280.

[7] See Appendix I.

an attempt to recreate the world of middle-class Cairo in three successive generations, roughly between the end of World War I and the end of World War II. This undertaking, unprecedented in Arabic literature, was accomplished in Maḥfūẓ's spare time, after office hours. Although a great proportion of the material comes from Maḥfūẓ's own memories, it certainly demanded some serious research to arrange the historical facts, dates, people and events. It seems that he spent at least a year on preliminary research and some six years in writing.[1] These years included, however, many interruptions, for Maḥfūẓ often had to go out on inspection for the Ministry of Waqfs.[2] Furthermore he suffered from an eye and skin affliction which allowed him to write only between the months of September and April every year.[3] On finishing the Trilogy, he once again was faced with the problem of finding a publisher for this voluminous book. It was not until 1956 that the first volume (*Bayn al-Qaṣrayn*) appeared on the book stalls. The second and third volumes (*Qaṣr al-Shawq* and *al-Sukkariyya*) were published in 1957.

The years following the publication of this work must have been among Maḥfūẓ's happiest. The Trilogy proved to be an instant success and critics all over the Arab world acclaimed it as the novel of the generation. In 1957 it brought him the state prize for literature. The three volumes, as well as the earlier works, soon went into several new printings.

His private life, also witnessed an important change. He married and became a father. He had also changed his occupation : at last he was given a job in the Department of Art which bears some affinity to his field of interest. In the last decade or so he was, first, head of the State Cinema Organization,[4] and then the advisor to the Minister of Culture.

The few years that elapsed between the completion of the Trilogy and its publication (roughly 1952-1957) marked, however, a severe personal crisis for Maḥfūẓ. In these years he refrained from creativity, and thought that he would write no more. He explains this pause

---

[1] According to Shukrī, *al-Muntamī*, p. 346, the preparatory work was done by Maḥfūẓ between Sept. 1945 and April 1946. The actual writing of the Trilogy stretched between the years 1946-1952.

[2] *Ibid.*

[3] *Ibid.*

[4] Le Gassik (*M.E. Journal*, 1967, No. 3, p. 145f); interview 'A.-al-Sharīf (*al-Ādāb* [Beirut], Mar. 1967), pp. 26-9.

by the fact that the Trilogy was completed a short time before the 1952 revolution, and, with the advent of that revolution, he no longer felt inclined to criticize the old society[1] (a criticism which, truly enough, constitutes the core of his realistic novels). "I felt," he tells us, "as though I now found an answer to an insistent question : 'What is the meaning of our life, and how ought we to employ it?' a question which lies behind every work of art whether overtly or covertly."[2] In other words we are called upon to believe that Maḥfūẓ instantly regarded the officers' *coup d'état* as a radical change in the Egyptian society; and furthermore, that he believed that the whole Egyptian social structure which had existed up to the *coup* had now disappeared. Such an explanation can hardly be accepted at its face value. The 1952 revolution was in its initial stages a predominantly political one. Its metamorphosis into a movement of social reform took some time to crystallize, and its adoption of radical slogans became dominant only a few years later. It is to be remembered, too, that most liberal and left-wing intellectuals could hardly be said to have applauded the *coup* from the outset.[3] Their joy at the fall of the hated monarchy was marred by the oppressive measures against all political organisations (including those of the left), and many of those intellectuals resorted to silent protest.[4]

What is even less conceivable is that Maḥfūẓ, well versed as he is in socialist thought, could believe that the whole society of the past (*al-mujtamaʿ al-qadīm*—not the *ancien régime* alone) could be erased or transformed in a trice. Lastly, Maḥfūẓ's novels and short stories up to that date, did not pivot solely around social injustice (*al-Sarāb*, for instance, can hardly be described as a sociological novel; the same applies to the Pharaonic ones), and being the per-

---

[1] Dawwāra, p. 283 : اذ حينما ذهب المجتمع القديم ذهبت معه كل رغبة في نفسي لنقده وظننت أنني انتهيت اديبا ، ولم يعد لدي ما أقوله أو اكتبه.

[2] Ṣabrī Ḥāfiẓ, "Waḍʿ al-funūn al-adabiyya al-rāhina," *al-Majalla*, 103 (June, 1965), p. 96 : وكأنما وجدت جوابا على سؤال ملح وهو : « ما معنى حياتنا وماذا نصنع بها؟ » وهو سؤال يكمن وراء كل عمل فني سواء على السطح اوفي الاعماق.

[3] See Abdel-Malek, *Egypte*, pp. 191ff; P. Mansfield, *Nasser's Egypt*, London (Penguin) 1965, pp. 211-12.

[4] Ghalī Shukrī, a young Egyptian critic, in an article in his book, *Thawrat al-fikr* (1965), p. 215, explaines Maḥfūẓ's silence to precisely such an attitude, describing him as the "vanguard of the silent battalion".

tinacious artist that he is, he could have resorted to general humanistic, psychological or historical-nationalistic themes.

It could be that this silence was due to other, more technical, reasons, or to a combination of such reasons. One explanation can rest on the fact that the period of silence followed several years of most exhausting work on the Trilogy, and having finished it, the author felt in need of a period of rest, in which he could read, find a publisher, prepare the manuscript for printing, etc. He might well have felt that he had had enough of the detailed naturalistic approach to his subject and enough of the extensive style (the third book of the Trilogy, foreshadows some important changes in style which are to dominate his works of the sixties), and thus searched for a new departure in technique.[1]

There is, however, a different explanation which emerges from his novels themselves (both before and after the pause), and which points in a different direction: that of a spiritual-metaphysical crisis.

As we have seen, Maḥfūẓ had believed in science and society, and embraced the novel because, among other things, he found it to be the adequate artistic form for the era of science. Kamāl, the protagonist of the Trilogy, develops in the second volume, *Qaṣr al-Shawq*, along somewhat similar lines. He comes to believe that "science is the real religion" and that it is "the key to the secrets and splendours of the Universe."[2] But a few years later, in *al-Sukkariyya*, his enthusiasm subsides and many doubts creep into his mind. In his thirties he questions the universal validity of scientific solutions,[3] but having lost his religious beliefs he feels absolutely distraught. There is no way back to belief, hard as his endeavour may be. The "sceptical disease" proves to be pervasive.

The representatives of the next generation of Kamāl's family are saved from such doubts by becoming immersed in political activity (one nephew becoming a Communist, the other a Muslim Brother). Kamāl, being basically inclined towards socialism (of a non-violent kind, that is) grows, towards the end of the novel, more attentive

---

[1] See al-Shārūnī, *Dirāsāt fil-adab*, p. 95; ʿAbd al-Ḥayy, p. 127.

[2] TR-II, p. 375.

[3] TR-III, p. 125: انه [العلم] دنيا مغلقة حيالنا لا نعرف الا بعض نتائجها القريبة؛ ثم اطلعت على آراء نخبة من العلماء يرتابون في مطابقة الحقيقة العلمية للحقيقة الواقعية وآخرين ينوّهون بقانون الاحتمال ، وغيرهم ممن تراجعوا عن ادعاء الحقيقة المطلقة ، فلم البث ان حركت رأسي مرتابا.

towards his Communist nephew, Aḥmad. The simultaneous arrest of both nephews renders him more militant, and his thinking undergoes an impressive change. He now accepts Aḥmad's argument that "man's universal duty is eternal revolution,"[1] and himself concludes that "mysticism is escapism, and so is the passive belief in science. Action is essential."[2]

Whether or not Kamāl provides an accurate portrait of Maḥfūẓ, it is clear that in the Trilogy the author's sympathies rest with the radical leftist solution, and that his more sceptical, morose mood is on the decline. One is tempted to conjecture that the subsequent works of such a writer would reflect more vividly this change of heart and portray "action" and "eternal revolution."

The change, however, did not actually take place. Instead there came that period of silence in the fifties, and when finally he came to the fore in 1959, he had become a different type of writer. Both in style and substance he took a rather unpredictable course. His works, especially *Awlād ḥāratinā,* formulate in quite articulate strokes a new view of life.

Awlād ḥāratinā is an allegorical novel, which portrays, as it were, the social and spiritual history of man from Adam to our days. Jabalāwī, who stands for the Creator, had retreated to his secluded mansion, making no effort to save posterity from cruel rulers, poverty and misery. A succession of rebels or prophets who come forth to rescue their oppressed peoples are always defeated by the rulers, either through outright destruction or by being turned into part of the bullying establishment. Finally a new prophet emerges, the scientist (referred to as a magician) who on attempting to uncover the ultimate secret (*sirr al-kitāb*) causes the death of the old Jabalāwī. Nevertheless, he not only fails to discover the secret, but also supplies the rulers with a destructive chemical weapon, and is in the end killed by those rulers.

'Arafa, the magician, who had believed passionately that his magic was worth more than anything that Jabalāwī had,[3] now understands that his inadvertent annihilation of that illustrious forefather was a great tragedy for all the people of the *Ḥāra.* Jabalāwī, he now perceives, was an indispensable symbol for the people, and his death

---

[1] TR-III, p. 392 : أما الواجب الانساني العام فهو الثورة الابدية

[2] TR-III, p. 391 : فالتصوف هروب ، كما أنّ الايمان السلبي بالعلم هروب

[3] AWL, p. 498.

leaves their lives barren and meaningless. So much so, in fact, that he decides to utilize all his magic in the hope of reviving Jabalāwī.[1] Furthermore he strives to liberate the people of the *Ḥāra* from their oppressors and exploiters, thus giving them every opportunity to become magicians like him, producing indescribable marvels. Although ʿArafa is, towards the end of the novel, destroyed by these oppressors, the story does not end with sheer pessimism, for the people of the *Ḥāra* are still awaiting the magician's surviving brother to come and save them.

If we accept this work as an artistic formulation of its author's thinking[2] we can conclude that a new philosophy had crystallized between the years 1952-1957. The main tenets of this world view is that science, which had killed God, did not offer a better alternative. Therefore belief in a mystical, supernatural power is essential. Such a belief can be obtained by self-purgation, love, and knowledge. But these goals are practically unobtainable for the individual in the present pattern of society (which of necessity involves exploitation, greed, misery, all of which render the human soul impure). There is a need for a new order, free from exploitation, whereby human relations will be based on love and mutual help. Only then can men aspire towards God. Furthermore, if all human energies are liberated from the yoke of evil social systems and steered towards scientific enquiry, the great secrets of nature and existence might one day be uncovered, and death suppressed.[3]

Maḥfūẓ describes the way of life that he aspires to as Ṣūfī-socialism.[4] What is remarkable about such philosophy is that it contradicts the general trend in Egypt. For just as the country as a whole is concentrating on scientific development, technology, socialism, and while certain writers who had been loudest in identifying themselves with the old society now pay as unreserved a homage to socialism, Maḥfūẓ, an old socialist and believer in science, had resorted to a

---

1 AWL, p. 503.

2 Maḥfūẓ himself refers to AWL as reflecting his thinking about the crisis of our era. See his article in *al-Kātib*, 35 (Feb. 1964) pp. 18-24, especially p. 21 : ... اولاد حارتنا
... في الواقع كانت صدى للتفكير في ازمة العصر الحديث

3 This delineation of Maḥfūẓ's new philosophic thinking is based mainly on AWL, but also on Maḥfūẓ's own formulations, such as those quoted by Ziyāda, *al-Ādāb*, Mar. 1962, p. 72; and al-Kharrāṭ, *al-Majalla*, Jan. 1963, p. 18; also in his own interview with Shukrī (*Ḥiwār*, Mar.-Apr. 1963), p. 74.

4 "Al-ṣūfiyya al-ishtirākiyya," al-Kharrāṭ, *op. cit.*; *al-Jumhūriyya*, Jan. 3, 1960.

highly introspective, mystical mood. Admittedly, neither did he not drop the word "socialism" from his vocabulary, nor did his respect for science disappear; but what is *new* is his increasing stress on metaphysical and spiritual moments, as *Awlād ḥāratinā* and the later novels confirm. Maḥfūẓ, to he sure, was always interested in problems of spirit, even in his earliest and most realistic works; but while in these early stories the spiritual questions were on the periphery, they have now occupied the centre of his world.[1]

Awlād Ḥāratinā was serialized in the daily newspaper *al-Ahrām* in the last months of 1959. It instantly aroused waves of welcoming interest on the one side and hostility on the other. Some Azharite quarters were lashed into fury. Their outcry was mainly directed against the "godlessness" of this work; more precisely against the profane portrait of the Prophet, the death of Jabalāwī, and the many deviations from the Koranic story. The same circles, who three decades earlier did their utmost to intimidate Ṭāhā Ḥusayn and 'Alī 'Abd al-Rāziq, for expressing non-conformist views, now tried to suppress a work of fiction. Some of them demanded that Maḥfūẓ be brought to trial. Friday sermons were used to arouse hostility against him.[2] But while in the twenties the obscurantist reaction indicated conservatism and intolerance, the case of Maḥfūẓ it showed besides all that, a total misinterpretation of the work, and a narrow-mindedness which clung to petty points and refused to be attentive to the central theme of the story (which is not anti-religious at all).[3]

Eventually a compromise of a kind was reached. The attacks came to a halt, thanks to intervention from above. On the other hand, the novel never came out in book form in Egypt.[4]

---

[1] In his article "Qirā'a jadīda li-Najīb Maḥfūẓ" (*al-Kātib*, Nov. 1965, pp. 55ff., esp. p. 61f.) the critic Aḥmad 'Abbās Ṣāliḥ obliquely implies that Maḥfūẓ was among those socialists whose belief was severely shaken by the revelations about the Stalin era. This is an important clue, since Khrushchev's famous speech falls in the period between TR and AWL. It is to be remembered that Mr. Ṣāliḥ, a prominent Leftist himself, has been for many years one of Maḥfūẓ's closest friends (see interview 'A. al-Sharīf, *al-Ādāb*, Mar. 1967, pp. 26ff).

[2] Stewart, p, 83.

[3] Aḥmad 'Abbās Ṣāliḥ, in his extensive critique of Maḥfūẓ's recent metaphysical attitude (*al-Kātib*, Nov., Dec. 1965; Feb., April, 1966), draws attention to the affinity of the philosophy emerging from AWL, (namely that there is no antagonism between science and religion), to that of medieval Islamic philosophers, such as Ibn Rushd.

[4] In 1967 the book was at long last published in Lebanon (Dār al-Ādāb, Beirut).

Characteristically enough, Maḥfūẓ refrained from taking part in the controversy around his work, and left it to his many friends to defend him. He accepted the blow with apparent calm, and was soon publishing variations on similar themes, mainly in the short stories which he resumed writing. These were first published in the same paper, *al-Ahrām,* and later collected into two books *Dunyā Allāh* (1963) and *Bayt sayyi' al-sum'a* (1965).[1]

These stories inaugurate a new style of writing which is to dominate the author's work ever since, a style which might be called symbolic or double-layered. The plots are not outright allegories. They are plausible in all their details. On the other hand, they embrace a more sophisticated theme, one that is not comprehensible at first sight. Many people or events have a significance that transcends the bare statement of experience. The language itself changes and becomes allusive and lyrical with unmistakably esoteric undertones.

One of these stories, "Za'balāwī,"[2] which was published in 1961, adequately represents this new thematical trend (man's search for God, after science has failed to quench his metaphysical doubt), as well as the evocative style.[3] Furthermore it contains a clear insinuation that the religious establishment has lost contact with God, that only the artist or ascetic can still communicate with Him. The phonetic similarity between "Za'balāwī" and "Jabalāwī" has not been lost upon Maḥfūẓ's readers; neither was his delicate, but devastating, counter-attack upon fossilized religious institutions.[4]

The novels and short stories of the sixties imply a further drift from the belief in science, a belief which still was powerful in *Awlād Ḥāratinā.* It looks as if the "spiritualisation" which started gaining impetus in the fifties did not reach its limit with the appearance of that allegorical novel. It was followed by a yet greater interest in the mystical experience. Most of the works that Maḥfūẓ wrote in recent years have at their centres Ṣūfī or semi-Ṣūfī people,[5]

---

[1] In subsequent years he was to publish four new collections of short stories, for which see Postscript.

[2] DUN, pp. 158-175. An English translation of "Za'balāwī" can be found in Denys Johnson-Davies' *Modern Arabic Short Stories,* O.U.P., London, 1967, pp. 137-47.

[3] See 'Abd al-Ṣabūr, *Ḥattā* pp. 215-18; S. Somekh in *JAL,* Vol. I (1970), pp. 24-35.

[4] Cf. *al-Adab* (Cairo), July 1961, p. 241-2.

[5] Cf. LISS, SUM, SHAH, THAR. Admittedly, Ṣūfī characters (e.g., Shaykh Rudwān al-Ḥusaynī in ZUQ) appear in earlier novels, but their Ṣūfism was normative, not "metaphysical." They are rather extraordinarily pious people who devote their thoughts

and the search itself becomes a dominant and ever-recurring theme.[1]

Between the years 1961-1966, five more novels of Maḥfūẓ were published : *al-Liṣṣ wal-kilāb* (1961); *al-Summān wal-kharīf* (1962); *al-Ṭarīq* (1964); *al-Shaḥḥādh* (1965); *Tharthara fawq al-Nīl* (1966).[2] These novels are all very short when compared not only with the the Trilogy, but also with its predecessors. Their characters and techniques will be dealt with in a subsequent chapter, but it can be said now that the influence of twentieth century fiction is evident. The "spatial form", the "flux" and the "stream of consciousness," are all here (though in a rather unobtrusive manner). Their lyricism is so tangible that it would not be far-fetched to suggest a direct connection between the change in world outlook and change in style. For, as in the pre-Trilogy period, when the belief in science initiated, as we have seen, the concept of a detailed, naturalistic story, so now the flair for mysticism necessitated the language of poetry : symbol, connotation, ambiguity, economy, and rhythm.

His output now averages a novel or a volume of short stories a year. These works are first serialized in *al-Ahrām* and shortly afterwards appear in book form. Each new work calls forth a wave of acclaim, and every respectable paper and periodical in Egypt gives it large coverage and at least one review. No less warm is the attitude in other Arab countries. Some of Maḥfūẓ's works have also received homage from European and American scholars.[3] One novel, *Zuqāq al-Midaqq*, has been published in an English translation[4], and a few into other languages.[5] It can be assumed that interest in Maḥfūẓ in

---

and deeds to the teachings of Muhammad. Furthermore, none of them occupied a central position in the story.

[1] Cf. TARIQ.

[2] In 1967 yet another novel—*Mīrāmār*—came out; see Postscript.

[3] An impressive treatment of Maḥfūẓ's fiction was written by Père J. Jomier and published in *MIDEO* (Cairo) IV, 1957, pp. 27-94. It comprises a detailed analysis of the Trilogy. AWL was also analysed at length by the Dutch orientalist, L.O. Schuman, in his inaugural lecture *Een moderne arabische Vertelling*, which was published as an independent booklet by Brill, Leiden, 1965.

[4] *Midaq Alley, Cairo,* translated and introduced by Trevor LeGassick, Beirut (Khayyāṭ), 1966.

[5] A few of his works were translated into French, Russian and Eastern European languages. Two novels were translated into Hebrew and published in Israel (ZUQ, trans. Isaac Schreiber, Tel-Aviv, 1969; and LISS trans. Menahem Kapeliuk, Tel-Aviv, 1970); also a great number of his short stories were translated into Hebrew.

the West will grow wider, and it is hoped that more of his novels will be translated.

At sixty, the most respected Egyptian novelist is still unable to make a living solely from writing, and has to carry on with his duties as a public servant [1]. Moreover, his official engagements have not diminished. The reverse is true. He had been given a more responsible position in the Ministry of Culture, entailing further involvement and initiative. He also wrote, a few years ago, some film scripts.[2] In the evenings, however, he sits down in his study and writes for an hour or two, then reads for a while. He has not given up the hope of liberating himself from the shackles of extra-literary occupations. In 1963 a journalist asked him whether he did not think of occupying himself exclusively with writing. Maḥfūẓ's answer was "I think of nothing else."[3] The persistence, then, which sustained him in his days of anonymity is still keeping him going in times when his name has become synonymous with the Egyptian novel.

---

[1] In the year 1972 Maḥfūẓ was supposed to retire after 33 years in the civil service.

[2] See Jomier in MIDEO VII (1962-1963), pp. 132ff; 'A. al-Sharīf (*al-Ādāb* [Beirut], Mar. 1967) pp. 26-9.

[3] لا أفكر الا في التفرّغ (interview Sarḥān, *al-Majalla*, Jan. 1953, p. 28).

CHAPTER THREE

EGYPT, OLD AND NEW

A. The Historical Novels

Maḥfūẓ's début in the field of the novel can hardly be regarded as a great literary event in itself. His first novels, the Pharaonic ones, though important in the context of contemporary Egyptian fiction, are amongst the author's least original. They lack both the accurate hand of a craftsman and the touch of a genuine artist. Admittedly, one would not demand virtuosity or artistic perfection from a beginner. Nevertheless in the case of a great number of artists, their early works impressed their readers as "an event" from the outset, or at least foreshadowed a fresh literary style and "vision". Maḥfūẓ's first novels do not strike us as such.

Maḥfūẓ was, for one thing, ill-equipped to write historical novels. His knowledge of ancient Egypt was fragmentary and his acquaintance with the western historical novel was slight.[1] Thus one is not surprised to discover that the outcome is nothing but a romantic reflection of the national past, full of marvellous occurences and stock characters. What these novels lack, to borrow G. Lukacs' words, is "precisely the specifically historical, that is, derivation of the individuality of characters from the historical peculiarity of their age."[2]

Furthermore these novels betray a meagre individual style and tone. True, many of the themes and ideas which are to become essential components of Maḥfūẓ's mature art are discernible in these early works (e.g., Fate, Death, social injustice, patriotic passion), but at this stage they are handled with little originality.

These qualifications apply to all three novels, but are especially true of *'Abaṯh al-aqdār* (hereafter cited as ABA), and *Kifāḥ Ṭība* (KIF), which are to my mind of a lesser order than *Rādūbīs* (RAD). The stress in these two novels is on the externalized action. They

---

[1] He tells us on one occasion that before engaging in historical fiction he had read novels of Sir Henry Rider Haggard drawing on Egyptian history. He also mentions Scott's *Kenilworth* and Michel Zévaco's popular novels (interview with S͟hukrī, *Ḥiwār*, 3, Mar.-Apr. 1963, p. 66).

[2] *The Historical Novel*, p. 15.

are crowded with detailed battles, breathtaking adventures and heroism. They have, it must be admitted, a certain thematic content (ABA—the invincibility of Fate; KIF—the patriotic passion). But these themes are rather naïve and all too transparent (the last chapter of ABA, for instance, is in a way a recapitulation of the main idea of the story : the dying Pharaoh admits that one should not defy Fate). The time span is long (ABA—twenty years or so; KIF—about thirteen); the action embraces the land of Egypt and the neighbouring countries; the characters are numerous (especially in KIF). Thus no room is left for adequate characterization, and the plot lacks focus. The situations are very often general, not particular (e.g., the conflict of duty versus love, cf. ABA chapter 32; KIF, pp. 239ff.). The love affairs are not necessarily an integral part of the story (especially in KIF). The hero is all kindness, but relentless on the battlefield. The story (especially in ABA) is based on a series of coincidences so frequent and so haphazard that they call to mind the techniques of the *Arabian Nights*.[1] Finally these novels are not free from historical and geographical inaccuracies[2] or anachronisms.[3]

It would not be fair, however, to deny these novels some merit. They form an ambitious effort to give a panoramic view of ancient Egypt with clear reference to the contemporary scene, adhering as far as possible to the cold historical facts, yet furnishing an imaginative framework. The allusions to the continuity of the Egyptian character and aspirations are neatly interwoven into the fabric of the narrative.

---

[1] In ABA, for instance, it happens that Pharaoh invites the fortune-teller on the day on which Dadaf is born. Furthermore that very day a child is born to the housemaid in the home of the priest (Dadaf's father), and it is this infant that is killed instead of Dadaf. Similarly, Pharaoh's party rescues Dadaf and Zāyā in the desert. Throughout his career, Dadaf is always lucky enough to be in the right place and at the right moment to rescue the Prince, King, etc. When he wins the battle of the desert, he brings back with his other captives his own mother of whom he knew nothing. Later Bishārū, his stepfather, arrives in the court at the right moment (Ch. 35), to make Pharaoh aware of the tricks of destiny. Admittedly, the very theme of the novel is "The Mockery of Fate," but the coincidences are too plentiful to be justified even in that context.

In KIF, too, the technique of the *deus ex machina* is employed injudiciously (e.g., pp. 134-6 : the Princess appears out of the blue to rescue Ahmose from sure death; later, pp. 201-2, he, in his turn, rescues the Princess from death.)

[2] Ahmose, the hero of KIF is thought to be Kāmose's brother, not his son as in the novel (cf., Gardiner, p. 73); the city of Ombos is, in fact, located to the north of Thebes, not, as in the novel, to the south (KIF, p. 156).

[3] The ancient Egyptian language is not alphabetical. Thus the Pyramid clerk could not have looked up the letter K (Kāf), as in ABA, p. 63.

The patriotic theme is introduced in an intelligent and calm way.

As opposed to these "thematic" novels, RAD is less straightforward, dealing with individual human beings rather than a period or an idea. It reveals a richer grasp of human emotions, and an ability to penetrate beyond superficial human appearances. Furthermore, this novel represents a mood and key more akin to that of the real Maḥfūẓ as he is to emerge : not heroic-flamboyant, but tragic-elegiac. The language is less rhetorical and assertive. True, both the themes of Fate and Patriotism are present in RAD as well, but they no longer occupy a central position. They are, rather, two of many components of which *love* is the most prominent.

What makes this novel more successful is the density of its structure, its intensity and concentration. The time-span is short (one year), the scene is narrow (one city) and the number of characters is kept to a minimum. They are more true-to-life : we no longer encounter mere puppets or supermen, and there is an attempt to develop genuine people whose inner selves are revealed to us through action.

We are told[1] that the character of Pharaoh Merenre' stands for King Farouk, and that the whole book is in fact, a covert criticism of the latter's corrupt regime. If this is the case we can only admire the more Maḥfūẓ's achievement as far as characterization is concerned; for he has not fallen into the trap of presenting a two dimensional character who is an outright wicked man (or, as in the case of the Hyksos King in KIF, a combination of nine parts wickedness and one part goodness). Merenre' is, in fact, not really bad at all. He is in the main a spoiled young man who cannot resist the call of his youth, but is by no means malicious or diabolical. At times he can even be truly pious.[2] He is not lacking in personality or courage and when in the last scene he strides unarmed to meet the rebellious throng, he appears superior to his foes and attracts our sympathy by contrast with the hysterical rabble.

Neither is Rādūbīs, with whom Pharaoh is infatuated, a detestable character. Admittedly this to a certain extent is the impression we

---

[1] Jomier, MIDEO IV, p. 31 (fn. 1).

[2] See e.g., RAD, p. 18 : وصلى فرعون صلاة طويلة ، واستغرق في العبادة ناسيا مجده التالد وعظمته الدنيوية. This is, by the way, the first mention of the theme of the "pious debauchee," a theme which we are to meet in later works, especially in the character of al-Sayyid in the Trilogy.

receive on first meeting her among her numerous rich lovers. She behaves in a rather schematic, puppet-like manner. But once she falls in love, a new image of her emerges : the heartless courtesan becomes a selfless lover, living only for her man. She grows more beautiful through love. Even her counselling of Pharaoh to raise a false alarm in order to subdue the restive element in his capital, does not strike us as evil. The situation is viewed from within : Rādūbīs is motivated solely by concern for the safety of her beloved and is terrified by the thought of what might happen to their love should Pharaoh's opponents gain the upper hand. Thus her act acquires the quality of self-defence. When Pharaoh dies, she refuses to run away and takes a step that only real love can promote : she puts an end to her life. In short, although we are aware of the flaws of these protagonists, we are at the same time made to sympathise with their love and mourn their death.

A very convincing character is that of Nitōcris, the forlorn queen. She is not a central figure, and does not appear on the scene of action very often. Yet she emerges as a vividly portrayed type. She is dignified and detached throughout her plight. Nevertheless we are not surprised when she takes the unseemly step of visiting, in disguise, Rādūbīs' house in an attempt to rescue her husband. (She is also anxious to have a look at the "other woman.")

It is this kind of fine insight that foreshadows the much more subtle artist that Maḥfūẓ is to become.

RAD however is far from being a faultless novel. There is no lack of set characters (Ṭāhū, the commander; the young sculptor). The author is omniscient and he takes advantage of that position to enter the selves of even minor characters—a technique characteristic of lesser fiction as opposed to articulate fiction, which tends to use a few (in many cases only one) characters through whom we view the events.

There are other primitive techniques in Rādūbīs. The story sometimes regresses in time, not to fulfil the demands of an artistic pattern, but simply to fill in some necessary details. One example can be found in the opening chapters. In the first Chapter we meet the courtesan at the Nile festival. In the second, Pharaoh sees her sandal, which was carried by an eagle, and is intrigued. Chapter three goes back to the intermediate period to relate how Rādūbīs arrives home and how the eagle lifts her sandal, carrying it to Pharaoh's court.

The dialogue in all these novels is far from natural : there is a stiff formality in practically every spoken sentence. This is undoubtedly due to the author's approach to the function of dialogue. It is, to him, yet another vehicle for furthering the narrative, and scarcely a mirror for the characters.[1] Furthermore the dialogue is written, as in all Maḥfūẓ's works, in literary Arabic (although it would be unnatural for a historical novel to have its dialogue in modern vernacular). But whereas in his later novels Maḥfūẓ is to develop the language of dialogue into a more flexible medium, the characters of the historical novels speak in an excessively formal—often antiquated—language.[2]

Such criticism can in fact be levelled at the language of the novel as a whole. It is, but for a few exceptional cases, devoid of creative images, crowded by a mass of clichés and hackneyed phrases.[3] On the other hand, many recondite—often Koranic—expressions are used, possibly to mitigate the drabness of a commonplace style.[4] The description of background is also commonplace and general and can hardly be said to serve an aesthetic end.[5]

---

1 This point is to be discussed later in this chapter, pp. 96ff. *supra*.

2 The following instances from RAD are all taken from the dialogue : بخ .. بخ ، (p. 13); ولما ألقيت عصا الترحال ... (p. 39); أن أكون اخا سفر ، جوّاب أرض (p. 38); لقد فقدت جناني ، (p. 74); فما عتمت ان وجدتني ... (p. 82); واني اقسم بحبي لاذهبن الغداة (p. 85); لماذا تجدّ مولاتي جدا ؟ (p. 88); سأذهب ريحهم (p. 158; cf. Koran 8/46).

3 The following are examples of the narrative language (all quotations are from RAD) : وأرسل ... نظرة امتنان وشكران (p. 42); وتأتي بالمعجز من الخفة والتثني (p. 55); واحتواها بوجد بين ذراعيه ، وطبع على شفتيها قبلة رطبت شفتيه برحيق (p. 85); عذب واصابها سهم سام في عزة نفسها اوسويداء عواطفها (p. 106); يشكو اليها بثه (p. 107); وخانها البيان (p. 149); وكأن على رؤوسهم الطير (p. 166); اخنى عليه القدم (p. 192); احست بطعنة نجلاء تخترق شغاف قلبها (p. 197).

4 For instance : مهطعين (RAD, p. 5; cf. Koran 14/43; 54/8; 70/36) يخلصون نجيا (p. 7; cf. Koran 12/80); المئون (p. 107 *et passim*); يولي كشحه الهموم (p. 115).

5 The lake in Rādūbīs' palace is described as follows (RAD, p. 36) : وانتهت بها قدماها الى بركة واسعة من ماء غير آسن ، ينطلق على شطآنها نبات اللوتس ، ويسبح على سطحها الاوز والبط ، وتغني في جوها الاطيار ، وقد انتشر شذى العطر وأريج الزهر وغردت البلابل. This as many other

B. The "Social" Novels

General

In the next group of novels, those published between 1945-1951. Maḥfūẓ's bent becomes clear. Life as embodied in these works is rather different from that of the historical novels. What distinguishes these five books is not merely the fact that they are all set in contemporary Cairo, and that they are populated, except for one case, with poor and simple people, not members of noble dynasties; it is above all their mood and underlying philosophy that gives the novels their distinct quality. Here we encounter, more than before, the pessimistic, often fatalistic, outlook. Four of the stories end in death—two of them in double death. There is a depressing atmosphere which is not mitigated even by the occasional humorous situation or utterance. A tragic air, that of an impending catastrophe, is ever dominant. Hope only produces a mirage. "Death is more pitiful than hope", says Ḥusayn, one of the characters in *Bidāya wa-nihāya*, "and this does not seem strange to me, for while death is a creation of God, hope is the offspring of our stupidity."[1]

It has often been professed that the gloomy vision has its roots in the stifling conditions prevalent in Egypt at the time, the very conditions that Maḥfūẓ wishes to portray.[2] But such a contention does not hold water. Many an author concerned with a depressing social scene has evinced a more sanguine state of mind. In Egypt itself, authors can be found whose view is not as pessimistic, even when they tackle the same scene. To mention one example—'Abd al-Raḥmān al-Sharqāwī, a member of Maḥfūẓ's generation, in his

settings in Maḥfūẓ's early works lacks the specific, the particular, and it is characteristic of it that the collectives and plurals are more often used than singulars :

الزهر البط الاوز بلابل اطيار شطآن

Note, too, the excessive use of parallel—well nigh synonymous—expressions, e.g. :

تغني .... الاطيار|| وغردت البلابل ; شذى العطر || وأريج الزهر.

(both phrases being anything but particular).

[1] BID, p. 230 : الموت ارحم من الامل. لست اعجب لهذا فالموت من صنع الله والامل وليد حماقتنا.

[2] See, for instance, Shukrī, *al-Muntamī*, Ch. III (pp. 77ff.). Maḥfūẓ himself (interv. with Shūsha, *al-Adāb*, June 1960, p. 18) takes this view in asserting that his sadness is, in fact, the only possible mood as far as his generation is concerned.

novel *al-Arḍ* (1953) describes the no less impoverished Egyptian countryside with much lightness and *joie de vivre*, though he is by no means less socially conscious than Maḥfūẓ. On the other hand, Maḥfūẓ's tone, even when he is concerned with wealthier classes, as in the case of *al-Sarāb*, is no less dismal. It would be safer, therefore, to conclude that this is an essential part of Maḥfūẓ.[1]

We shall concern ourselves in the following pages first with the four novels which can be described as "social". *Al-Sarāb* will be treated separately for, as we shall see, it is unique in its theme and setting as well as in its structure.

All four novels depict the lives of the poor or lower middle-classes, mostly those living in the old squalid alleys of Cairo. They are oppressed and helpless. A host of overwhelming forces—poverty being only one—seem to coalesce to perpetuate the misery of these men and women, and to inflict yet greater tragedies. Everything works to trample them down, to starve and humiliate them.

Al-Qāhira al-jadīda (hereafter cited as QAH) is the story of a young student from a humble provincial family who, on the very point of starvation, finishes his university training in Cairo only to discover that society is not interested in decent intelligent people. He finds out, moreover, that unless he consents to stoop to moral corruption he will be unemployed and destitute. Being a nihilist by inclination he "sells his soul to the devil", and marries the mistress of a prominent Bey; but his immoral path leads him, before long, to a *débâcle*.[2]

In *Bidāya wa-nihāya* (BID), a family is left to face extreme poverty brought about by the sudden death of the father, a minor civil servant. They all live in very austere circumstances in the hope that the younger sons will graduate from school and bring financial relief. In the meantime, the eldest son takes to a life of crime; the daughter, to prostitution. When things eventually begin to change for the better, a sudden catastrophe befalls the family. The police capture the

---

[1] The author's inexorable pessimism can be further illustrated by his own account of the history of writing BID. According to this account, this novel, by far the most depressing of his works, was originally conceived as a humorous story, through which he intended to satirize a family which he knew in real life, and whose conduct struck him as bizarre. In the course of writing, however, the story swerved off its path and turned into a tragedy, (والتوت القصة في يدي اثناء الكتابة الى مأساة) see *al-Ahrām*, 7 Nov. 1958.

[2] For more detailed resumés of the plots of this and other novels see Appendix II.

daughter in a brothel and subsequently both she and her youngest brother commit suicide.

In *Khān al-Khalīlī* (KHAN), we are introduced to another hapless lower middle-class family. Aḥmad ʿĀkif, the middle-aged son, has given up his ambition, accepted a minor position in the civil service and refrained from marriage—all in order to help his parents and, particularly, to enable his younger brother, Rushdī, to graduate from college and obtain a respectable situation. But just as the future begins to look rosier, and Rushdī is promoted to a position in Cairo—the family is shattered : Rushdī, their sole hope, falls ill with consumption which results in his death.

Zuqāq al-Midaqq (ZUQ) is a story of an entire alley in one of those poverty stricken districts of Cairo. Its people are tempted to take the opportunity offered by World War II to salvage their lives from want. The result, however, is catastrophic. Ḥamīda, the beauty of the alley, is beguiled into prostitution to entertain the foreign soldiers. Her fiancé, who leaves the alley to become a barber in a British army camp, is killed by the drunken soldiers when trying to rescue Ḥamīda.

The social theme then is dominant in these novels. They can truly be said to belong to the literature of social protest.[1] The characters themselves are often aware that they are oppressed by an unjust social and political order. Ḥusayn, the pious son in BID, sums up this awareness. "As a matter of fact," he says to his brother, "we go too far in making God responsible for our numerous hardships. Can't you see that even if He is responsible for our father's death, He is by no means to blame for the meagreness of his pension?"[2]

Moreover, there are also representatives of a revolutionary solution, such as ʿAlī Ṭāhā in QAH and Aḥmad Rāshid in KHAN, who have

---

[1] It would be unfair to contend, as did the Marxist critic, Maḥmūd Amīn al-ʿĀlim (al-ʿĀlim and Anīs, p. 168), that these novels are backward-looking, because, as he puts it, they reflect basically a nostalgia for the glorious past and only disgust *vis-à-vis* the ugly present. It is true that the major theme embodied in them is that "there is something rotten." It is also true that these are not "propaganda novels" in that they do not put forward overtly and forcefully, an alternative. Nevertheless, their main effect on the reader is first and foremost to shake him out of his lethargy, and bring home to him the urgent need for change.

[2] BID, pp. 31-2 : والحق اننا نغالي في تحميل الله مسئولية مصائبنا الكثيرة الا ترى ان الله اذا كان مسئولا عن موت والدنا فليس مسئولاً بحال عن قلة المعاش الذي تركه ؟

a clear vision of the sources of social evil; and although such characters are never central in these novels, they constitute foci of dissatisfaction with the present, stressing the need for a new social order.

The tone of these novels is restrained and neutral. Ostensibly the author does not take sides. Yet his very interest in the poor and oppressed shows where his sympathy lies. Maḥfūẓ, to be sure, shows a special relish in portraying exotic characters and scenes (e.g., Zīṭa and "Doctor" Būshī in ZUQ; Nūnū, the calligrapher, in KHAN; old and picturesque cafés and alleys); but such characters are, again, marginal, and not, as in the works of Taymūr, Lāshīn and Kāmil, in the centre of action.[1] Furthermore, the people are very often portrayed from within; and seeing them in this manner we more often than not have our sympathies on their side. In fact, the neutral stance is only a disguise under which the author is able to elicit sympathy for his people in a more subtle way. There is no doubt whatever that his heart is with them, although he is occasionally cruel to them (as we shall see in the case of Aḥmad 'Ākif). On the other hand, whenever representatives of the wealthier classes make an appearance (e.g., the Bey in QAH; Aḥmad Yusrī in BID; Salīm 'Ilwān in ZUQ), they are ignoble.

It is this attitude to his unfortunate protagonists that distinguishes Maḥfūẓ's art from that of the Naturalists, who regard their characters as specimens and their plots as cold studies, or even "case studies" to illustrate their so-called scientific theories. There are a few qualities, however, which link these novels to the practices of the Naturalists, rendering it untrue to say that they are *solely* concerned with social criticism. There is a certain emphasis on the role of inherited qualities. This trend is to become more prominent in the Trilogy, but is discernible here as well.[2] The environment too, plays a certain role;[3] sexual impulses are important in the make-up and subsequently in the fates of a great many characters.[4] But while these elements appear only in the background of the novels discussed, there is one theme which is ever present and which comes out nearly as strongly as that

---

[1] See *supra*, Ch. I.

[2] ZUQ, p. 119 (Ḥusayn and his mother); BID, p. 16 (Nafīsa and her mother; the brothers and their late father.)

[3] In QAH Iḥsān's deterioration clearly reflects her parent's dubious past; in ZUQ and KHAN, the physical environment receives a special attention, and has an unmistakable effect on the people.

[4] Nafīsa in BID; Salīm 'Ilwān, Kirsha in ZUQ; Nūnū in KHAN, *et al.*

of the social theme. This can be called fate, accident or chance. The theme of the "Mockery of Fate," which in the novel bearing that name (*'Abath al-aqdār*) was treated in a rather naïve and didactic manner, is now introduced stealthily but forcibly. It is ever-present, omnipotent, and devastating.

This theme is played to its extreme in KHAN.[1] The family moves precipitately to Khān al-Khalīlī to escape the air-raids. It is in this place and within a very short period that they lose their beloved son. Furthermore, Rushdī is attacked by consumption just as he decides to mend his ways and marry a young neighbour. Earlier Rushdī, who has worked in the provinces, is transferred to Cairo at the very moment that his elder brother falls in love with that same young woman. The young brother unwittingly deprives Aḥmad, whom he loves and respects, of long-anticipated happiness.

The novels BID and QAH have as their starting points the sudden death (in BID), or paralysis (in QAH) of the head of the family, bringing about a sequence of events culminating in catastrophe. These sudden events would not have brought about such hardships had it not been for the unjust social order. Nevertheless, these and other examples point to the acute awareness of the role of accident or Fate. In ZUQ, to take yet another instance, Ḥamīda is about to become the second wife of Salīm 'Ilwān, but at that very moment, the man falls prey to an ailment which leaves him unfit for sensual pleasures. Consequently the marriage does not take place. The reader is inclined at first to think that this is nothing but an easy trick employed by the author to dispense with 'Ilwān in order to leave Ḥamīda exposed to the machinations of her seducer. On second thoughts, one finds some deeper significance in that incident. For one thing, it is, in a way, an example of poetic justice : Ḥamīda had earlier jilted her poor betrothed to accept 'Ilwān's offer. Her foster-mother, in fact, had warned her beforehand, though half-heartedly, of the dire consequences of going back on the *Fātiḥa* (i.e. the symbolic ceremony of betrothal).[2]

---

[1] Sayyid Quṭb, in his review of KHAN (*Kutub*, pp. 171-7) elaborates this point with much eloquence. He describes the theme of this book as "the story of feeble Humanity in the hands of formidable Fate," but he goes on to suggest that the author, on writing his novel, was so busy depicting the characters and events, that he was unaware of the greater significance of the story (*idem.*, p. 176). This is a very dubious observation, considering Maḥfūẓ's insistent preoccupation with this topic throughout his literary career.

[2] ZUQ, p. 154.

Accident then has a significance beyond its mechanical usage in the plot. Its role is integral in the fabric of human life. On the other hand, it can be noticed that these accidents are not treated in a vacuum, but rather as part and parcel of the social tragedy. They are, to a certain extent, instrumental in underlining the frailty of the social structure : the lives of the protagonists need nothing more than a little unexpected jolt to deteriorate and end in *débâcle*. In a different social order Nafīsa, Ḥasanayn, Maḥjūb, even Ḥamīda, might not have been crushed in the wake of their respective "incidents".

Characters

1. *Men*

So far only the external factors affecting the fates of Maḥfūẓ's people have been outlined. This should in no way blur the fact that Maḥfūẓ is meticulous and industrious in sketching those people from within, and in expounding their psychological and emotional development. It would be greatly misleading to suggest that external pressures are solely responsible for their tragedies. The author is at all times aware that his art is one which has characterization as a basic medium of expression. Thus all the protagonists are given their fair share of attention and more often than not that events follow on logically——possibly too logically—from the nature of these characters. There is always a flaw in the protagonist which largely contributes to his fall, and in this sense Maḥfūẓ is undoubtedly a scrupulous tragedian in Aristotelian terms.

What characterizes many protagonists can be described as overambition. This is especially true of Maḥjūb (QAH), and Ḥasanayn (BID). In fact there is evidence to suggest that the latter character is probably a revised version of the first, although their circumstances are different. There is little doubt that in the latter work (which appeared some five years after the first), the art of characterization is finer and the hero more tragic.

The story of the ambitious young man who is unable to see the external limitations and who finally winds up in a resounding disaster, has fascinated many a novelist in different cultural environments. Maḥfūẓ might have learned something from such works as Stendhal's *Le Rouge et le Noir*, and Dreiser's *An American Tragedy*.[1] But on the

[1] Indeed Ḥasanayn, the hero of BID, is in more than one point reminiscent of Clyde Griffiths, the protagonist of Dreiser's novel.

whole, his characters, especially that of Ḥasanayn, can stand in their own right, revealing a genuine insight and artistry.

Ḥasanayn — Ḥasanayn is a protagonist who unfolds before us. He is a lively and real young man, developing with admirable freedom, even though the plot itself is a stifling one, with the impending catastrophe always in the air, allowing little opportunity for the characters to behave with any degree of freedom.

We first meet him on the day of his father's death. He is a seventeen year old schoolboy, fond of gymnastics and other such innocent pastimes. At the same time he is greatly concerned about the family's "dignity", afraid that people should find out how destitute his family is. Even at his father's funeral he does not stop worrying lest their friends discover the extent of their poverty. He contrives the boldest lies in order to keep up appearances.[1] He is also extremely selfish and has no qualms in accepting the sacrifice of his whole family to promote his future. When the mother decides that Nafīsa, his sister, should become a seamstress, he protests loudly. But we soon discover that his concern is not so much for his sister's dignity as for his own. "My sister will never become a seamstress," he cries. "No. I shall never be a seamstress' brother."[2]

In fact he is always ready to rebel when his personal interest is involved. In the wake of his father's death he is all set to rebel against Fate. "He who surrenders to Fate", he tells his brother," is in fact encouraging it to impose a yet tougher tyranny."[3] But his brother reminds him that it is futile to rebel against such a formidable force. Later on, visiting the villa of Aḥmad Yusrī, he reverts to the theme of revolt.

> He glanced, startled, at the manifestations of wealth surrounding him and in a low voice asked his brother : "Would the death of a man like Aḥmad Bey arouse sorrow in his heirs ?"
> "Wouldn't we have been bereaved at our father's death even if he had been rich ?" answered Ḥusayn, half consciously.
> The youngster frowned thoughtfully. "I think so," he said, "but it seems that sorrow is of varying degrees ... Oh why wasn't our father rich !"
> "This is a different question."
> "But it is everything. Tell me, how did this Bey become rich ? ..."

---

[1] See, for instance, BID, p. 33 (Ch. 9); p. 267 (Ch. 65); pp. 285-6 (Ch. 70).

[2] BID, p. 24 : لن تكون أختي خياطة ، كلا ، ولن أكون أخا لخياطة

[3] BID, p. 30 : ان من يستسلم للاقدار يشجعها على التمادي في طغيانها

"He was probably born rich."

Ḥasanayn's brown eyes brightened. "We all must be rich," he said.

"And if not ? !"

"Then we all must be poor."

"And if this is not possible ? !"

"Then we must revolt," he answered angrily, "kill, plunder ..."

"That's what we've been doing for thousands of years," answered Ḥusayn smilingly.[1]

At first sight we are tempted to assume that Ḥasanayn's remarks constitute an unrefined, and somewhat naïve, revolutionary approach. It might have been so were it not for the self-centred overtones.

When Ḥasanayn remarks on another occasion that "some people make money without the sweat of their brow,"[2] we again might detect nascent class militancy. The envious tone, however, is blatant here as in many of the young man's other utterances.

In the course of the novel his egotism grows continuously and upon entering the same villa a year later, he no longer reflects on what "all people" should or should not have. His only thought now is "would I ever be able to acquire such a villa ?"[3]

His dreams of a quick change in fortune now dictate the rhythm of his life. On discovering the luxurious life of the rich he is enraged and protests to God "questioning, in a challenging manner, the secret of His wisdom that created the world as it is."[4] The daughter of the Bey appeals not so much to his sexual as to his possessive instincts. "How wonderful it would be to possess this villa and lie upon this girl ... It is not a matter of desire alone, but also of power and glory."[5]

He becomes still more aware of his own wretched conditions on entering the military academy and meeting the rich, spoiled cadets. On graduating as an officer he is determined to draw "a thick curtain over the past," and to cross the barriers to the "other society." He develops an obsessive hatred for his poor environment, jilting his

1 BID, p. 181.

2 BID, p. 240 : ثمة أناس يكسبون دون أن يعرق لهم جبين

3 BID, p. 244 : هل يمكن أن اقتني يوما فيلا كهذه

4 BID, p. 257 : فلم يجد من متنفس الا في أن يناقش ربه الحساب ، متسائلا — فيما يشبه التحدي — عن أسرار حكمته التي جعلت الدنيا ما هو كائن!

5 BID, p. 245 : ما اجمل أن أملك هذه الفيلا وأنام فوق هذه الفتاة. ليست شهوة فحسب ولكنها قوة وعزة.

fiancée, whom he no longer finds suitable to his ambitions, and becoming haughty even in his conduct at home. On moving to the new flat in Heliopolis, he even orders his mother and sister to refrain from befriending the neighbours lest the latter discover their commonness. He is prone to depression and melancholy whenever he encounters an obstacle in the way of his ambition. He is especially upset about the "profession" of his brother Ḥasan (smuggling drugs, etc.)—the same brother who was so helpful in time of need, and whose generosity enabled Ḥasanayn to become an officer. When, towards the end of the novel, the injured Ḥasan arrives home seeking shelter from the police, we are presented with an acute psychological insight into Ḥasanayn's mercurial and conflicting sentiments.[1] He is torn between fraternal affection and hysterical fear, and intermittently wishes that his brother was dead. At the end of the novel he forces his sister to commit suicide not so much because of her sin, but because she has jeopardized his own future. It is only after her body is removed from the Nile that he feels remorse and reflects with pain :

> I'm the worst member of the family. Everyone knows that. If the world is ugly, my own self is the ugliest thing in it. I've never found in this self of mine anything but a desire to destroy those around me. How did I allow myself to become judge when I am the worst of criminals? I am finished.[2]

Note however, the last sentence. He is still concerned with the collapse of his own expectations. The eternal "I" is unsuppressed even at that moment of revelation.

What makes Ḥasanayn an immensely tragic figure is the fact that in spite of all his detestable qualities, we are not made to hate him at the outset. His buoyancy and restlessness make him a very live character, and his transformation from a playful—though selfish—youngster into a dangerously anti-social opportunist, is so depicted that we are not inclined to be too harsh in our judgement. His obsession with glory and fortune is no less of a reaction against the harshness of society as a product of his inborn over-ambition. He is in a way rebelling, albeit in a perverted fashion. His depression and often recurring feeling of impotence against the prevailing order of things make his fall even more painful.

---

[1] BID, Chs. 86-8, esp. pp. 354-5; 358.

[2] BID, p. 381 : اني شر الاسرة جميعا. حقيقة يعرفها الجميع ، واذا كانت الدنيا قبيحة فنفسي أقبح ما فيها. ما وجدت في نفسي يوما الا تمنيات الدمار لمن حولي فكيف أبحت لنفسي أن أكون قاضيا وأنا رأس المجرمين ! لقد قضي عليّ.

Maḥjūb — Maḥjūb ʿAbd al-Dā'im, the protagonist of QAH is a less tragic figure than Ḥasanayn. Neither is his agony as pathetic nor his end as shocking. Furthermore, he is less successfully portrayed; and although he shares many a trait with the hero of BID, his overall portrait tends to be that of a type, not of a living human being.

It has already suggested that Maḥjūb is in a way an earlier "version" of Ḥasaneyn. Both stories are concerned with the rise and fall of an over-ambitious young man. Maḥjūb's tragic course starts with the sudden paralysis of his father which leaves him in great trouble (cf., the death of father in the beginning of BID). He too is self-centred and cynical, but is no less of a proud man (he would not ask his friends for help even though they are capable and willing to do so). He is as resourceful and imaginative, and as good a liar. He too discovers the luxurious life while visiting a rich home (that of Ḥamdīs, a relative of his mother) to ask for help. It is there that he meets Ḥamdīs' daughter Taḥiyya, who does not appeal primarily to his senses, but immediately arouses in him such thoughts as "such a girl is indeed a magic key which will open well-locked doors and perform miracles."[1] On seeing the girl he, too, refrains from making his request to her father so that she will not see him in a humiliating position.[2]

More examples could be cited to illustrate the similarity between the two characters. It would be more useful however, to dwell upon the differences between them. In other words : to find out what it is that makes the hero of QAH a lesser character than that of BID.

The salient weakness of QAH lies in the fact that its characters do not develop in the course of the action. What is more important is that they are not revealed to us through the action at all. The characters are at first introduced to us in great detail. Each personality is described in full in the opening chapters of the book, before the plot unfolds. Thus we are fully aware of their psychological make-up at the outset.[3] When the story finally gets under way, we are very

---

[1] QAH, p. 60 : ان فتاة مثلها لحقيقة بأن تكون مفتاحا سحريا يفتح الابواب المغلقة ويصنع المعجزات.

[2] QAH, Ch. 13; cf. BID, Ch. 70.

[3] Thus the first two chapters of the novel introduce, in a rather theatrical manner, the world outlooks of the three friends. Ch. 3 is an account, by the omniscient author, of Ma'mūn's character; Ch. 4 describes both ʿAlī and Iḥsān in much the same manner; Ch. 5 acquaints us with Maḥjūb. It is only in Ch. 6 that the real plot commences (a letter arrives breaking the news of the father's illness).

seldom surprised by their actions and conduct. Their demeanour is in accordance with what we have already learned about them from the author. They are, in short, static characters.

This applies both to secondary figures (Ma'mūn, 'Alī) as well as to Maḥjūb and Iḥsān. Maḥjūb, the author informs us, believes that "it is both naïve and stupid for him to let principles or values be obstacles in the way of his happiness."[1] "His irony," we are told, "has at all times an element of malice about it."[2] "He preferred darkness," we further learn, "and loved secrecy."[3] Lastly, we are reminded that he was "a poor immoral young man, biding his time, ready to attack with unlimited audacity."[4] Four times at least, we are assured that he was a man with great self confidence.[5]

Having been introduced to Maḥjūb in this way, we are by no means shocked when he accepts the shameful offer to marry the mistress of the Bey. In fact we are surprised that he should hesitate at all before accepting it.[6] When his career ends in scandal, we are even inclined to feel that this is not an unjust punishment for such a man.

As opposed to such static characterization, Ḥasanayn develops, as we have seen, in the course of the novel, and his personality crystallises in a reaction to external challenges that the plot itself releases.

Maḥjūb, again, is inferior in that the author left him with no freedom to behave in his own fashion. Admittedly, in all the novels in question, the characters are virtually barred from freedom of action; overwhelming forces subdue them only too often. Yet some characters are given at least the opportunity to make their own decisions. In most cases they are, truly enough, eventually crushed and beaten. Yet this very partial freedom serves to underline their tragedy. Maḥjūb, on the other hand, possesses all the qualities that allow him to make decisions. But the plot of QAH provides no opportunities for him to exercise his will. He is, rather, a puppet operated by a ruthless fate. His immoral choice (i.e., accepting the offer of becoming

---

1 QAH, p. 25: ولذلك يرى من الجهالة والحمق أن يقف مبدأ أو قيمة حجر عثرة في سبيل نفسه وسعادتها.

2 QAH, p. 24: فسخريته تضمر دائما حقدا

3 QAH, p. 24: الا أنه يؤثر الظلمة ويحب الستر

4 QAH, p. 27: ومضى في سبيله شابا فقيرا بلا خلق يرصد الفرص ويتوثب للانقضاض عليها بجراءة لا تعرف الحدود.

5 See QAH, pp. 41, 61, 144, 197.

6 QAH, pp. 107, 111.

an "official" husband in return for employment), is not an act of free will. He is, to all intents and purposes, left with no alternative. He has reached the point of starvation; his hopes of any kind of employment have been finally eliminated; his advances to Taḥiyya prove to be a devastating blunder (he also loses hope of her father's help). Finally al-Ikhshīdī's machinations are so well contrived that the young man is in reality trapped even before giving his consent.

To sum up, Maḥjūb has initially all the qualifications for committing evil. He commits that evil, not so much because of the flaw in his character as because he has no option. The author places the wrong character in the wrong plot, thus missing his mark. We agree with ʿAlī Ṭāhā when he describes his former friend—after the latter's fall—as "at once the beast and the prey."[1] Yet the interplay of these two attributes is not as artfully employed in QAH as in BID.

Aḥmad — Now we turn to a different kind of protagonist—Aḥmad ʿĀkif, the main character in KHAN ,who is neither young nor ambitious. He is a forty year old bachelor, skinny, untidily dressed; the edge of his tarboosh is soiled with sweat and dust; his teeth are yellow from smoking. He has long since relinquished his dreams of literary fame, scholarship or success of any kind. Long years of frustration have made him recoil from society, somewhat bitter, incessantly lamenting his wasted talents, grumbling against Egypt for not appreciating his genius. In the past he had some success with women, but by now he has given up marital hopes. For many years he has lived "without hope, without a friend, without a heart, neither enjoying life, nor appreciating the pleasures it offered. Despair of a successful career made him turn to solitude; and despair of love—to prostitutes."[2]

On moving from al-Sakākīnī to Khān al-Khalīlī, he is at first utterly disgusted with the "low-brow people" of the new district. His exaggerated sensitivity over his class dignity (i.e., of a civil servant as opposed to the uneducated people of the Khān) makes itself evident in such utterances as, "Oh, most of them [the residents]

---

1 QAH, p. 213: وصاحبنا البائس وحش وفريسة معا

2 KHAN, p. 40: وعاش بلا أمل ، بلا حبيب ، وبلا قلب ، لا يأنس بالحياة ولا يدرك معنى افراحها ، فدفعه القنوط من النجح الى العزلة ، ودفعه القنوط من الحب الى البغاء.

are common people, yet among the dwellers of the new blocks there are many who belong to *our* class."[1]

He soon, however, discovers the many pleasures which the Khān offers its inhabitants. He is enchanted by the Ramaḍān festivities and processions. He makes friends (some "inferior," but some quite his "equal"), with whom he spends enjoyable evenings in the local café. He once even participates, though half-heartedly, in a hashish session. But his greatest pleasure turns out to be Nawāl, the young neighbour whom he finds responsive, even audaciously so, to his timid looks. His long-slumbering heart is awakened. Yet life, once again, fails to treat him kindly. His young brother wins the girl's heart and, to make things worse, he even asks Aḥmad to be his emissary to her father. The shock is great, but Aḥmad soon recovers —or imagines he does—adding yet another frustration to the many he had suffered. His ordeal does not end at this point. He is to witness the slow death of his brother and subsequently to move out of the Khān in panic, barely a year after arriving there. The last chapter of the book, which describes the bereaved family, Aḥmad's last meeting with Nawāl, and his departure from the district are among the most touching scenes in the book, and indeed in any of the author's novels.

Aḥmad is not a tragic character in the classical sense. There is no dramatic "fall," neither is his plight precipitated by a flaw in his character. Furthermore his portrait is, generally speaking, delineated with less rigidity in comparison to other of Maḥfūẓ's protagonists. There are, as we shall see presently, some ostensible inconsistencies in the rendering of the portrait. Yet we are presented with a very successful character.

It might well be that the very success of Aḥmad's portrait is partially due to this relaxation in the structural patterns, to the spontaneity with which Aḥmad moves in the novel; in the way he defies his author and in the course of the novel refuses to comply with the characterization offered as *de rigueur* in the first few chapters.[2]

[1] KHAN, p. 118: — أوه ... غالبيتهم من أهل البلد ولكن كثيرين من سكان العمارات الجديدة من طبقتنا.

[2] This spontaneity might, curiously enough, stem from the fact that originally Maḥfūẓ had possibly intended to make the younger brother Rushdī, the hero of KHAN. He tells us (*al-Ahrām*, 7 Nov. 1958) that the idea of the novel germinated in his mind when visiting a sanatorium in Ḥulwān and encountering an inmate suffering from fatal consumption. It looks as if Aḥmad's part in the plot was conceived as secondary, and

Indeed, to echo E.M. Forster, he is capable of surprising in a convincing way.[1]

For in these first chapters he is introduced not always in a favourable manner. There is often a mocking undertone, and for a while something of a caricature emerges. Aḥmad's frustrations are portrayed as obsessive; he is stingy, suspicious, and conceited. His past adventures as scholar-*manqué* and a lover-*manqué* are not altogether amiably presented. The titles of his rejected articles, for example, are "The Crime of Poverty Against Genius," "The Insignificance of Literature"[2] (this latter article, it is to be remembered, was written after all his earlier ones had been rejected by the editors). There is also a ridiculous story about Aḥmad's experiment in the field of magic which all but drove him to insanity.[3]

Furthermore the author comes out with such remarks as "... this does not necessarily mean that he is stupid. In fact he is of average intelligence;"[4] or, "eventually he suffered from mental indigestion;"[5] or, "the insomnia which afflicted him for a period of six months was, no doubt, among the causes of his mental barrenness."[6] These remarks, coming as they do from the omniscient author, make a misleading introduction to a character which the story proves to be warm, lovable, and not devoid of intelligence. Were such comments on his personality made, for instance, in a conversation between other characters of the novel (neighbours, for instance), we would not be surprised when the story later belies them. But for an author not to know his protagonist is indeed a different thing.

The initial failure, however, is well redeemed by the rest of the novel. When the portrait of Aḥmad unfolds, we discover a character which is far from being a caricature. He is capable of many more

---

rather humorous, as the first chapters of KHAN might suggest. It is, one might conjecture, in the course of writing the story that Aḥmad "usurps" the main role.

[1] *Aspects*, p. 85.

[2] KHAN, p. 18: تفاهة الادب؛ جناية الفقر على النبوغ

[3] KHAN, p. 21. The account of Aḥmad's intellectual vicissitudes can be found in KHAN Ch. 2 (pp. 13-22).

[4] KHAN, p. 20: وليس يعني هذا حتما انه غبي ، والحقيقة انه كان عادي الذكاء.

[5] KHAN, p. 20: وأصابه سوء هضم عقلي.

[6] KHAN, p. 20: ولا شك أن الارق الذى مرض به نصف عام من حياته كان من جملة الاسباب التى عقم بها عقله.

humane actions than we would expect. He is basically good-natured and his early arrogant stance towards the people of the Khān melts away as he comes to know them better. He soon finds himself mixing with these people, much to his pleasure. He enjoys—in spite of his austere veneer—their festivities and joy of life. His short-lived affair with Nawāl shows him at his best; he is thirsty for and ready to indulge in love, but, on the other hand, he is childishly shy and naïve. Later his dignified reticence when Rushdī attracts the girl, renders him worthy of our admiration. Finally his predicament throughout Rushdī's heartbreaking sickness, his devotion and generosity, wipe out whatever adverse statements were made about him.

Aḥmad is not a flamboyant character entangled in breath-taking adventures. He is quite passive and, for a while, when his young brother comes to the fore, he even recedes to the background. Yet his portrait is as deep and lively as any in Maḥfūẓ's works. He does not change or develop in the course of the plot (he is, to be sure, too old for that), but he is constantly revealed to us by the action, increasingly eliciting our sympathy and understanding. He is one of those heroes of fiction whose shortcomings it is easy to criticize, but whose impact on the reader is not easily forgotten.

2. *Women* :

Being a socially orientated author, Maḥfūẓ is at all times aware that the Egyptian woman is a doubly-oppressed human being. The women in his novels are not a complementary element; often they are in the very centre of action. In BID the female protagonist is equally as important as the male; in ZUQ Ḥamīda is possibly more prominent than any of the other people presented in the novel. Furthermore, all the female characters are genuinely Egyptian. The author is not tempted, as are many Egyptian novelists, to "borrow" women who are totally European in behaviour in order to facilitate the love story.[1] Instead he goes into much trouble to contrive his plots in such a manner as to make the love story plausible in the Cairo of the thirties and forties. Thus the love scenes are seldom romantic nor are the lovers carefree. Their meetings often take place in dark staircases,[2] damp shelters,[3] or even grave-yards.[4] All the lovers have

[1] See Ch. I of this book, e.g. p. 16 *supra*.

[2] ZUQ, p. 116 (Ch. 13).

[3] KHAN, Ch. 14.

[4] KHAN, Ch. 27.

before them an obstacle course of social and psychological taboos to tackle before even getting to know or speak to each other.

But while the oppressed men are in some cases able to revolt by becoming selfish or anti-social, the women have little if any outlet. They are subject to a life-long imprisonment. The mothers suffer greatly, but suffer quietly. Sometimes they are resourceful (as in BID), but in the long run they can do very little in the face of overwhelming odds. As a rule, the older women accept the order of things without much complaint.

Of a different order is the plight of the younger women. They have matured in a rapidly changing world, but belonging as they do to the poor or lower middle-classes, they remain subject to severe medieval restrictions. If they are lucky and attractive, they can hope to gain a relative freedom through marriage; otherwise they face the prospect of becoming spinsters or of being married to old or illiterate men. They have no means of rebelling against this vicious circle, and in the few cases in which they try to do so, end up in prostitution of one kind or another.

Indeed this extreme form of degradation of woman seems to take up a great deal of Maḥfūẓ's attention. Two of the heroines in the novels discussed (ZUQ and BID) take to outright prostitution, a third (in QAH) becomes the concubine of a statesman. In fact these three women are the main female characters of the novels in question.

The function of these women is, then, to underline with greater intensity the depressing social conditions. Their characterization, however, goes beyond illustrating these conditions. As in the case of the male protagonists, Maḥfūẓ goes into extensive elaboration of their psychological make-up, and is at all times labouring to maintain their verisimilitude. In all these cases his characterization impresses one as being an answer to a challenging, nagging question: how does a young woman become a prostitute?

Nafīsa — Nafīsa, of BID, is probably one of the fullest of Maḥfūẓ's characters and also one of the most tragic. She is an unattractive but good-natured girl of twenty-three, who suddenly finds herself deprived of the protection of a father. She grows apprehensive for her own future. The agonies of poverty are aggravated by the fact that she is obliged to work as a dress-maker, preparing the wedding trousseau for happy brides. Having no real matrimonial prospects, she responds to the advances of Salmān, a semi-literate and dull grocer, hoping that he will marry her. She is well aware, however, that her family would object to such a marriage as being degrading for "they are proud people. I cannot believe that poverty will subdue their vanity."[1] Yet she will not relinquish her only visible hope; and having in the meantime developed a liking for Salmān, she surrenders herself to him. But no sooner does he get his way than he marries another girl. Nafīsa is trapped. Her despair, coupled with strong sexual compulsions, make her fatalistic enough to give way to other men, gradually accepting meagre sums of money (which the family desperately needs) in return for her favours. All of this, of course, is made possible by the fact that she is free to be out of the house to carry out her dressmaking orders. When at last her family is better off, and she no longer has to be the bread-winner, she continues her secret meetings with men : she is by now too entangled and too interested. Eventually she is caught by the police and subsequently commits suicide in her brother's presence.

All the steps which lead Nafīsa to prostitution are so carefully depicted that her downfall is more than convincing. Her portrait is so meticulously drawn that it sometimes seems too logical to be human.

To make her infatuation and subsequent surrender to Salmān plausible, we are repeatedly reminded of how unattractive, poor, hopeless, and sexually demanding she is. On the fateful evening, when she goes with Salmān to his house, all those forces come into play, in addition to the following :

> ... She opened her mouth to speak, but an approaching figure attracted her attention and her blood froze in her veins. She groaned in fear and was about to run away when the pedestrian passed under the streetlight and his face was illuminated. She sighed in relief. Salmān was puzzled by her behaviour. "What is the matter?" he asked. "I thought it was my brother Ḥasan," she answered, gasping for breath. The young man took the opportunity to declare a long cherished wish. "We won't be free of fear," he said, "as long as we continue to stroll in these lanes. Listen to me : Why can't we go to our [i.e. Salmān's] house where we can spend a while away in privacy."[2]

This scene has been quoted *in extenso* because it is typical of many fateful stages in Nafīsā's downfall. Once the psychological background is laid out, there comes a sudden occurrence (such as the sharp fear

[1] BID, p. 73 : انهم جميعا ذوو كبرياء ولا أظن الفقر بغالب على كبريائهم

[2] BID, p. 99.

described here) which leads her to a new stage in her downfall. (It must be remembered what an unusual step it is for a girl in Egypt —still more in the 1930's—to slip into a man's home.) Of course, Maḥfūẓ is too clever a writer to believe or have us believe that this shock would, by itself, be sufficient to bring about such repercussions. The scene is continued with her resisting at first to go with him. Then after she is in the house, we watch her struggling with her "anxious, troubled and tense" self, until she finally surrenders. Nevertheless, the mechanism of cause and effect is too transparent.

The cold planning of the character's fall does not mean that the character itself is lifeless. On the whole Nafīsa is portrayed with much competence. There are certain scenes where acute poetic insight is displayed by the author. On the very night of her surrender to Salmān, when she returns home, she hears "the voice of her brother Ḥasanayn reading his lessons aloud in the midst of prevailing silence, leaving on her a strange impact of fear or pure sadness—which it was, she could not say."[1] The prophetic tone of this sentence(which foreshadows the final scene when she is forced by her brother to commit suicide) is refreshing after the too prosaic narration which precedes it.

Iḥsān — Iḥsān is a fairly marginal character in QAH. Furthermore, her relative value in the gallery of Maḥfūẓ's characters is unimpressive. She is rather superficially portrayed, and although she goes through many ups and downs in the course of the story, she nonetheless remains a flat character. It would nevertheless be useful to comment on this character if only because she is so different from Nafīsa. She is a beautiful girl of eighteen, of relatively adequate education (but a "lower" class background, her father being a poor tobacconist). She is loved by the student ʿAlī Ṭāhā, who intends to marry her as soon as is practicable. On the face of it, she lacks many of the basic motivations that led the heroine of BID to prostitution. Yet Iḥsān, too, falls. "How did it happen?" asks the author,[2] and at once begins to analyse all the aspects of the problem.

Iḥsān too is a victim of social conditions and certain inherited and

---

[1] BID, p. 105: وفي السكون الشامل ترامى اليها صوت حسنين وهو يطالع فترك في نفسها أثرا عجيبا لم تدر ان كان خوفا ام حزنا خالصا.

[2] QAH, p. 116: كيف وقع هذا؟

psychological factors. She surrenders to the Bey's advances for the following reasons :

a) her parents are immoral people who encourage her, nay push her, to sell her beauty and bring home some money which will sustain them and their eight children;

b) she has inherited some immoral traits from her parents who both have a dubious past (the milieu ! the heredity !); she is herself fond of luxury and wealth, and hates poverty;

c) though her attachment to 'Alī Ṭāhā saved her for a while from falling, her love for him is nevertheless "not a love that blinds and deafens one; not a love that would withstand violent tests and furious temptations;"[1]

d) lastly, she is faced with a cunning, experienced and rich hedonist who has developed an elaborate technique of seduction. Somehow he entices her into his car and then into the villa which he keeps for his amorous adventures (alleging an imaginary breakdown in the car), where he makes her drink champagne (assuring her that it is a soft drink), etc.

The logical formula is, then, employed once again, and as before, serves the character ill. What makes Nafīsa a more convincing character is that while the psychological background of the character is laid down by means of "telling," the actual transformation is "shown" while happening.[2] In the case of Iḥsān the story, including the actual moment of surrender, is briefly related by the author *after* it has taken place, as it were to fill a gap in our knowledge.[3] Her character is as close as anything can be, to a "case history."

One is tempted here, as in the case of Maḥjūb—Ḥasanayn, to conclude that the author himself was not altogether satisfied with the character of Iḥsān and tried his hand again in producing a liveleir version.

Ḥamīda — Turning to Ḥamīda, the heroine of ZUQ, we find ourselves encountering a portrait whose vitality and spontaneity by far surpasses that of other female characters in this group of novels.

---

[1] QAH, p. 116: ولكنه ليس الحبي الذ يعمي ويصم. ليس الحب الذي يصمد للتجارب الشديدة والمغريات العنيفة.

[2] The terms "telling" and "showing" are here used in the sense elaborated by Wayne C. Booth in *The Rhetoric of Fiction*, pp. 3-20; 211-40.

[3] QAH, Ch. 25 (pp. 113-18).

The stiff mechanism in characterization is here reduced to a minimum, and there is greater freedom of interplay in circumstances versus individual traits. Admittedly, Ḥamīda too stoops to prostitution by force of overwhelming circumstances and external factors. Yet she is by no means a formula wherein causality and social factors are all-powerful.

Ḥamīda was born out of wedlock, in poverty. Her mother died soon after her birth, and she was brought up by a poor female matchmaker. She is a beautiful shrew, sharp-witted and opinionated. She is also an ambitious person who cannot visualize her future in the alley and who dreams of wealth and happiness. She despises the uncouth manners of the alley people, and is disgusted with prospects of poverty, filthy children and eternal slavery at home. The "new world,"[1] that of the modern quarters of Cairo, is the epitome of her dreams. She envies her girl-friends who have become factory workers and are thus both relatively emancipated and well-off. The local barber, 'Abbās, has long wanted to marry her. He is, however, the very opposite of Ḥamīda; calm, frugal and easily contented. He prefers the alley and its people to anything else in the world. Ḥamīda is aware that 'Abbās is the best man for whom she can hope from among the people around her; but he comes nowhere near her image of her future husband. When he proposes to her, she shows no enthusiasm. It is only on hearing that he is leaving to work for the British army that she gives her consent, hoping that his new occupation will change his fortunes. However, once he is gone to the distant army camp, he is out of her mind and heart. Thus when the merchant Salīm 'Ilwān asks for her hand, she repudiates her earlier commitment without any qualms. Subsequently when her engagement to Salīm is broken off, following his illness, Ḥamīda is no longer able to consider 'Abbās as a possible husband : the merchant's proposal has enhanced her ambition to the point of no return. At that juncture, the pimp Faraj enters the picture, luring the girl into his snare.

Ostensibly, here again the rigid planning is discernible. Everything happens at the right moment to further the story; everything coalesces to divert her from her path. However, the distinctive facet of Ḥamīda's character is the wide scope alloted to her individuality in determining her fate. There is a greater freedom in the movement of life. Ḥamīda is, to start with, "frighteningly eccentric,"[2] as her foster mother

[1] See ZUQ, p. 202 : الدنيا الجديدة

[2] ZUQ, p. 151 : وعاودها شعورها القديم بأن ابنتها فتاة شاذة مخيفة

sees her. Furthermore, her interaction with the other people is never simple or unequivocal. Her complex attitude towards 'Abbās for instance, is fully, though economically, portrayed, and we are always conscious of the ambiguity of her feelings. Even on the eve of his departure, when Ḥamīda feels that "never before had she had such an emotional experience as that evening on the staircase. In one brief moment she lived through a long life loaded with emotions, feelings, and warmth. Her life, she thought, was forever bound to his"[1]—even at such a moment the reader is aware that things are not so simple. Thus the author's later remark—on the occasion of her "change of heart"—that "her abandonment of 'Abbās was not as abrupt as her mother thought"[2]—seems unnecessary in view of what we have already learnt about Ḥamīda.

The most illuminating part in the portrayal of Ḥamīda is undoubtedly that which falls between the appearance of Faraj and her eventual elopement. Faraj is indeed a professional seducer who is well-trained in identifying candidates for his "school" (i.e., the premises on which he trains his recruits in the art of love) and to isolate those young women who are, in his words, "born prostitutes." His skill in analysing Ḥamīda's mind and accordingly attacking the weak points is faultless. On the face of it, the girl is doomed the moment he sets his eyes upon her.

Yet Ḥamīda, once again, proves to be anything but a stock character. The pitfall of mediocrity is avoided by the fact that Ḥamīda is viewed from within : we see things through her own eyes, and in the course of action. She is shrewd enough to detect something sinister about Faraj from the beginning—that he is "a tiger waiting for an opportunity to leap."[3] Yet he attracts her by the very fact that he is a man of the "new world" and her venturesome temperament is challenged. She is out to fight a "battle of giants" unaware that he is always capable of outwitting and outflanking her. As the days pass she is speedily enmeshed. Ḥamīda, however, is not altogether a pathetic prey : unconsciously she is willing to be trapped. The duel

---

[1] ZUQ, p. 116 : لم يبلغ بها الانفعال يوما ما بلغه هذا المساء على السلم ، حيت في دقيقة قصيرة حياة طويلة مفعمة بالاحساس والعاطفة والحرارة ، وحسبت أن حياتها قد ارتبطت به الى الابد.

[2] ZUQ, p. 152 : لم يكن تحوّلها عن عباس الحلو بغير تمهيد كما ظنت أمها

[3] ZUQ, p. 180 : فقلبها يحدثها بأنه نمر يتحين فرصة للوثوب

between Faraj and Ḥamīda is recorded with much insight and subtlety. In one of her outings to "wrestle" with the pimp we are presented with a moment which shows the full complexity of Ḥamīda's motives :

> ... they walked away, side by side, with Ḥamīda making no attempt to move away from him, aware of how she had lain in wait for him so recently, intent on punishing him in this very street. However, now her thoughts centered on the fact that she had forced him to let go of her hand. Perhaps if he were to try again she would not prevent him; after all, hadn't she left her house for the sole purpose of meeting him? Anyway it annoyed her that he should show more daring and self-confidence than she did and so she walked by his side, unconcerned about what passers-by might think. She could scarcely wait to see the envious astonishment his appearance would cause among the factory girls. The thought filled her with feelings of superiority and a desire for life and adventure.[1]

Her obsession with dominating and impressing others is coupled with the unmistakable desire to defy her own social environment and to challenge its moral values. When she is about to enter Faraj's flat for the first time she remembers the saintly man of the alley and ponders : "What would Ruḍwān al-Ḥusaynī, for example, say if he were to see her enter this apartment house. A smile played on her lips and she had a strange feeling that today was certain to be the happiest one in her whole life."[2]

Later, when she discovers that Faraj is nothing but a pimp, she goes mad with rage. She curses and swears, yet "her wrath was caused by the surprise and disappointment, but not by the immorality—a subject with which she had not, as yet, had to come to grips."[3]

Her rage abates very quickly. When she is again at home after that visit we promptly learn that "she had already made up her mind unconsciously. The choice was made in the man's arms, in his own house. Outwardly she was angry, while inwardly she danced with joy. Her face had gone pale with rage while her dreams and hopes breathed new life and happiness."[4]

---

[1] ZUQ, p. 198.

[2] ZUQ, p. 204 : وما عسى ان يقول السيد رضوان الحسيني مثلا لو رآها تمرق الى هذه العمارة؟ وارتسمت ابتسامة على شفتيها ، وداخلها شعور غريب بأن هذا اليوم هو أسعد ايام حياتها على الاطلاق.

[3] ZUQ, p. 210 : وان كان غضبها للمفاجأة التي دهمتها والخيبة التى ادركتها منه لا للفساد الذى لم تعتد أن تثور له!

[4] ZUQ, p. 214 : ... بل الحق أنها اختارت سبيلها بالفعل وهي لا تدري ،

Of course, she makes up her mind not to give way without putting up a token resistance. When she sees her shoddy underwear she resolves not to surrender to Faraj "until she had changed these shabby clothes for new, glamorous ones. This idea appealed to her. Being unable to love without putting up a fight, she was now filled with joy."[1]

Ḥamīda's story is cut off soon after her elopement to Faraj's school. When we next meet her some two months later she is outwardly a different woman, an accomplished prostitute. She is impenitent, and though apparently unhappy, she has no interest whatever in the old alley. She is concerned when 'Abbās's tone suggests that he might try to forgive and reclaim her.[2] Her hatred towards that world for which he stands is as strong as ever. Her only interest in 'Abbās is to manipulate him to take revenge—not too harshly!—on Faraj. Her grudge against the latter is not so much for making her a prostitute as for being untruthful in his declaration of love.[3] This last appearance of Ḥamīda sheds yet another light on her earlier motivations and gives her portrait a final touch.

The success of this character is particularly due to the technique of presentation. There is a happy co-ordination between "showing" and "telling", the two being used continuously in juxtaposition. Even when the author interferes and speaks in his own voice (as in some of the examples quoted above), his remarks do not constitute the main source of information. They are, rather, interpretative, and their aim is to recapitulate and help the reader grasp in full a situation which has already taken place before him. Such remarks are often redundant, but they do not damage the fabric of narration.

Equally noteworthy is the vividness of the visual portrait the author presents. Ḥamīda's physical appearance is dynamic and plays its part in the progress of the story. Her beautiful black eyes,

---

ووقع اختيارها عليه وهى بين يدي ذلك الرجل ، فى بيته! كان لسانها يهدر
غضبا وأعماقها ترقص طربا ، كان وجهها يربد ويعبس وأحلامها تتنفس وتمرح!
[1] ZUQ, p. 217: واربد وجهها وهاج صدرها ، فصممت على ألا تسلم اليه
حتي تستبدل بهذه الثياب الرقيقة أخرى جديدة زاهية. وطاب لها هذا
الرأي ، وصادف من نفسها — التي تأبى الهوى الا في حومة العراك والعناد
— هوى ولذة.

[2] ZUQ, p. 292.

[3] ZUQ, Ch. 31.

framed with kohl, are at all times a mirror of her inner self, reflecting her determination and ferocity. This reflection of severity, the author tells us, "is for some a flaw in her beauty, while for others it is an enhancement."[1]

Her long black hair too, is not a static item. In Ḥamīda's first appearance in the novel her mother criticises her for having her hair full of lice.[2] Thus Ḥamīda's hair epitomizes the utter poverty and filth of her environment. But its beauty also serves as a subtle reminder of her potentiality in the white-slave market, a trait which is later recognized by the pimp.[3]

Even her voice is made use of as a medium reflecting her character. At least three times we are reminded that her voice is unpleasant, the weak point in her beauty. In each of these cases, however, the mention of the voice is functional. The first time—in the parting scene on the eve of 'Abbās's departure[4]—it is used as a dissonant chord, as a reminder that the tenderness which she shows towards her fiancé is ephemeral. In the second instance—her first conversation with Faraj[5]—she lowers her voice so as not to reveal its harshness to the suave stranger. In the third case, it is mentioned in conjuction with a new and delicate "Pharaonic" name—Tītī, which was given to her by Faraj to appeal to the English and American soldiers. Ḥamīda herself, in that scene, wishes she could replace her coarse voice with a soft one more suited to the new environment.[6]

Structure

Having considered some of the chief characters in these novels. and the manner in which they are portrayed, we can now proceed to such problems as technique, setting, and language. It goes without saying that these aspects of the novelist's craft constitute, together with characterization, one and the same network, and it is next to impossible to try to reduce a novel to elementary ingredients. We cannot understand a character in a story unless we see it in conjuntion

[1] ZUQ, p. 43: وكانت عيناها الجميلتين (sic) تنطقان احيانا بهذا الشعور نطقا يذهب بجمالها فى رأي البعض ويضاعفه في رأي البعض الآخر.

[2] ZUQ, p. 27.

[3] ZUQ, p. 207.

[4] ZUQ, p. 93.

[5] ZUQ, p. 177.

[6] ZUQ, p. 232.

with other characters in the same work. Neither can we evaluate properly the merits and faults in portraying a certain character without casting a glance at its place in the general arrangement of the material, and its position in relation to its setting. Similarly we are likely to miss our mark if we fail to examine the language with which the character speaks or is spoken of, or to consider the use of language in the work as a whole.

The structure of our novels is, on the whole, a simple one, combining straightforward narration with dialogue and description. There is no attempt at making use of those techniques which came to prominence in the West mainly in the twentieth century. Such devices as the stream of consciousness, or *le style indirect libre*, are never employed and the connection between the past and the present is done explicitly by intervention on the part of the author.

Each novel is a self-contained "slice of life" which, without exception, culminates in a traumatic occurrence. BID and QAH also begin with a tragic incident (death or paralysis of the fathers), while KHAN has a definite starting point of a different kind (the family's moving to a new area). ZUQ is exceptional in that it has no dramatic beginning and only its end resembles that of the other novels. Nevertheless it is no less self-contained as far as plot is concerned, as we shall presently see.

The focusing of the plot is frequently achieved through a technique that can be described as that of a "shut-in arena,"[1] wherein the fates of characters are closely linked and their stories interrelated.

The best example of this technique is BID. This novel has at least five active characters (the mother and her four children), of which two can be described as protagonists (Nafīsa and Ḥasanayn); and although each of the children conducts his own life, and moves in different circles, the plot as a whole is neatly streamlined. It is the story of the family. The fates of its members are inter-dependent : Ḥasanayn's destiny and ambitions are determined by his brothers and sister, and vice versa. Even the older brother Ḥasan who chooses to desert his mother's home in search of a different way of life, returns at the end of the novel to his family, wounded and helpless.

In order to achieve the delicate balance between the story of the family as a whole, on the one hand, and the intermediate stories (of Ḥasan, Nafīsa, Ḥusayn and Ḥasanayn) on the other, Maḥfūẓ

[1] Muir, p. 61.

applies a mechanism which may be compared to that of the human heart, with its different arteries continuously circulating blood, carrying it away, but finally bringing it back to its starting point. The family scene (the hub of which is the mother) stands in the very centre. The sons and daughter depart from it to pursue their daily lives, but come back, converge and disperse again. One interesting device which helps Maḥfūẓ implement this pattern is a quasi-family council that spontaneously meets to face some crucial issue or to discuss the future of one of the sons. This "council" recurs in different stages of the book (mainly Chapters 6, 12, 29, 44, 79, 81) to give the plot a symmetrical shape.

To what extent the fate of the family forms the main interest of this story can be illustrated even by the Ṭanṭā section (Chapters 48-56). Here Maḥfūẓ takes us for a while away from his usual Cairo scene to track the steps of Ḥusayn. It is significant that these chapters contain no description of the new scene of activity. The only fragments of physical background mentioned are Ḥusayn's hotel, his new room, his office. Ḥusayn's life in Ṭanṭā is pursued only to the extent that it bears upon his family's destiny. These chapters by no means constitute a sub-plot. They contribute to an understanding of the mother's character (when she comes to visit her son), and, of course, to Ḥusayn's. The moment that Ṭanṭā has no more bearing on the family's story, the spotlight is rather abruptly shifted back to Naṣralla Close in Cairo.

Another example can be found at the beginning of Chapter 34 where the action takes place after the showdown between Nafīsa and Salmān. A full page[1] is devoted to an account of how the cowardly Salmān was panic-stricken by Ḥasan's visit before he finally realized that Nafīsa's brother, unconscious of his sister's relations with him, came only to ask for the job of singing at his wedding. The function of prolonged description of Salmān's fears and soliloquy is not, however, to show another side or trait of Salmān's personality. Its sole purpose is to underline with greater force the deriding fate of Nafīsa, of Ḥasan, and most important, of their *family*—a lower middle-class family which is fighting fiercely to retain its status, while in reality, "an ugly beast-like, cowardly" grocer's son has not only seduced their daughter, but is now witnessing the humiliation of another member.

The time element in BID is also worth considering. Ostensibly

---

[1] BID, pp. 132-3.

the plot duration is relatively lengthy, for while in the other Cairene novels the plots last a year or less, BID's time span is about three and a half to four years. But this is not to the detriment of clarity or focus : it allows the author ample room to pursue the developments and changes in his characters. The prolongation is especially important since the plot is one in which the past does not really play a very important part. The father's death not only brings about new economic and social hardships, but it marks the start of a different life for each member of the family. The past is dead and a new reality commences. Ḥasanayn, for example, on feeling (towards the end of the novel) that "the heavy hammer of his past hangs over his head and constantly threatens him"[1] does not allude to a past which exists beyond the limits of the actual plot. It is a "past" which is created in the course of the novel by the new circumstances. Certainly one can argue that the background of these occurrences goes back to earlier years in the sense that nothing emerges from the blue; that the family's new economic situation has its roots in the period preceding the father's death; that Nafīsa, Ḥasanayn, and the rest display in the course of the plot qualities which already existed in them formerly and are only intensified or brought to light under the new circumstances. Admittedly this is the case; but structurally we are presented with a self-contained set of occurrences. No elements of the "remote" past (that is, before the father's death) play a definite part in the plot. Furthermore, we are not told any facts about the childhood and early adolescence of Ḥusayn, Nafīsa, and Ḥasanayn (and only a superficial reference is made to Ḥasan's relationship with his father).[2]

A similar device—that of a family-centred plot—is also adopted in KHAN. This design is instrumental in keeping the unity of the plot in spite of cleavage caused by the appearance on the scene of the brother Rushdī (see *supra* p. 77, fn. 1). Another factor which brings the story into focus is that the plot is enclosed at both ends no less tightly than in BID : it starts with the family's appearance on the Khan's scene and ends with their disappearance a year later.

There is a difference, however, between the structure of these two

---

1 BID, p. 344 : كان يشعر دائما بأن مطرقة ثقيلة من ماضيه معلقة فوق رأسه تهدده في كل حين.

2 BID, Ch. 11.

novels. Unlike BID, KHAN tends to be concerned less with the fate of the family than with that of one of its members. Aḥmad, as we have seen, "usurps" the central role, leaving the others in the shade. Consequently every detail which adds a line to Aḥmad's portrait becomes vital to the story, and we feel no diversion when the author follows Aḥmad's steps into his office or into a hashish session : these scenes have considerable bearing on the main character. Furthermore the love scenes of Rus͟hdī and Nawāl (of which Aḥmad knows very little) are not felt as extraneous to Aḥmad's story : Nawāl herself is a part of Aḥmad's predicament. However, when the author indulges in describing Rus͟hdī's friends, their gambling parties, and the gambler's psychology at large,[1] the impression is that we have drifted too far from the centre : these scenes have no visible reference to Aḥmad's story. They would have been relevant had Rus͟hdī been given as important a role as his elder brother.

In ZUQ, a novel with many characters and ostensibly divergent stories, the coherence of the plot is achieved by means of a strict spatial enclosure. The great majority of the situations take place in that narrow close, Zuqāq al-Midaqq, and the people, but for one or two exceptions, are those who occupy its few old houses.

Furthermore, the fates of these people are not in the least independent of each other. The same circumstances and occurrences affect them all in a chain reaction. The World War disturbs the lives of all the young: Ḥamīda, 'Abbās, Ḥusayn Kirs͟ha and the girls working in the factory. Salīm's sudden malady has repercussions on Ḥamīda and subsequently on 'Abbās, and so on. Even minor characters are interrelated. Saniyya, the landlady in whose house Ḥamīda lived, faints on hearing the news that "Doctor" Būs͟hī and Zīṭa have been caught by the police digging up graves to steal gold teeth : she had just had a new set fitted for her by that "dentist" in readiness for her marriage to a young man (the match-maker being Ḥamīda's mother). Similarly, when shaykh Ruḍwān al-Ḥusaynī decides to make the pilgrimage to Mecca, he explicitly connects the trip with the outrages of Ḥamīda, Būs͟hī and Zīṭa.

This conception of the alley as a crucible is carried out with much consistency, saving the story from fragmentation. Everything that happens in the alley is thus relevant to the story. On the other hand,

---

[1] KHAN, pp. 124-5.

the few scenes set outside the alley tend to pale. The author has been wise enough to cut short Ḥamīda's story soon after her desertion of the alley. It would probably have been better had he omitted altogether the scenes in which Faraj acquaints Ḥamīda with his "school"[1] or that of their quarrel two months later.[2]

Salīm 'Ilwān, to take another example, belongs to the "shut-in arena" as long as he is physically present (he has his business in the neighbourhood, but he does not live there). It is also relevant when the author devotes a whole chapter[3] sketching his past and present family situation or even when he penetrates summarily into his inner self to describe his desire and misgivings vis-à-vis Ḥamīda.[4] The moment he falls ill, however, and his offer is nipped in the bud, he ceases to be important to our story. Thus the later chapter[5] depicting his life after Ḥamīda's disappearance—and especially his quarrels with his own family—is totally unnecessary.

These minor structural faults apart, the author shows good control over the different situations presented in ZUQ, moving between the numerous people and episodes with admirable freedom.

The structure of QAH is of a different nature. It is a story with one protagonist, Maḥjūb, in relation to whom all the other characters are secondary. It is *his* story with which the novel is concerned. Yet this work is far less well-focused than any other of Maḥfūẓ. Its design is rather lop-sided. The first chapters introduce the three friends with equal emphasis, thus suggesting that they are all central characters. Yet no sooner does the reader become interested in 'Alī and Ma'mūn, than their stories are all but discontinued. Surely these two friends of Maḥjūb are brought in as representatives of possible solutions (Leftist and Islamic) to the problem of the "lost generation" for which Maḥjūb stands. The fact, however, that they both fade away leaving the scene entirely to Maḥjūb, renders them rather ornamental, not integral characters. Their role as foils is presented more as an abstraction than as a part of a dramatic juxtaposition.

This is not the only point in which QAH is inferior to that of the other Cairene novels. We have seen that both Maḥjūb and Iḥsān

---

1 ZUQ, Ch. 26.

2 ZUQ, Ch. 31.

3 ZUQ, Ch. 8.

4 ZUQ, pp. 74-7; 142-3.

5 ZUQ, Ch. 29.

are lesser characters when compared to other of Maḥfūẓ's protagonists. Furthermore, there are many artificial scenes (such as the imbroglio in the concluding chapters). The time element is not altogether clear (cf. the other novels where the reader is at all times aware of the dates of the occurrences, of the passage of time, and of the plot span as a whole).

It can therefore be summed up that at this stage Maḥfūẓ achieves better results when he tackles more complex plots with two or more closely linked central characters. It should be added however, that QAH and KHAN are the earliest of the author's Cairene novels, while BID, the most impressive as far as structure is concerned, is the fifth in the series (SAR being the fourth). There is a distinct and continuous progress in the author's art no less in structure than in characterization.

Language and Dialogue

The language in general is now more functional. There are fewer hackneyed cliches than in the historical novels, yet the author's individual turn of phrase is not always distinguishable. Idiosyncracies of style are difficult to find. This is especially evident in the dialogue (as we shall presently see), but it is also true of the language generally.

The background descriptions are, on the whole, admirably short and illuminating. In the opening chapters of ZUQ a vivid idea of the picturesque close is conveyed in two pages.[1] Ziṭa's filthy dwelling is described with equal brevity.[2] The author is at his best when he reflects the background through the minds of his characters, thus welding outside scenery into the dramatic action. Ḥamīda's sarcastic comments, in soliloquy, about her neighbourhood, at once illustrate her present mood, her feeling towards her environment, and last but not least, delineate that environment itself.[3] In KHAN, again, pictures of the old alleys of Cairo are not conveyed in a static manner, but through Aḥmad's bewildered eyes. The visual scenery intermingles with the hustle and bustle and smells of the K͟hān. Above all, it is the fact that these scenes have an immediate effect on Aḥmad's moods that they become so lively.[4]

[1] ZUQ, pp. 5-6.

[2] ZUQ, p. 60.

[3] ZUQ, pp. 31-2; 216.

[4] KHAN, pp. 24; 32-3; 63.

The author however, is less successful in conveying emotions and moods through action or evocative words and images. Very often the reader is overwhelmed with hosts of plain statements in which the author *informs* him of the mood. In BID, to take one example, the tragic atmosphere is introduced not by means of poetic symbols, but by a long series of words all denoting "sorrow."[1]

Another quality which characterizes these novels is the great passion for precise detail. Often we find, for instance, lengthy enumerations of local foodstuffs.[2] The practice of meticulous description is, of course, an essential part in the art of the realistic-naturalistic novelist. Yet when he tends to become repetitious such details are no longer advantageous to the novel. Repetitions not only reduce the dramatic tension, but they might cause us to overlook some important details.

Consider the following example from QAH : When Maḥjūb receives the letter summoning him to al-Qanāṭir, he promptly "wrapped his gallabiyya in an old newspaper and left the house." (p. 30). As his train arrives at his destination we are again reminded of that parcel : "then the train stopped in al-Qanāṭir; Maḥjūb picked up his parcel and got off" (p. 34) Finally when he reaches his parents' house he "put his gallabiyya on a table and entered the room." (p. 35).

This is clearly a case where the author's meticulous eye for detail serves his art ill. The gallabiyya has no obvious function in the story. If its purpose is to underline his extreme poverty, it adds nothing new, since his lamentable financial situation is vividly elaborated upon throughout the novel. Furthermore the first mention of the parcel would suffice as a reference to the poverty theme.

Such stylistic redundancies seem to originate in a certain reluctance on the author's part to leave anything to the reader's imagination. Every act and deed has to be elucidated and interpreted. The dialogue is often extended beyond the scope of normal speech in order to explain any possible ambiguities. Furthermore, no sooner does the conversation come to an end, than the author enters to explain and comment. This practice has already been alluded to (see *supra* pp. 85, 87). The following scene from BID will further illustrate it.

Ḥasanayn has recently finished his secondary schooling. His mother

---

[1] In the last thirty lines of Ch. 25 of BID, for instance, we come across the following words : حزن (twice) ؛ تعاسة (twice) ؛ أسى ؛ كآبة ؛ قنوط ؛ شقاء ؛ فجيعة ؛ هموم ؛ تأثر ؛ صمت ثقيل.

[2] See KHAN pp. 77-9; 83; 131-2; BID pp. 111; 261.

suggests that he should join a teacher's training college where students are exempt from paying fees. The following conversation ensues :

"I would hate to become a teacher," said the youngster, disgusted, "and I would hate the more to join an institute which charges no fees."

"But you don't object to enrolling in the military school free of charge."

"There's a great difference between an institute which is free to all and one which might exempt *me* from fees wholly or partially. People will say, in the first case, that I studied gratis, while in the second it will be impossible for anyone—save for the school clerk—to know of it."

The mother shook her head dubiously. "But the question is more serious than that," she muttered.

"Nothing is more serious than that. I hate poverty and its implications and I do not like to bow my head when amongst people of dignity."[1]

Formal as it is, this dialogue supplies a precious piece of information, which can help us construct a clear notion of Ḥasanayn's psychology. But the author feels that he should not depend too much on the reader's intelligence, for he adds in the following line : "This was not the only motive for his preference. In fact he aspired to the military school, driven by an inherent thirst for domination, power, and dashing appearance."[2]

This last statement, which is conspicuously redundent, is repeated all but *verbatim*, on another occasion in the book.[3]

It may well be that the author's mistrust, as it were, of dialogue stems from his awareness of the shortcomings of the very language he puts in the mouths of his characters. For unlike certain Arabic novelists, who prefer to use the spoken language (*ʿāmmiyya*) in their dialogue, Maḥfūẓ is adamant in translating all the utterances of his characters from the Cairene idiom into literary Arabic (*fuṣḥā*).[4]

---

1 BID, pp. 233-4.

2 BID, p. 234 : ولم يكن هذا فحسب دافعه الحقيقي الى هذا الاختيار ، والواقع أنه طمح الى المدرسة الحربية مدفوعا بنفسه الظمأى الى السيادة والقوة والمظهر الخلاب.

3 BID, p. 251 : كان طموحه الى الحربية يتفجر من صميم روحه الملهوفة على السيادة ...

4 According to M.A. al-ʿĀlim, certain friends of Maḥfūẓ explain his attachment to the *fuṣḥā* by the fact that when he wrote his early novels he had his eye on the prizes offered by the Language Academy, an institution which recognizes only that language (*Fil-thaqāfa al-Miṣriyya*, p. 172). But while such an explanation may be relevant to the novels of the forties it fails to explain why the author continued to use the *fuṣḥā*

Needless to say, this choice of language accounts for much of the formality and stiffness in the dialogue of these novels. But it is not the sole reason. One should not overlook the novelist's own faults. Often he chooses to register a formal situation by means of dialogue (this originates in the author's insistence on presenting "complete scenes" which start from the moment two people meet).[1] Some conversations are trivial and downright redundant. They include too many lengthy comments on events and even semi-philosophical speeches.[2] The author is fond of recording "verbal duels," many of which contribute little to the understanding of the characters.[3]

Above all, Maḥfūẓ's characters express themselves not in their own words, but rather in those of their author. The reader is very seldom capable of identifying a character of Maḥfūẓ when confronted with only one or two of its utterances. The same standard language is spoken by learned and ignorant, young and old.[4] Indeed the use of *'āmmiyya* would have made such a differentation easier to accomplish. Yet Maḥfūẓ himself, in his later novels, proves that it

in the later novels, when his fame made it unnecessary for him to comply with such rules. Above all, such a proposition is belied by the fact that the author's early short stories—his very first attempts in the field of fiction—have the same language of dialogue. One would be on safer ground to assume that Maḥfūẓ has chosen this language of his own accord. He is later to explain this choice by two factors : a) the national motive, i.e., the historical attachment to the language of the ancient Arabs and the fact that it is at present the common language of all Arabs; and b) Maḥfūẓ considers the dialect as inferior to the *fuṣḥā*; authors, he believes, should strive to shape a modern language which is basically the written Arabic enriched by vernacular expressions (sse interview, al-Bannā, *al-Adab* (Cairo), July 1960, p. 237).

The question of the language of dialogue has been a matter of much controversy for at least three decades. Consequently a great number of essays have been written on that subject. A useful survey of the history of this problem, together with bibliography, can by found in al-Shārūnī's book *Dirāsāt adabiyya* (n.d.), pp. 127-257 (esp. pp. 186-218).

[1] See for instance, KHAN, Ch. 5; QAH, Ch. 5.

[2] For example, ZUQ, Ch. 33 (Ruḍwān al-Ḥusaynī's pious philosophy).

[3] For instance, ZUQ, pp. 136ff. (Zīṭa and Ḥasaniyya); KHAN, pp. 125ff. (Rushdī and his friends).

[4] The mother in BID, who is presumably ignorant, is made to speak in such an elevated style as حدثني فريد افندي محمد عن معهد التربية الابتدائي فوجدت فيه ميزات تستحق التقدير، فمدة دراسته ثلاث سنوات بالمجان تضمن بعدها وظيفة مدرس (BID, p. 233) أراك كعادتك نافذ الصبر متعجلا للمتاعب، ونصيحتي لك الا تخلط أفراحك الحقيقية بافراح وهمية لا أهمية لها ... (BID, p. 278).

is often possible to convey the sense of individual identity while still using the *fuṣḥā*.[1] In these early novels, however, the author, in using the standard language, is unable to convey idiosyncracies of language, local idioms, slang and the like.[2]

The tension between the different levels of speech (or between *fuṣḥā* and *ʿāmmiyya*), which is often employed by novelists to produce effects, humorous or otherwise, is virtually non-existent except when explicitly indicated by the author.[3] In fact Maḥfūẓ, like many writers who use the *fuṣḥā* in dialogue, very frequently resorts to introductory remarks describing the speaker's tone, mood, gesticulations.[4] The use of these remarks, it is true, is a technique employed by practically all novelists. But the excessive recurrence of "stage direction" in Maḥfūẓ's novels is tantamount to an admission on the author's part that his dialogue cannot by itself convey modulations or similar effects.

All this having been said, it must be pointed out that the language of these novels is not entirely devoid of elements of the spoken language. Many lexical items are used which are taken from the Cairene dialect

---

[1] See the language sections in Chs. IV, V, VI of this book.

[2] To specify a special local dialect spoken by a character, the author would supply such remarks as وسمعت الام صوتا يقول بلهجة ريفية (BID, p. 218).

[3] In BID, pp. 255-6, the author tells us that the army officer, when addressing the new cadets, spoke *ʿāmmiyya*, but a *fuṣḥā* expression العقاب الصارم punctuated his speech : وكان يخطب باللغة العامية بصوت أجش يوافق ما ارتسم على أساريره من الصلابة والعنف ، وكان يفصل بين كثير من جمله بهذه العبارة « العقاب الصارم » حتى صارت كضربات الايقاع وملأت القلوب رهبة وحذرا.

[4] The following are a few instances—chosen at random—of such introductory remarks : QAH, pp. 6-7 : وقال بنبرات خطابية؛ قال ... بلهجة انتقادية؛ فقال ... بلهجة تقريرية.
KHAN, p. 155 : وقال بلهجته الجدية؛ فاستدرك ... قائلا بأسف؛ .. فقال بانكار؛ وقال بلهجة ساخرة.
ZUQ, p. 221 : قال بلهخة تنم عن التسليم؛ قالت بسرعة وحدة؛ ثم قال لها بسرور وفخار؛ فغمغمت تقول وقد تورد وجهها.
BID, pp. 166-7 : وسمعته يقول ضاحكا في زهو؛ فقالت بعجلة واضطراب؛ فقال بدهشة وفتور؛ وقالت بلهجة المستصرخ؛ وتساءلت في قلق؛ وسألها بلهجة ذات معنى.

(and which are, therefore, not necessarily comprehensible to readers in other Arab regions). But these colloquialisms are by no means confined to the dialogue, often occurring in the narrative style itself. Such words and expressions belong in the main to the field of *realia* (food products[1] and similar local items).[2] Occasionally a saucy local expression makes an appearance.[3]

More interesting is the "hidden" vernacular which is to be found mainly in the dialogue. Occasionally one can detect, behind the *fuṣḥā* veneer, syntactical structures typical of the spoken Arabic of the Egyptians.[4] In many cases the colloquial constructions are rendered literally since all their words are of the common type (common, that is, to both the spoken and written languages). The resultant sentences thus worded are only outwardly *fuṣḥā*. A closer scrutiny, however, will reveal that they do not comply with the norms of classical Arabic. They constitute, in fact, a stylized version of the *ʿāmmiyya*.[5]

---

1 Examples : ابوفروة (BID, p. 51); كستليتة ، ممبار ، موزة (BID, p. 111); بسبوسة (ZUQ, p. 6); صينية فريك (ZUQ, p. 73); النقل ، الكنافة ، القطائف (KHAN, p. 77); مفتقة ، موغات (ZUQ, p. 28).

2 Examples : وابور الزلط (ZUQ, p. 62); تعميرة على الجوزة (KHAN, p. 28); [لعب] الكومي (ZUQ, p. 15); حانطور (ZUQ, p. 7); [حفلة] زار (KHAN, p. 27).

3 Examples : يا هوه (BID, p. 112); دقة قديمة (BID, p. 267; ZUQ, p. 40); ابن القديمة (BID, p. 208); يا عكروت (ZUQ, p. 247); معلهش يازهر (ZUQ, p. 270).

4 Instances of such structures are the repetition of the vocative *yā* in : ياخراب بيتك يا اختي (BID, p. 11); ياخسارتك ياحميدة (ZUQ, p. 32). The following sentence is conspicuously remiscent of the Cairene idiom : ستي تسلم عليك يا ستي وتقول ان هذا فطير القرافة (BID, p. 45).

5 Such cases are the adjectival (or predicative) construct والهانم طول الشبر (BID, p. 266); كريمة بلك قد الدنيا (BID, p. 345); طربوش نصف عمر (ZUQ, p. 134); درجة ولا كل الدرجات (ZUQ, p. 128); or the adjectival use of *kam* (in the sense of "a few") in the following sentence (BID, p. 39); ولست طامعا فما تريد الا اللقمة والسترة وكم كأسا من الكونياك ، وكم نفسا من الحشيش ، وكم امرأة من النساء.

A remarkable reflection of the Egyptian Arabic can be found in the following example : أصل شعبنا اعتاد الجوع (BID, p. 226).

These reflections of the spoken language render the language of the dialogue more lively and vibrant. They are, however, few and far between. Furthermore they do not seem to follow a pattern : they are not confined, for instance, to a certain type of people (say, uneducated). Indeed simple people, as we have already seen, can speak in a most literary language. Moreover in the great majority of cases, the author is meticulous in using the forms and features of classical Arabic, even when there is a way of replacing these features with ones which are less remote from the spoken language. Very often the dual[1] or the passive tense[2] occur in the speech of simple people. In matters of vocabulary, too, there is a tendency to use—in the dialogue—words which exist only in *fuṣḥā* in preference not only to vernacular equivalents, but also to words of the common type.[3]

C. A Cairene Oedipus : al-Sarāb

Unlike the four novels discussed above, *al-Sarāb* (SAR) cannot be described as a social novel. Admittedly, it is contemporary, presenting people and scenes from twentieth century Cairo. Yet the sector of society which it portrays bears no resemblance to that familiar to Maḥfūẓ's novels. Most of its people are of Turkish origin, well-off and rather secluded from the world surrounding them.

Of equal importance is the fact that the theme of this book is exclusively psychological, being an account of the mental development

---

1 Examples : ماخطبكما (BID, p. 81, the speaker being the mother !);
حسبكما (BID, p. 7, the same speaker);
أن تتحملا (BID, p. 5);
انهماخارجان (BID, p. 94).

2 Examples : ولن تُحرق الدنيا (BID, p. 263) هذا خيرما يُفعل (BID, p. 330); ان تُقترفَ جريمة (KHAN, p. 104); أن تُحرم من نعمة النوم (KHAN, p. 116); مُنحت اجازة. (ZUQ, p. 267).

3 Thus : حسبي (BID, p. 66) instead of the common root كفى;
لنعد (BID, p. 101) instead of the common root رجع;
نافذة (BID, p. 251) instead of the common شباك;
واخجلتاه (ZUQ, p. 126) instead of the common roots عيب , حياء;
أمقت (ZUQ, p. 197) instead of the common root كره.

of Kāmil Ru'ba Lāẓ, son of divorced parents, whose excessive attachment to his mother throughout childhood and youth makes him sexually erratic and of somewhat dull intellect. Some Freudian theories are well reflected in every chapter of the book.

In many ways this novel is a refreshing experiment, an attempt, albeit ephemeral, to break loose from the familiar faces and scenes. In fact it makes Maḥfūẓ's world richer and more diversified. Furthermore the author proves his admirable capacity for adopting and mastering new techniques. His first attempt at a novel in the first person[1] is surprisingly free from technical faults. He maintains throughout this relatively long work (about 100,000 words) a distance between the protagonist-narrator and himself. He views all events from within, never forgetting that it is through Kāmil's eyes that we follow the story. When, at the age of seventeen, Kāmil contemplates suicide, he reflects : "Just a few moments, and it is eternal peace. I was unaware of the punishment inflicted in the world to come upon those who commit suicide, so I had no doubt that I was embarking on a life of repose."[2] It is this kind of reflection that can prove or disprove the author's command of the technique, for he could have easily forgotten for a second that the protagonist-narrator, who is relating the story many years after the event, is still an unsophisticated believer. In other words, a less cautious author might have written something like "I thought so because I was unaware at the time of the punishment *which is said to be* inflicted, etc."

Yet, while on the technical level, the subtleties of form are maintained, there is often a feeling that Kāmil expresses some *ideas* which are too complex to be his own (it is to be remembered that he was regarded by everyone as being far from brilliant). This applies especially to the profound observations that Kāmil makes on matters of psychology. He is at all times capable of laying his finger on the precise nature of his psychological and sexual problems. He arranges the material of his confession in a manner which only one who is versed in psychological literature can do.[3]

---

[1] In HAMS, the collection of the author's early short stories, two stories ("al-Sharīda" pp. 28-46; "Ṣawt min al-'ālam al-ākhar," pp. 300-317) are in the first person, but in the first, the narrator is a witness, not a protagonist.

[2] SAR, p. 59 : دقائق معدودات ثم الراحة الابدية. ولم يكن لدي علم عن عذاب المنتحر في الاخرة، فلم أشك في أني أستهل حياة مطمئنة.

[3] Admittedly Kāmil tells us (p. 78) that he studied the elements of psychology

Of course a novel in the first person, though offering a more focused picture and a stronger illusion of reality, deprives its author of some of the vantage points which are the basic privileges of the omniscient author. The protagonist-narrator can only record things he has seen or heard, and is only credible when he talks about matters he knows well. Thus it is understandable that in SAR only the portraits of the mother and grandfather and, of course, of Kāmil himself, are represented in depth. Similarly it is only natural that the other members of the family, such as Kāmil's brother and sister, are only lightly touched upon : having lived with their father, they are only in the periphery of Kāmil's world.

A more difficult case is presented by the character of Kāmil's wife, Rabāb. Throughout Kāmil's prolonged courting and during the few months of their married life, she impresses us as the epitome of kindness, modesty and fidelity. Thus when we suddenly discover that she has been unfaithful to her husband, her whole portrait becomes incoherent, her actions unexplained. True, we have only seen her through the eyes of her naïve and loving husband who lived with her for a relatively short period, and is therefore likely to miss some pointers in her conduct which would make her betrayal more credible. In short, the form of this novel can be blamed, to a certain extent, for the shortcomings in her characterization. However, a novel in the first person is not devoid of the means for making such points clearer. For instance, her fall could have been elucidated retrospectively through a remark dropped by her lover or mother.

The main criticism which can be levelled against this novel is that it is too much of a psychological report. Psychology, in many parts of the book, ceases to be a tool in the service of the novelist; rather, it becomes an end in itself.

Some critics find this very point praiseworthy and pay homage to Maḥfūẓ for introducing modern psychology into Arabic fiction.[1] Surely the novel attests its author's wide acquaintance with that field of knowledge, but the mere introduction of scientific or semi-scientific theories into literature is not by itself an artistic achievement. The novelist can assimilate the knowledge provided by psychologists into his art,[2] but the essence of his work is far removed from

---

in school, but that cannot account for such a well-arranged and highly sophisticated introspection as can be found in SAR.

1 Rāghib, p. 216.

2 Many critics, in fact, connect the rise of the twentieth century techniques in the

that of the psychologist. The latter tries to sift his cases and regiment them into clear-cut categories while the novelist is especially interested in portraying those situations, mental or otherwise, which cannot be pigeon-holed. It is in the nature of the artist's trade to relish ambiguities and reflect ironic incongruities.

SAR impresses one as being a story tailored to suit one such psychological concept—the Oedipal situation. Kāmil grows up with his divorced mother, who had been deprived of her other two children (they lived with the father who forbade them to see their mother). The mother becomes attached to Kāmil in a manner which the latter describes as "an unnatural love which went too far. Her wounded motherhood found solace, comfort and remedy in me."[1] When her son became a young man, she could not bear the thought that one day he would marry.[2] The son himself is far from detesting such a relationship : he enjoys being cosseted and protected. He is utterly dependent on his mother and even shares her bed until he is twenty-six (and would not have thought of getting a separate bed, were it not for his grandfather's rebuke).[3]

But this is not the only source of Kāmil's emotional anomaly and, consequently, his tragedy. A fixation of a different kind is implanted in him in his early youth : an ugly housemaid teaches him, at the age of eleven, the secrets of sex.[4] The mother discovers the affair and expels the girl. The incident, however, has repercussions on Kāmil's sexual preferences throughout his manhood : he is only aroused by women as ugly as that maid.[5] He is, to be sure, capable of loving a good-looking young woman, as happens in the case of Rabāb. Yet when it comes to sex he finds himself virtually impotent unless confronted with ugliness.

Such was the psychological (or clinical) background against which Kāmil's tragedy unfolds. He marries the attractive and intelligent girl, Rabāb, but finds himself incapable of satisfying her. Later his wife arouses his suspicion. He sets out to spy on her to find out whether

---

novel, as in other artistic fields, with the theories propagated by Freud and his disciples. See Allen, *The English Novel*, p. 327; Kettle, vol. 2, p. 60; West, p. 90.

[1] SAR, p. 18 : ... كان حنانا شاذا قد جاوز حده ... كانت مصابة في صميم أمومتها فوجدت فيّ أنا السلوى والعزاء والشفاء.

[2] SAR, p. 53-4 : 55-6 : 109-110; 184-9.

[3] SAR, p. 102.

[4] SAR, p. 49.

[5] SAR, pp. 55, 77, 289, 310, 313.

there is another man in her life, but in the meantime another woman enters his own life. 'Ināyāt, an ugly widow, much older than he, at once becomes mother and lover to him. Having discovered his sexual abilities through 'Ināyāt, his suspicions vis-à-vis Rabāb are pushed out of his mind for a while. Finally his wife dies while undergoing a secret abortion. It turns out that she was trying to get rid of the child of another man (who was himself the doctor performing the abortion). This news drives Kāmil out of his senses. He insults his ailing mother who dies that night.

The plot, therefore, is constructed on the scaffolding of the complexes which dominated the protagonist's personality. Some parts of the book have no obvious function other than to demonstrate these complexes. Kāmil's affair with 'Ināyāt, for instance, has little bearing on the fate of the triangle, Kāmil—his mother—Rabāb. Her appearance in the novel constitutes, in fact, a separate development in Kāmil's story. It looks as if 'Ināyāt was brought into the book to personify Kāmil's sexual fixation (his inclination towards ugly and elderly women). That, of course, explains in more explicit terms, the sources of Kāmil's sexual failure in the case of Rabāb, but each of the two stories remains self-contained.

There are also in the novel certain scenes and remarks which are reminiscent of popular clinical books dealing with sexual problems of young people (e.g. the problem of masturbation,[1] the first night of a virgin couple).[2]

The novel, however, is by no means devoid of colourful people and cleverly laid situations. Kāmil's long-hidden love for Rabāb is presented with much sensitivity. The grandfather, a retired army officer, is anything but a stock figure. Especially interesting is the portrait of Kāmil's father, whose few short appearances in the course of the novel (and particularly, the first, when the grandfather takes Kāmil to meet him)[3] are amongst the most lively in SAR. The sudden metamorphosis of the father from a dull and stupefied drunkard into a shrewd egotist, is delineated succinctly, but with great insight. Lastly one cannot but admire the irony with which Kāmil's entanglement with 'Ināyāt is presented : it is precisely when he is out

---

[1] SAR, pp. 55, 77, 90, 236, 238.

[2] SAR, Ch. 40.

[3] SAR, Ch. 12.

to find proof of his wife's infidelity, that he himself plunges inadvertently into infidelity.[1]

Occasionally the author is capable of mitigating the over-prosaic, sometimes edifying, tone of the novel by evoking the more "spiritual" facets of Kāmil's self. There are moments of religious aspiration, of closeness to God.[2] At times we have a vague feeling that Kāmil is looking for something beyond the adjustment of his emotional and social defects. Mystery-laden words like *sirr* and *lughz* ("secret" and "enigma" respectively) occur all too often in his language.[3] Finally in the last pages of the book, Kāmil is overwhelmed by an urge for self-purgation and feels that he was born for nothing but *taṣawwuf* ("mysticism," "pietism").[4] That moment, of course, comes in the wake of a severe traumatic experience which befalls him, namely the discovery that he had been cuckolded, and the death, within hours of each other, of the two people he loved most. In that sense one might suspect the author of reverting, here too, to psychology, i.e. of being interested not in the spiritual experience, but in a certain state of mind.

[1] SAR, p. 309.

[2] SAR, pp. 56-7; 107.

[3] See, for instance, SAR pp. 125; 128; 145; 194; 205; 220; 347; 348; 349.

[4] SAR, p. 366.

CHAPTER FOUR

THE CHANGING RHYTHM

The Trilogy—General

No sooner did Maḥfūẓ publish the first volume of his Trilogy in 1956 (*Bayn al-Qaṣrayn* [TR-I]), than it became clear to many readers that this was the beginning of a great literary event. With the appearance in 1957 of the second and third volumes (*Qaṣr al-Shawq* [TR-II] and *al-Sukkariyya* [TR-III]), these expectations proved to be fully justified. The author was now unanimously acclaimed as the foremost novelist of modern Egypt.

The work, an enormous personal testimony, portrays the political scene of Egypt, and the daily life of the middle-class Cairene through a period of twenty-seven years (1917-1944). No future student of Egyptian politics, society or folklore will be able to overlook the material embodied in Maḥfūẓ's Trilogy.

The portrait of the 1919 Egyptian revolution is, for one thing, more accurate, and at the same time more lively than that of any previous attempt in the field of literature (not excluding that of Tawfīq al-Ḥakīm).

The change of social patterns is not less admirably recorded; the rapid rejection of time-honoured social norms, the slow emancipation of woman from medieval shackles, the spread of education and scientific thinking, the increasing influence of western culture, the decline of religious adherence among the urban middle-class.

But while the process of change is at the forefront of this work, the world of yesterday, that which is rapidly losing ground, receives no less meticulous a treatment. It is delineated with great competence and love (sometimes even with a tinge of nostalgia). Throughout the pages of the Trilogy, and especially its first part, this world is recalled in its minutest details. The people of Cairo in the early twenties come alive before us, as do their habits, entertainments, songs, prejudices, dress and furniture.[1]

Yet it cannot be stressed too strongly that this is not a sociological

---

[1] In *al-Majalla*, March 1958, pp. 99-106, an article by Fawzī al-ʿIntīl enumerates such features of social habits and folklore as can be found in TR-I.

or historical study. Neither is it a body of social or political criticism in the guise of narrative. Maḥfūẓ's Trilogy, is, above all, a *novel* and a very enjoyable one at that.

The many, ever-widening circles which constitute the material of this work are at all times under control, and one has to look very hard if one is to discover discrepancies or inconsistencies. Similarly the reader finds no difficulty whatever in following the comings and goings of the numerous protagonists. The tension is nearly always kept at a high pitch and there are very few dull passages in the whole of the 1500 pages comprising the Trilogy.

The Trilogy admittedly draws on autobiographical material, yet it is by no means an autobiographical novel. Neither the social background nor the personages are fully identifiable with those of Maḥfūẓ's own life. The main character, Kamāl, resembles the author in more than one detail, but the two differ in many others. Certain fragments of the author's own story are delegated to other characters.[1] The general tone is detached and balanced, so different in fact from that of many confessional novels.

In more than one way the Trilogy can be compared to Thomas Mann's first major novel *Buddenbrooks* (1901). Both novels deal with the history of a family through several generations. Both are characterized by patient accumulation of detail, and combine autobiographical and imaginary material; above all, both describe, albeit the difference in background, the decline of the merchant and the appearance of the intellectual.[2]

None of the stories embodied in the Trilogy are simple and there are no happy endings. Life is a complicated web where tragedy lies in every corner. On reading the Trilogy one is continually shocked by the most cruel manifestations of life and human relations. In this way it is saved from being one of those middle-brow family

---

[1] Aḥmad Shawkat, for instance, is undoubtedly representative of Maḥfūẓ's socialistic inclinations. Furthermore the meeting between Aḥmad and 'Adlī Karīm (TR-III, Ch. 13) has an accurate parallel in Maḥfūẓ's life—his first meeting with Salāma Mūsā. The "authenticity" of this chapter was confirmed by both Maḥfūẓ and Mūsā (see Shukrī, *al-Muntamī*, pp. 40-1).

Even minor physical features of the author are bestowed upon certain characters of the Trilogy, not necessarily Kamāl : the prominent mole on Maḥfūẓ's left cheek is transferred to Amīna (TR-I p. 6).

[2] A. Kettle, *An Introduction*, II, p. 87.

chronicles. In discussing Galsworthy's *Man of Property*, Arnold Kettle provides us with a useful characterization of that brand of chronicle :

> Though permitted to titillate with the mention and even the occasional vision of the unmentionable, [middle-brow literature] must never fundamentally shake, never stretch beyond breaking point, certain secure complacencies. It is worth making this point because it would be quite wrong to see 'middle-brow' literature as merely qualitatively mediocre, better than bad literature but worse than good. Its distinctive feature is not its quality but its function.

The function of Maḥfūẓ's Trilogy is precisely "to fundamentally shake."

I have mentioned one novel to which the Trilogy bears some resemblance and which could have influenced Maḥfūẓ. Egyptian critics have found some threads leading to other masterpieces of the *roman-fleuve.*[1] Surely any novelist writing a novel of generations must have learned something from other masters. Maḥfūẓ is no exception and indeed we hear from him about his acquaintance with such works at an early stage.[2] On the other hand he has for many years practised, with considerable success, the family-based novel, though none of these spans many years or covers several generations. We have also seen that he has always been interested in portraying "complete worlds." It would not then be an exaggeration to suggest that this Trilogy emerged as a natural development, as a culmination of its author's earlier experiments, and that it is a natural extension of his former literary experiments. What Maḥfūẓ has learned from the western masters does not exceed the general framework, and it would be more profitable to point out its links with other works of Maḥfūẓ, particularly as both characters and events are unmistakably Egyptian and the local colour is ever-present. The structure and technique are, to anticipate further discussion, in harmony with the intrinsic qualities of the characters. The novel's rhythm is dictated by the changing pace of life in Cairo.

It has often been said that this is a Naturalistic novel. If by Naturalism is meant a meticulous portrayal of life and its seamy side in particular, such a description would fit the Trilogy to a certain

---

[1] Dr. 'Awaḍ mentions Zola's Rougon-Macquart cycle (see *Maqālāt*, p. 369ff); Gh. Shukrī makes a comparison between Maḥfūẓ's Trilogy and that of Sartre, *Les Chemins de la liberté* (see *al-Muntamī*, pp. 9ff.).

[2] See *supra* p. 45.

extent, for its author shows here, more than in the other Cairene novels, a great passion for the minute details of life. Nothing is left in the dark, however unappealing it might be.

But one should be more sceptical if by Naturalism is meant a philosophy of life, or in the words of Edmund Wilson, a doctrine which

> ... was put into practice by novelists like Zola, who believed that composing a novel was like performing a laboratory experiment : you had only to supply your characters with a specific environment and heredity and then watch their automatic reactions.[1]

In fact this is precisely what one Egyptian critic, Dr. Louis ʿAwaḍ claims.[2] He cites a few examples in TR-I to illustrate his view. The most convincing of the examples—which in any case are not numerous—is that of Yāsīn, the son of al-Sayyid by his first marriage. ʿAwaḍ reminds us that throughout the novel Yāsīn's sexual excesses, which border on obsession, are linked with the fact that both his parents were overly inclined to sensual pleasures.[3]

Admittedly, the case of Yāsīn bears a resemblance to certain characters in Naturalistic novels, yet it does not determine the nature of the whole work. In a way he functions in the Trilogy as a foil to his father who is far more central in the work. Yāsīn is consistently portrayed as a vulgar, unrefined version of al-Sayyid. In this manner the father's image gains much of the dignity and charm that the author intended it should have. His acts and excesses become, when compared to those of his son, much less distasteful than they would otherwise look.[4] To mention but one example : the simultaneous affairs of both the father and son with Zannūba, the *ʿūd*-girl, which culminates in the latter falling into disgrace while the former escapes—albeit by the skin of his teeth.[5]

In the third volume of the Trilogy, we can find another example of the formula "heredity plus environment equals character," again

---

1 Wilson, *Axel's Castle*, p. 13.

2 ʿAwaḍ, *Maqālāt*, p. 369 : وهي ليست عملية « مسح » كما يذهب بعض النقاد ولكنها تجربة علمية على طريقة زولا واشياعه في آثار قوانين الوراثة الاجتماعية ...

3 *Ibid.*, pp. 370-3.

4 See *infra* p. 117.

5 TR-II, esp. Chs. 25-30.

connected with Yāsīn. Ruḍwān, his son by his first marriage, shows certain homosexual inclinations. He shuns women and is disgusted by the very thought of marriage. These qualities are expressly seen as a result of his anomalous upbringing, his father's excesses, etc.

Yet such characters in the Trilogy should not mislead us into viewing the whole work in a Naturalistic light. After all Yāsīn and Ruḍwān are only two in a large gallery of characters who populate the three volumes of this novel. There is no feel of the laboratory in these characters and even in the two cases just mentioned, it can be said that the stress on environment and heredity does not constitute the sole point of departure.

Above all it can be noticed that there is much less determinism here than in Maḥfūẓ's other novels. In fact the stress is not on the perennial, the static, the immutable. On the contrary : the main theme of the Trilogy is precisely the *change*. It is in fact a study of a rapidly changing human community, a change which finds expression in every aspect of the lives and values of these people.[1]

The change, it must be added, is not confined to superficial aspects of life. In this respect one should not make the mistake of seeing the Trilogy as a political novel as indeed a few critics have done.[2]

True, the interest in politics is here, as in practically all of Maḥfūẓ's works, a central issue. This is especially true of TR-I and TR-III. The death of Fahmī in the first volume and the emergence of a generation of political activists in the third, tend to create the impression that the whole work is basically a commentary on the Egyptian political scene. The major political events are at all times recorded with great accuracy. Many of the important upheavals in politics have parallels in the life of al-Sayyid's family. The very day of Sa'd Zaghlūl's death witnesses the death of 'Ā'isha's husband and two sons (TR-II, Ch. 44). There are even certain political figures who make an appearance in TR-III (e.g. 'Adlī Karīm, the Leftist journalist who represents the well-known author and activist Salāma Mūsā; the corrupt 'Abd

[1] The stress on the theme of change can only be seen clearly when viewing the Trilogy as a whole, with special reference to TR-II and TR-III. The first volume, in fact, deals mainly with the old society, which is only the starting point of the work. Dr. 'Awaḍ, to be sure, bases his judgement chiefly on TR-I (as he himself admits at one point, see *Maqālāt*, p. 346).

[2] E.g. Shukrī, *al-Muntamī*, pp. 15-70; 218-30; J. al-Sayyid in *al-Kātib*, Jan. 1963, pp. 70-79.

al-Raḥīm Pasha 'Īsa, who has many prototypes in the *ancien régime*). One can also agree with M. Jomier that :

> Il a cependant souligné de temps à autre le parallélisme que l'on constate entre l'évolution des moeurs familiales et l'évolution politique de l'Égypte. Tandis que les enfants échappaient petit à petit au despotisme de leur père, l'Egypte échappait elle aussi à la domination des Anglais.[1]

Yet a closer look at the work—again as one entity—will reveal that politics is only one of many facets. A great number of protagonists of al-Sayyid's family, and to a certain degree Kamāl himself, are only marginally politically minded. Furthermore, although a certain bias towards the Left is discernible in the third volume, the novel is far removed from what is known as socialist-realism. It has no "positive hero" (Fahmī, the only one who comes near to that description, disappears as early as the first volume). It has no easy way out to offer and does not end in either resounding triumph or defeat. Politics, in a word, is brought into the novel only to the extent that it constitutes an integral part of the life-fabric of the urban Arab (and the Arab intelligentsia in particular).

To see politics in the Trilogy in its right perspective let us return to Fahmī. His death is undoubtedly the climax of the first volume. But the political quality of his heroism is intermingled with the eternal "Mockery of Fate" theme. He dies at the "wrong" moment! Having weathered the severe storms of revolution and survived the bloodiest of battles, he is killed when marching in a peaceful demonstration in honour of Zaghlūl's release.

His death is naturally a traumatic experience for the whole family. It affects their lives—especially that of the mother—immensely. But one of its repercussions is, in fact, to keep them away from politics and it is only twenty years later that political activists rise in their midst. Moreover, when viewed in the context of the work as a whole, the death receives a different connotation. It is only one of a series of tragic events (and the only one to have any political significance). At least six other members of the family die in the course of the novel in addition to a dozen or so minor characters. The total effect of the recurring deaths, some no less tragic than that of Fahmī, is to further emphasize the tragedy of life, and to underline the existential question. Indeed the "non-political" aspect of Fahmī's death is forcefully

---

[1] *MIDEO* IV, p. 28.

brought to prominence by Kamāl when he recollects an incident which occurs to him shortly after his brother's death. (He remembers these events seven years after they occurred, in a soliloquy, hence the second person):

> Immortality, you said? ... Do you remember that experiment which you performed at the age of twelve, in order to find out what would happen to him [i.e., the dead Fahmī]? Oh, painful memory! You caught a bird in its nest, strangled it, then shrouded it. Then you dug a small grave for it in the backyard of the house, near the old well. There you buried it. A few days —or weeks—later you dug out the corpse from the soil, and, ho,what you saw, what you smelt! You rushed to your mother, enquiring about the fate of the deceased, any deceased, and Fahmī in particular. Only her tears turned you away.[1]

Politics, then, is only one of many manifestations of life which Maḥfūẓ tackles in his Trilogy. The question might now be asked: Is there one central point around which the whole work pivots? Is it a philosophical "inquiry" into the effect on human beings of time, death, and fate? In a way it is. These issues are ever-present and no reader can fail to notice them. But as has already been pointed out, the author, while greatly interested in all matters philosophical or metaphysical, is always aware of the basic demands of the art of story-telling. His main concern is to tell the *story* of his own world, past and present, mundane and spiritual. Having lived in an age of dramatic change, of seething revolution, he is fascinated above all by the process of that change. He dwells upon the fate of his nation, groping for a quick way out of the medieval world and, at the same time, fighting to rid itself of foreign domination. He is fascinated by the *rapidly changing rhythm of life*. It is this changing rhythm, as we shall see later, that determines the structure and style of the whole work.

Each one of the features—social, political, or otherwise—embodied in this novel deserves a special study, and indeed numerous articles have already been written on it, some with considerable insight, by Egyptian critics.[2] It will not be possible in the context of this chapter to cover all or even most of these points. On matters concerning the social and religious scene, one can refer to Jomier's essay, which at

---

1 TR-II, pp. 410-11.

2 See the articles mentioned in the Bibliography appended to this thesis. (List "C"—under "The Trilogy").

the same time, serves as a very useful introduction to the main characters of the novel. The following remarks will be confined to a discussion of selective questions of characterization, structure and language.

Characters

The Trilogy has no single character who can be described as the chief protagonist. The family of al-Sayyid as a whole is the hero of the work. Nevertheless there is in every volume one figure who dominates it.

TR-I pivots around al-Sayyid. His forceful personality overshadows all the rest. TR-II is mostly concerned with Kamāl (although its title *Qaṣr al-Shawq* is unfortunate in that it implies that the scene is that of Yāsīn's house). In TR-III Kamāl is still very important but no less prominent are the members of the third generation of the family, particularly Aḥmad, the youngest of al-Sayyid's grandsons.

Besides the members of the family and their direct posterity, there is a host of characters; but these are, in most cases, portrayed with quick strokes. The author's tone is, with very few exceptions, warm and friendly; there are very few caricatures to be found.[1]

It would be next to impossible to try to discuss all or most of these characters here. There are as many as fifteen members of al-Sayyid's family, at least that number of secondary yet important ones (e.g., the sons-in-law, al-Sayyid's bosom friends) and twice as many peripheral men and women. We shall have to confine our remarks to those who seem most important to us.

al-Sayyid — On the face of it, the portrait of Aḥmad 'Abd al-Jawād (al-Sayyid) is not altogether new in Maḥfūẓ's fiction. It has many of its beginnings in the characters of earlier novels. The hedonistic merchant was already presented in ZUQ (Salīm 'Ilwān); the pious debauchee in RAD (Merenre').

Moreover the technique by which this character is presented in the Trilogy is basically the same—general introductory remarks followed

[1] It is to be noted that there are many characters of Turkish descent. Sometimes they are referred to—by other characters—in mildly derogatory clichés ('stubborn,' 'lazy'). Nevertheless there is, as far as the author is concerned, none of the anti-Turkish feeling, so conspicuous in al-Ḥakīm's *'Awdat al-rūḥ*. The Shawkats, for instance, are for all their sluggishness, kind-hearted and compassionate, and so is Muḥammad 'Iffat, al-Sayyid's life-long friend who is, furthermore, a sworn Egyptian patriot.

by a set of occurrences in which the character participates and where the generalizations are shown in action. It is only then that the character starts playing its proper role in the story. Nevertheless, this is one of the most impressive of Maḥfūẓ's characters, possibly his greatest achievement.

Its importance lies not only in its quality, which is undoubtedly superior to its rudimentary prototypes. The very "quantity"—the variety of the situations with which al-Sayyid is confronted, the accumulative wealth of personal traits—is impressive in itself.

Al-Sayyid dominates the whole of the first volume of the Trilogy. But he is also a very active figure in the second—and, until his death, is still important in the third. Through him we are acquainted with a representative (an individual representative, that is) of that colourful old race of patriarchal merchants. As a father he is despotic yet loving; as a merchant, astute yet generous; as a lover, indulgent yet majestic. The richness and many-sidedness of his personality are represented with great competence, mostly by means of action. Throughout these situations we get a full view of the world that surrounds al-Sayyid : his middle-aged friends, their *samar* parties, their amorous affairs with prominent *'awālim* (plural of *'ālima*—'a female singer'); their different attitudes towards family affairs, business, etc.

So much for the "quantity" of al-Sayyid's portrait. It is the "quality" that deserves most attention. Al-Sayyid is not merely a vehicle through which the dense layers of colourful details are delivered. He is a great dramatic figure : complex though crystal clear; lovable in spite of possessing many traits which are repulsive to our tastes.

The richness and complexity of this character can be demonstrated on two different levels : the psychological and the dramatic. Psychologically we know very much about his "accumulated experience" since, as we have already noted, there is a comprehensive introduction to his character in addition to recurring "introductions" by the author to different situations in which he is placed. His motivations are always complex, never one-sided, even when tackling trifling issues. There is always a certain dialectic in his "decision-making process" wherein, to vulgarize a well-known Hegelian concept, thesis is followed by anti-thesis, resulting in synthesis.

Consider, for example, the following situation in TR-I in which al-Sayyid has to decide on a course of action vis-à-vis his wife Amīna, who has disobeyed his orders and gone to visit a nearby mosque.

This outing, it will be remembered, results in a minor road accident in which Amīna is involved. While his wife is convalescing, al-Sayyid remains silent, apparently in a benevolent mood. No sooner does she recover, however, than he orders her to leave his house without delay. This scene of expulsion is followed by a lengthy analysis of the internal reasoning which led him to decide whether to punish her or not:

> As for al-Sayyid, with his last words he had been set free from the burden of thought which had stirred his brain throughout the past three weeks. The struggle had begun at the moment when the woman, confined to bed and weeping, had admitted her offence. At first he could not believe his ears. Then the odious reality of the challenge to his pride and self-importance began to dawn upon him. However until he saw the true nature of her injuries he postponed his rage for, truth to tell, he was unable to think about the challenge to his pride and conceit, because a deep anxiety bordering on fear and pity for the woman he was fond of and of whose virtues he thought highly—took possession of him. His compassion for her made him lose sight of her error, so he asked God for her well-being. His rigour receded in the face of her imminent danger. The abundant compassion which lay dormant within him was awakened. That same day he returned to his room, sad and dispirited. His face, either in front of her or any of his children, betrayed nothing of the struggle within him. Once he saw her firm steps to recovery, however, he very soon recovered his peace of mind. He proceeded therefore to reconsider the whole affair, its causes and its consequences, with a new eye—or to be exact with the old eye with which he was accustomed to look at his household. It was unfortunate, unfortunate for the mother that is, that he should have reconsidered it quietly, in solitude, and that he should have been convinced that if forgiveness triumphed and the call of compassion was obeyed, which was what his heart leaned towards, then he would forfeit his dignity, his honour, his tradition, everything; the reins would slip from his hands and the family, which he insisted on ruling with firmness and severity would fall apart.
>
> Aḥmad ʿAbd al-Jawād could not see himself in that situation at all; he could never be satisfied to be anyone but himself! It was most unfortunate then that he should have reconsidered the matter quietly, in solitude, for if he had been given the chance to vent his anger when she confessed, his anger would have been quenched and the incident would have passed over without trailing behind it such serious consequences. But he could not be angry at the time just as his pride would not permit him to manifest his rage immediately after her recovery, after a calm lasting three weeks, for this would have been more in the nature of a forced scolding than a genuine anger. Since his anger usually broke out both by nature and design and since the natural side had not found an outlet at the time, then from the point of view of design he was duty bound, having been given the opportunity to think it over calmly, to find a practical way to re-assert himself in a manner which corresponded to the gravity of the offence.[1]

[1] TR-I, p. 223-4.

This is a typical example of the manner in which al-Sayyid's mind works. It is highly complex and individual, yet it has nothing to do with the near-clinical psychology that we encountered earlier.

The complexity of this character can be further demonstrated by the fact that he is a man of many faces. He is one person at home (*wajh ḥāzim ṣārim*, 'a resolute, severe face') and another with his friends (*wajh bassām, mus͟hriq*, 'a smiling, radiant face'). He is, again, different when facing his God (*wajh k͟has͟hiʿ*, 'a submissive face'). He is a genuine and naïve believer, even though he would not refrain from commiting numerous acts which, he knows very well, cannot be approved by his Maker.

This last point brings us to the subject of *ambiguous morality*. In a way al-Sayyid represents a character that had long since intrigued the author—that of the pious sinner; how can belief and blasphemy, holiness and profanity dwell side by side in one human soul? "What a man you are," exclaims one of his mistresses, Zubayda.[1] "Outwardly you are respectable and pious; inwardly you are nothing but debauchery." This is too much of a simplification. In fact he is not only ostensibly pious. He is absolutely sincere in his devotions. His prayer is that "of passion, and genuine feeling."[2] It is a "spiritual pilgrimage which carries him around in the ample precincts of the Lord."[3] The author explains these ostensible discrepancies as follows:

> Was he two separate men in one personality? Or was his belief in the divine grace such that he did not believe that it would prohibit those joys? Even if they were prohibited, God's mercy would forgive the wrong-doers so long as nobody was harmed. It is more likely that he accepted life with his heart and senses without thought or introspection. He found in himself strong impulses. Some of them craved God; these were channelled by means of worship. Others pursued pleasure; and they were sated through amusement. He mingled them all within himself, confident and trusting, without bothering to reconcile them.[4]

But it is not this kind of explanation, so often supplied by the author, that makes al-Sayyid such a breathtaking example of the pious debauchee. Both sides of his ego are seen in live action throughout

---

[1] TR-I, p. 106: يا لك من رجل مظهره الوقار والتقوى وباطنه الخلاعة والفجور ...

[2] TR-I, p. 23.

[3] TR-I, p. 23: هكذا كانت الفريضة حجة روحية يطوف فيها برحاب المولى

[4] TR-I, pp. 51-2.

the book. Furthermore in both cases he is constantly contrasted with his son Yāsīn—an animal in his sensuality and an insincere adherent to his faith. Consequently the two outwardly incompatible features of the father are made much easier to accept.

Al-Sayyid's portrait is not a static one. The richness of his psychology and background motivations are not an end in themselves. They are instrumental in producing the tragic climax in which he is eventually placed. Thus he should not be evaluated on the basis of the first volume alone. For in this volume he is a great invincible giant. His word is undisputed. His spell on women is unsurpassed. To his household he is almighty, infallible. He is capable of solving any problem—at least this is the way people think of him (in fact he is more often than not unable to solve these problems and only imagines or suggests to people that he is). Yet already in TR-I there are signs that his world is not as unshakable as it seems to be. His children are beginning to rebel, each in his own way. They even persuade their mother to take a "rebellious" step—one which she has never taken before throughout her life with al-Sayyid (and which brings upon her much sorrow). Outside his house, the new political and social processes are too dynamic for him to understand fully. The pace of life in general is already too quick for al-Sayyid to cope with. TR-I ends with the death of Fahmī which results in al-Sayyid's forswearing most of his cherished pleasures. When, after a period of five years, he is prevailed upon to join his friends in their pleasures, he very soon discovers that time has already taken its toll. But it is not for him to give in without putting up a fight. He takes upon himself the challenge of "conquering" a young *'ūd*-girl, Zannūba. But the woman senses at once that his days of glory are gone and that he is now easy prey. She deliberately shows little enthusiasm, in the hope of squeezing as much as possible out of him. Finally she refuses to have any dealings with him unless he marries her.

Al-Sayyid is not unaware that he is fighting a losing battle. The reader is even more aware of this. He knows, unlike al-Sayyid, that Zannūba has in the past been the mistress of his son Yāsīn. Later she "betrays" the father to spend a night with the son.

Truly enough al-Sayyid is saved by whatever common sense he has from the humiliation that marrying this girl would have brought upon him. But the whole affair causes him great anguish. The scene of the aging man roaming around the houseboat that he himself rented for Zannūba and finally discovering her liaison with his own son, is amongst the most touching in the work. He is later to suffer the further indignity of having to accept Zannūba as his daughter-in-law. He is above all tormented by the feeling of his own helplessness in the face of events.

By the time of World War II he is an ailing, bedridden and desolate old man who has lost even the company of his life-long friends. His death itself is wrought with humiliation : he is carried back home from an air-raid shelter on Kamāl's shoulders, like a child. That night he dies.

Al-Sayyid is among the few characters who are not passive in the face of events. He is a man of action and will. Furthermore he is one of the few joyful people in Maḥfūẓ's novels : his humour would not desert him even in the most desperate hours of crisis. It can be said that it is these two qualities which render his decline and fall so poignant. He is strong-willed, but helpless against the tyranny of Time; he is fond of life and pleasures, but these, alas, never last.

Kamāl — Kamāl, sharing as he does some of the author's own experiences, provides those interested in the intellectual history of Egypt with rich material. He can be viewed as an important "specimen" of the sophisticated new generation, as the Egyptian breed of the "outsider" (*al-lā-muntamī*[1]) or as one critic prefers to put it, "the crisis-stricken insider" (*al-muntamī al-ma'zūm*).[2] The love-hate affair of the Arab intellectual with the West is portrayed through Kamāl with the utmost vitality.

As an artistic accomplishment, however, this character is rather uneven. In TR-I he is a perceptive and well-developed boy. The discrepancies between his powers of imagination on the one hand and his lack of positive action on the other, are already evident (for instance : in his imaginary story about the bus-conductor[3] or his behaviour at the time of the demonstration).[4] Yet one is often surprised that such an intelligent boy of twelve should show a curious lack of intelligence when witnessing Fahmī's flirtation with Maryam[5]

---

1 See al-Rā'ī, *Dirāsāt*, p. 272.

2 See Shukrī, *al-Muntamī*, pp. 68 *et passim*.

3 TR-I, Ch. 9.

4 TR-I, Ch. 55.

5 TR-I, Chs. 10; 21.

or when completely misunderstanding what marriage means.[1] In TR-II Kamāl is undisputed as the central figure. It is in this volume that the most poignant moments of his life unfold before us : his painful awakening to the realities of religion, love, and life in general. A succession of crises leave him pathetically irresolute. He loses faith in God, but is unable to find another haven of belief or idealism. His agonizing first love for the aristocratic 'Ā'ida leaves him with more than one open wound. He loses his self-confidence, becoming afraid of love and marriage, suspicious of friendship and helplessly aware of the prevailing social injustice and political perfidy. His literary ambitions are also frustrated and the pangs of love, far from igniting his imagination, suppress whatever creative ability he might possess. Nevertheless he refuses to let himself slide into cynicism or to become anti-social. This stage of his development is the most convincing and at the same the time most poetic.

In TR-III however, we witness a static Kamāl already fully shaped. His literary aspirations are reduced to occasional articles summarizing world philosophical trends. His great passion for "a life of ideas" which induces him to join a teacher's college, end in the unrewarding post of teacher of elementary English at a junior school. He is a bachelor and has not the courage to change his position when a sudden opportunity arises. Thus when, towards the end of the work, he becomes convinced that action is essential, his conversion does not impress us as being other than superficial.

It is only natural that the static image of Kamāl in his mid-thirties is less appealing, less interesting than that of TR-II or even TR-I. Ian Watt discussing Richardson's art, remarks as follows :

> ... compared to the drama or epic, the novel has tended to choose young protagonists whose developing reactions to ordinary human life are interesting precisely because they embody the psychological drama whereby the ego is formed. Once formed surely such characters like Pamela in the second two volumes will become flat. Only if they are involved in great events—such as befalls Ulysses or Macbeth—are full formed characters likely to interest us as such.[2]

Kamāl, to be sure, is not a flat character, even in TR-III. Yet he is, in a way, an anti-climax. The forceful portrait which emerges from TR-II is somewhat wasted. The author, had he so wished, could

---

[1] TR-I, Ch. 40.

[2] [Watt and others,] *The Novelist as Innovator*, pp. 12-3.

have eliminated him in one way or another in order to keep his overall image strongly focused. But a closer look convinces us that he is deliberately kept in the forefront of events in spite of his unchanging posture, as though the author wants to underline the tragedy of a man who comes to an impasse through inaction. Kamāl is in more than one way the reverse of his father. He is highly intelligent but devoid of will-power. He lacks the humour and joviality of al-Sayyid. He is tormented by the feeling of sterility and helplessness.

In that sense he is a precursor of a line of protagonists in later works by Maḥfūẓ who reach a point of absolute passiveness. It is this very awareness of his impotence which is now the centre of interest. Characters in later novels resort in one way or another to a rejection of human society and often take to mysticism. Kamāl does not reach this stage but he frequently refers to *taṣawwuf* in conjunction with himself.[1] When he is confronted by the bravery of his nephews and impressed by their active role in life, he reflects, as though criticising his own spiritual tendencies, that "mysticism (*taṣawwuf*) is escapism, so is a passive belief in science."[2]

Kamāl is no mystic but his thoughts and attitudes become more and more contemplative, seeking the ultimate secrets. The words *lughz* and *sirr*, which we have already encountered in earlier novels, now become the key words in his inner world. At first in TR-II those two words, when used by Kamāl, indicate the curiosity of youth, the inquisitiveness of the intelligent adolescent.[3] Yet in the static stage in TR-III they begin to assume a deeper significance.[4] Certain utterances by our character sound esoteric.[5]

---

1 E.g., TR-II, p. 206; TR-III, pp. 131, 231, 340.

2 TR-III, p. 391 : على ذلك فالتصوف هروب ، كما أن الايمان السلبي بالعلم هروب.

3 Examples; TR-II, p. 197 : هذا الذى جعل السعادة سرا تتيه فيه العقول والافهام...

TR-II, p. 283 : وفغمه شذا ياسمين ساحرا آسرا ولكن ما هويته؟ ، ما أشبهه بالحب في سحره وأسره وغموضه ، لعل سر هذا يفضي الى ذاك ، ولكنه لن يحل هذا اللغز حتى يأتي على تراتيل الحيرة.

4 Examples; TR-III, p. 44 : يسأل في الصباح عن معنى كلمة وهجاء أخرى ويتساءل بالليل عن معنى وجوده ذلك اللغز القائم بين لغزين.

TR-III, p. 303 : ... ضجره وسقمه وحيرته أمام ألغاز لاتحل

5 TR-III, p. 135 : اذا ضحكت بلا سبب فاعلمي أن الاسباب أجل من أن تذكر

Sometimes, however, he would entertain more "constructive" views, such as, "It would probably be wrong for us to search in our world for a meaning. Rather, it is our duty to create that meaning."[1] But such reflections never lead him to action.

True, the very last page of the novel sounds like a call to action. Kamāl's last words in the novel asking the salesman for a black tie, in mourning for his mother, can also be taken to indicate that his whole past is dying and a new era is being born. But the author's subsequent works, far from indicating the rise of a "new type of Kamāl," are full of passive, musing characters. Often these characters retreat into the world of mystical literature or adopt Ṣūfī attitudes. Kamāl then foreshadows the tragic hero whose tragedy does not rise—as in the social novels discussed in Chapter III—solely from the external strains and stresses. They are, to use the words of Murray Krieger,[2] "tragic visionaries" whose tragedy echoes the crisis mentality of our times. Hence they are much akin to the characters of such authors as Conrad, Kafka and Camus. It is their inner world which is irredeemably shattered.

The art of presenting the character of Kamāl is in itself an innovation, compared with the author's earlier works. There are very few examples wherein the "telling" technique is applied. Instead the image is revealed through action and through the character's introspection (which in itself is a way of "showing"). This technique is made possible by, among other things, the fact that Kamāl grows and matures before our eyes. We accompany him on a long journey throughout his boyhood and youth, sharing his observations, revelations and crises at first hand. In this manner the need for "briefing" as to his motivations vis-à-vis specific issues which arise later is eliminated.

To cite but one example : Kamāl's inaction, his timidity in the face of violence are seen in their rudimentary forms in his boyhood. Later we witness the frustration of his early youth which further inhibits his will to act. Thus when in TR-III (Ch. 4) he shelters in a safe café at the time of a violent demonstration, there is no need for the author to engage in a lengthy description of his state of mind as he would most likely have done in the case of the other characters.

---

[1] TR-III, p. 257 : ربما كان الخطأ أن نبحث في هذه الدنيا عن معنى بينا أن مهمتنا الاولى أن نخلق هذا المعنى.

[2] *The Tragic Vision*, pp. 3ff.

Suffice it for him to allude tersely to a similar occasion in Kamāl's childhood, when he ran away from a similar demonstration and sheltered in a little pastry shop.[1]

Other means of information is procured through the continuous self-searching internal monologue. Kamāl's introspective activity is marked by a genuine immediacy and natural flow. Possibly this stems from the semi-autobiographical nature of Kamāl. The author, as it were, is reflecting on his own inner self.

These techniques, though restricted in the Trilogy mainly to Kamāl, are adopted and fully developed by Maḥfūẓ in his short novels of the sixties, as we shall see in Chapter VI.

Other Characters

1. *Men : The Third Generation*

The three main representatives of the third generation—the two sons of Khadīja and one of Yāsīn—are men of action. They are entangled in a variety of interesting situations, yet the overall impression they leave is rather superficial. This apparently is due to hasty characterization. Although they come to the forefront of events at an early age (they are all under seventeen when the last volume opens) they are, however, fully shaped, each having already chosen a distinct course in life. In their first appearance in TR-III 'Abd al-Mun'im Shawkat is already under the influence of Muslim fundamentalism,[2] while his brother Aḥmad behaves in a manner which betrays an early attachment to the ideas of socialism-cum-atheism.[3] Lastly Ruḍwān is enchanted by "politics" i.e., by a political ambition which is not necessarily motivated by idealism[4] (before long we are also to discover his abnormalities in matters of sex). In the course of this volume each of the three develops along somewhat well-trodden paths, a fact which makes them less of individuals than representatives of the Muslim Brotherhood, Communism, and opportunism respectively. Needless to say, this is very similar to what happens to the three friends in QAH. TR-III is, as it were, a new, slightly improved version, this time in the context of one family. However, in TR-III the stress is not on the "negative" character, Ruḍwān, but on the two idealists, Aḥmad and 'Abd al-Mun'im.

[1] TR-III, p. 47; (the reference is to the story in TR-I, Ch. 55, [pp. 418-20]).
[2] TR-III, p. 37.
[3] TR-III, pp. 33, 37.
[4] TR-III, p. 38.

Aḥmad is attracted to revolutionary ideas at an early age (unfortunately we are not told when, where and how). His path to Marxist socialism and active Communism is fairly casual : it involves no intellectual or spiritual tremors. Neither does his atheism arouse unduly painful situations vis-à-vis his family or society. To a certain extent, he is viewed through the admiring eyes of Kamāl, who is inclined to regard his nephew as the epitome of positive actions, of progressive aspirations. No wonder then that he emerges as a rather favourable character.

On second reading however, we might discover that as a fictional character he lacks depth. His characterization is patchy and rather over-simplified, often following a generalized pattern. His disenchantment with the aristocratic girl ʿAlawiyya Ṣabrī does not go deep : her rejection of his love on mercenary grounds leaves but little emotional residue in Aḥmad's feelings. Later, when he joins the editorial board of the Leftist journal and falls in love with the Communist Sawsan Ḥammād, there is again little depth to his feelings. (Sawsan with her ice-cold reactions to his advances and her incessant doctrinaire remarks makes us wonder whether, after all, he has chosen the right woman as a wife.)

Aḥmad can be said to combine admirable features of both al-Sayyid (whose name he shares) and Kamāl. On the one hand he is resolute and active. On the other he is intellectually scrupulous, with a great flair for modern ideas. Yet, compared with the latter two portraits, Aḥmad comes out rather pale, thus lacking the ability to serve as a "corrective" to either of his two predecessors.

His brother ʿAbd al-Munʿim is not made to look particularly inspiring, even though he is as idealistic and as active as his younger brother. He is even more hastily sketched. Sometimes he is ridiculed by the author by the juxtapostition of his antiquated religious fanaticism to the more liberal ideals of the other members of his generation. Yet there is one episode that adds dimension to his otherwise externalized portrait. This is the scene wherein his deep religious feelings spoil his moments of pleasure with a girl living in their house. His agony ends when the "spirit" wins : he shuns the girl and instantly asks his father to find him a wife so as to free him from temptation.[1]

[1] TR-III, Ch. 17.

Ruḍwān, their cousin, is even more of a two-dimensional figure, yet in his case we at least have a ready-made psychological background which renders his acts plausible. He is the son of a broken marriage; he has grown up in abnormal circumstances, hence his aversion to marriage, his preference for the company of men, and finally his unbridled ambition. But it is to be stressed that his acts and motivations amount again to a *type*, a skeleton of a character which is poorly covered with sinew and flesh.

Many critics have noticed the relative inadequacy in the characterization in TR-III. Some, like Jomier,[1] tend to attribute this to the fact that these young characters only reach their manhood towards the end of the novel; hence there was insufficient room for the novelist fully to delineate them. This explanation is far from convincing. The three younger men appear in TR-III for a period of nine years. Aḥmad, for example, is sixteen when the volume commences and twenty-five when it ends. Surely these are the most revealing years as far as characterization is concerned (cf. Kamāl in TR-II).

Fahmī

Furthermore, in the Trilogy itself, or rather, in TR-I, there is one character, Fahmī, who dies at the age of eighteen, only two years after the novel opens. Yet he is a fully developed, impressively profound character. In fact, this character deserves more than a brief mention. His short appearance is one of the most forceful. The outline of his story is fairly commonplace : his love for Maryam is frustrated by the despotism of his father, which leaves him broken-hearted. Subsequently he joins the national struggle, exposes himself to danger and is finally killed when leading a peaceful demonstration. Yet in Maḥfūẓ's hands he does not become just another stereotyped martyr. He is, for one thing, an obedient and devout young man who impresses one as anything but a revolutionary. There is nothing ostentatiously heroic in his daily conduct or even in his struggle. He does not really revolt against the tyranny of his father, and when the latter is both angry and frightened on hearing of his involvement in the struggle, Fahmī would do anything to abate his wrath. (He refuses, however, to swear on the Koran that he would stop his activities). Although his participation in a mass-movement strengthens his spirit and

[1] *MIDEO* IV, pp. 76ff.

helps him withstand his emotional plight, he never becomes a "typical" hero. Even in the midst of the battle he is not without fear or doubts. Often he even regards himself as a coward.

When the British soldiers camp in their street, al-Sayyid forbids Fahmī and his brothers to leave the house. Fahmī, of course, is unhappy at this development, as it means that he is unable to carry on his political activity. Yet "his courage failed him to argue with his father lest he should arouse his anger. On the other hand he found in the latter's order forbidding him to leave the house an excuse to quieten his conscience, which taunted him for not going out into the road occupied by soldiers thirsty for students' blood."[1] These and many other similar incursions into the hero's innermost thoughts lend his heroism a genuine humanistic nature. His activism, compared to that of his nephews some twenty-five years later, is infinitely more appealing.

Yāsīn

There are, of course, many other important characters in the novel whom we shall be forced to leave undiscussed. Nevertheless one cannot avoid mentioning one of the most interesting. Yāsīn has been mentioned above as being a poor imitation of his father, but it should be emphasized that he is not only that. He is by all standards an important character in his own right. He occupies considerable space in all three volumes of the work, the scandals of his sex-life punctuating every part of it. He is interesting as a social type and sometimes as an individual character with his own distinct features. Some of his adventures are portrayed with great ability and humour.[2] Yet at times one feels that they are frivolous. His three marriages (and two divorces), his assaults on two different aged servants in his father's house, his constant pursuit of big women—such scenes are very enjoyable at first but their repetition is frivolous. In all, Yāsīn notwithstanding his carefully elaborated background

---

[1] TR-I, pp. 427-8: لم تواته شجاعته على مراجعة أبيه خشية أن يغضبه من ناحية ، ولانه من ناحية أخرى — وجد في أمره بمنع مغادرة البيت عذرا يبرّربه أمام ضميره امتناعه عن الخروج الى الطريق المحتل بالجنود المتعطشين الى دماء أمثاله من الطلبة.

[2] A singularly funny scene is that described in TR-II, Ch. 11, wherein Yāsīn visits Umm Maryam ("an adolescent at fifty") to ask for her daughter's hand, and winds up with a liaison with the mother.

(again divorced parents; obsession with his mother's indecencies, etc.) is not a deep character[1]. All in all, if we accept E.M. Forster's definition that the flat character is constructed round a single idea or quality, then Yāsīn is a flat character. The quality around which Yāsīn is constructed is sex obsession. "His temperament made him crave the body of a woman, neglecting her personality. Furthermore his attention is always focused on certain parts of her body, never the body as a whole."[2]

2. *Women*

The women in the Trilogy are numerous. Their variety amounts to a fascinating catalogue of characters ranging from the saintly Amīna to the worst of the Cairene bawds; from the tragic 'Ā'isha to the carefree Zannūba; from homely types of the twenties to the sophisticated students of the forties. This is no doubt a great departure from the narrow range of women whom we meet in Maḥfūẓ's early Cairene novels. Furthermore their characterization is much more natural and spontaneous. Such colourful women as Khadīja, and Mrs. Shawkat, though not always portrayed in depth, play a large role in enlivening the novel.

Amīna

Undoubtedly the most important female character in the whole novel is Amīna. She is the first character to appear in the novel, and her death marks its end. She is definitely the axis around which the whole Trilogy revolves.

Through her we meet the Egyptian mother of yesterday, enslaved and demeaned. As an individual, however, she is a woman with great personality and dignity. She is also the cement that keeps the family whole and serves as a buffer against al-Sayyid's tyranny.

She is incredibly naïve and outwardly submissive. Yet she is not without a will of her own. The author gives us a clue to her character when he remarks on one occasion that "it often looks as if the total submission which characterizes her behaviour, a submission stripped of any weapon, is a brand of passive courage."[3]

---

[1] But cf. M. Peled, "Yāsīn fātiḥ al-abwāb", *al-Sharq* (Jerusalem), June-July 1972, pp. 77-82.

[2] TR-I, p. 279 : اذ تأدى به مزاجه الى التهالك على جسم المرأة متجاهلا شخصيتها ثم الى تركيز العناية في أجزاء من الجسم متجاهلا جملته.

[3] TR-I, p. 209 : وكثيرا ما يبدو هذا الاستسلام في سلوكها — الاعزل من كل سلاح — كأسلوب من أساليب الشجاعة السلبية.

Al-Sayyid's rough treatment, especially when he temporarily expels her from his house following her outing to pray in the mosque, never leaves in her any residue of ill-will. When, after the death of her husband, she recollects scenes from their life together, the only part of that incident which she remembers is al-Sayyid's "forgiveness" of her and his allowing her to return to her children.[1]

There are many points in Amīna's portrait which show a great insight on the part of the author. Her naïveté is striking. Early one morning, for instance, she discovers that the soldiers have camped near the house; she is terrified : "'I'll wake up your father and tell him what hapened' [she tells her son Fahmī] she said these words as if al-Sayyid, who solved all her problems was capable of solving this one too."[2]

Throughout TR-I her demeanour is never tinged with the slightest trace of malice. When she discloses to al-Sayyid that Yāsīn has taken his wife to a cabaret show, news which is sure to enrage him, she instantly regrets having done so "as if [the author comments] she divulged the news solely for the sake of regretting what she had done."[3]

But time does not leave her unchanged. After the death of Fahmī she turns into a stiffer, less magnanimous person. She nurses a grudge against Maryam, Fahmī's sweetheart, for no conceivable reason, and later would not forgive Yāsīn for marrying her. (It is only after many years have elapsed and after Yāsīn has divorced Maryam that they are reconciled).

Amīna is a character to whom Maḥfūẓ devotes more attention than any other female character. She is also one of his greatest achievements.

Structure

At first glance the Trilogy might look structurally unsophisticated. There is no visible preoccupation with technique, as can be discerned, for instance, in the works of such novelists as Flaubert and Henry

---

[1] TR-III, p. 274.

[2] TR-I, p. 424 : — سأوقظ والدك لاخبره بالامر .. قالتها المرأة كآخر ما عندها من حيلة ، كأن السيد الذي يحل لها جميع مشكلات حياتها كفيل أيضا بأن يجد حلا لهذا المشكل.

[3] TR-I, p. 358 : ثم غصت بالندم على ما بدر منها ، ندم عاجلها مبادرا عقب البوح بسرها مباشرة كأنها لم تبح الا كي تندم.

James. Equally, the modern pursuit of the life-like flow is not prominent.

Furthermore there is an apparent lack of concentration and unity in the Trilogy. It stretches over a long period of time, bringing in many different milieus which are not necessarily compatible. There is a mixture of technique in the delineation of characters (cf. Kamāl and al-Sayyid respectively). Even the language undergoes a visible change in the course of TR-II and TR-III.

In short, the author appears at times to have drifted from his original concept of the work, or still worse, to have had no sound plan in the first place.

It is common knowledge that a neat form in itself does not make great literature. Conversely, a lopsided construction can be encountered even in great works of art, and fiction is no exception. Even the greatest of novels, Tolstoy's *War and Peace*, has been sometimes criticised for its "unsound" form.[1] Yet the reader ought to ask himself on reading a novel so enjoyable as Maḥfūẓ's Trilogy : how, after all, did the author succeed in interesting us throughout? He will soon discover that the answer does not simply lie in the fact that there are plenty of fascinating scenes and characters in it. In fact, just because so much material is amassed into a work of art, it is inconceivable that no deliberate design existed for it. Without a design it would have become chaotic, and therefore boring. I shall try to show in the following pages that the very lack of unity in technique and style is functional—in other words, that it is a design in itself.

We have already seen that the major theme of the novel is that of the change in life and society. The first volume describes people who are prisoners of medieval values and norms. They are kept secluded from an outer world moving towards certain changes, by fences that al-Sayyid has erected around them. This applies not only to women, but to the men as well. Yāsīn is anything but modern. Fahmī, despite his revolutionary passion, is deeply religious, tending to conform, in matters of the family, to the old order. The boy Kamāl is stuffed with the worst medieval superstitions.

In TR-II the entire household is infinitely less in the father's grip. Amīna, having lost her son, is no longer confined to the house. The two sisters have left home and live with their undomineering husbands. Yāsīn lives in his own house. More important, Kamāl

[1] See Liddell, *A Treatise*, pp. 26-42.

has by now gradually severed his links with everything that signifies the medieval past. He is enchanted by scientific and liberal thinking, and although he lives under the strict eye of his father, he is capable of defiance by electing to join the teachers' college.

In TR-III the break with the past is total. The young generation (not excluding the Islamic revivalist) view their world from a different angle. The institutions of the past are decaying : young women go to school and even to the University; the pace of life is no longer that of a slumbering patriarchal society.

Thus each of the three volumes of the Trilogy describes a different world as far as the pace of life is concerned. No wonder, then, that there is a considerable difference in the respective techniques and styles. TR-I follows a rather orthodox style of narration. The movement is relatively slow. The portrayal of environmental and psychological background is painstaking. Any section of the TR-I will provide us with a good example of its slow pace. Chapter 35, for example, begins with the appearance in al-Sayyid's house of their neighbour Bahīja. Then follow three pages describing the traditional exchange of courtesies which finally brings the visitor to the object of her visit (she has come to intercede on behalf of al-Sayyid's exiled wife). The dialogue is followed by a long analysis of al-Sayyid's attitude to women in general and to Bahīja in particular (she is later to become his mistress). The chapter winds up with complimentary remarks bringing the visit to its end.

Similarly, Chapter 49 opens with al-Sayyid in his shop. In comes his friend Muḥammad 'Iffat to obtain his signature on a petition supporting Sa'd Zalghūl and his comrades. The two men exchange some comments on the political situation. 'Iffat takes his leave. This scene is followed by two pages describing al-Sayyid's political affinities and the place of politics in his life. Here the description of his inner reasoning and attitudes is done by means of a semi-reflective style, in other words, in third person, but reflecting a sequence of thought in the man's mind. When the author feels that he has given us an adequate summary of al-Sayyid's "philosophy," the movement is resumed, but not before reminding us in an explicit manner that these were al-Sayyid's own thoughts.[1]

Needless to say, this is a legitimate technique used to this very

---

[1] TR-I, p. 380: وانه ليفكر في هذا كله اذ اقترب منه جميل الحمزاوي وهو يقول...

day by many novelists. But when TR-I is compared to the two other volumes of the Trilogy, one can hardly fail to notice that the technique allows the pace to become quicker and the representation more immediate. In TR-II there is already a less distinct division between dialogue and description. Here we encounter the language of *style indirect libre* which often replaces the externalized method of telling us what is going on inside the character. A conversation is occasionally stopped in order to introduce an internal monologue, using the first or second person, often mixing both or all three persons.

This technique is employed particularly when dealing with Kamāl[1] but it is at times employed with the other chief characters as well.[2] Furthermore the scenes are not rounded off as completely as those just cited from TR-I. The language itself tends to become livelier and less formal.[3]

In TR-III the movement is further accelerated. The part played by the dialogue is considerably greater and the "montage technique" is employed more often than ever. Above all, the language becomes more connotative and consequently more economical.

The change in tempo can be further illustrated by considering the time element in each of the three volumes. The time span in relation to the number of pages is as follows :

---

[1] For instance, TR-II, Ch. 2 (pp. 19-22); Ch. 3 (p. 46); Ch. 37 (pp. 410-1); Ch. 42 (p. 444), *et passim*.

[2] For example : Amīna : TR-II, Ch. 2 (pp. 13-14); al-Sayyid : TR-II, Ch. 2 (pp. 14-15); TR-II, Ch. 8 (pp. 102-7); Yāsīn : TR-II, Ch. 25 (pp. 294-5).

[3] One feature which typifies the traditional Arabic prose style is the use of long cycles of independent—or consecutive—sentences, clustered together by means of conjunctions (esp. *wa, fa*). In modern Arabic, however, there is a growing tendency to keep away from such cycles. (This is especially evident in the language of journalists).

In some passages in TR-II these cycle-making conjunctions are eliminated altogether. This produces a quicker—often dizzying—effect.

The following example (TR-II, p. 90-1) will illustrate this phenomenon :

نهض السيد احمد ليخلع الجبة ، قام علي عبد الرحيم ليتولى — كعادته — مهمة الساقي ، صدرت عن أوتار العود همسات غير مؤتلفة للاختبار ، دندنت زبيدة في غمغمة ، سوّت جليلة بأناملها خصلات شعرها وطوق الفستان فيما بين ثدييها ، تابعت أعين بتشوق يدي علي عبد الرحيم وهو يملأ الاقداح ، تربع السيد أحمد في مجلسه وهو يجيل بصره في المكان والناس حتى التقت عيناه اتفاقا بعيني زنوبة فابتسمت الاعين تحية ، قدم علي عبد الرحيم الدفعة الاولى من الكئوس ، قال محمد عفت ... قالت جليلة ... قالت زبيدة ...

TR-I	1½	years (Nov. 1917-Apr. 1919)	579 pages
TR-II	3	years (1924-1927)	464 pages
TR-III	9	years (1935-1944)	395 pages

To this one must add that the number of active characters increases in each volume, leaving the author with even less space for developing his characters.

The correspondence between the changing life-rhythm on the one hand and the change of technique and style on the other, maintained as it is throughout the novel, can hardly be accidental. It is instrumental in creating the mood of the work at large. The style and technique in each volume serve to consolidate its dramatic movement and characterization, and vice versa. The major theme of TIME-CHANGE is therefore expressed not only by means of plot and character, but also by the style and internal rhythm of the work. All these components are skillfully orchestrated to produce an ultimate harmony.

Apart from the "grand design" just described, there are other links which maintain the unity of this immense novel. Firstly, there are the "frame characters," i.e., people who appear throughout the work, such as Amīna, and Kamāl. Secondly, the very fact that it is a family-based novel is important;[1] although the family branches out, its heart stays in Bayn al-Qaṣrayn. The afternoon gatherings of the family (when al-Sayyid is away in his shop) around the coffee-pot recur in different parts of TR-I and II and in the early chapters of TR-III,[2] thus providing a focus at which the divergent lines of the action meet.

The method of parallelism between different characters and scenes, abundantly used through different volumes, adds yet another element of coherence and continuity. Al-Sayyid's juxtaposition with Yāsīn has already been referred to as being a means by which a profounder characterization is achieved. This parallelism is no less advantageous to the *structure* of the novel. Examples of such parallelism are numerous. The following are only some of them :

a) The affair of Fahmī and Maryam, which takes place near the fence that separates the roofs of their houses,[3] has a second version

---

[1] Cf. *supra* Ch. III, pp. 89ff.

[2] See Tr-I, Chs. 9, 24, 42, 45-6, 52, 64; TR-II, Chs. 3, 5, 10, 15; TR-III, Ch. 3.

[3] TR-I, Ch. 10.

in TR-II with only one difference : the suitor this time is Yāsīn.[1] Kamāl witnesses both affairs.

b) In TR-III Kamāl and his nephew Aḥmad become contributors to different periodicals, each according to his bent. The correspondence between the two is underlined by the two visits paid by both men to their respective papers and described in adjacent chapters.[2]

c) The affair of 'Ā'ida and Kamāl in TR-II has two parallels in TR-III : the first being that of Kamāl himself and 'Ā'ida's younger sister;[3] the second that of Aḥmad and the rich student 'Alawiyya.[4]

Similarly there are many scenes and characters, the recurrence of which at intervals amounts to a leitmotiv. For instance :

a) The repeated dough-kneading in Amīna's kitchen, each time signifying the beginning of a new day.[5]

b) The appearance, again and again, of the holy man Mutawallī 'Abd al-Ṣamad, throughout the novel.[6]

There are also certain characters who disappear in the course of volumes one and two, and suddenly turn up in volume three. Their reappearance serves as a reminder of past events and, again, they contribute to establishing the unity between the different parts of the story. Such characters are Maryam, who disappears when Yāsīn divorces her around 1925,[7] not to emerge again until 1941 working in a bar which caters for the British soldiers.[8]

Another such case is the police officer who in the first stages of TR-I wanted to marry 'Ā'isha, around the year 1918.[9] He sinks into oblivion for a quarter of a century, until we meet him again towards the end of World War II.[10]

---

1 TR-II, Ch. 5.

2 TR-III, Ch. 13 (Aḥmad) and Ch. 15 (Kamāl).

3 TR-III, Chs. 41-2; 45.

4 TR-III, Chs. 25 and 29.

5 TR-I, the opening of Chs. 3 (p. 19-21), Ch. 54 (p. 408); TR-II, Ch. 2 (p. 12).

6 TR-I, Chs. 7, 67; TR-II, Ch. 42; TR-III, Chs, 2, 18, 37, 54. This character has a significance, in fact, that surpasses that of a mere structural device. His appearance, more than anything else, marks the passage of time. He is also one of the precursors of the ageless men whom we shall meet later (e.g. in AWL and THAR), a man who has many of the attributes of the Almighty himself. Cf., his assertion that : (TR-I, p. 46) : أغيب كما يحلو لي ، وأحضر كما يحلو لي ، ولا أسأل عن السبب

7 TR-II, Chs. 26-7.

8 TR-III, Ch. 30 (pp. 228-9).

9 TR-I, Chs. 5, 22-24.

10 TR-III, Chs. 52-3.

Finally there are some parallel scenes in the beginnings or endings of different sections of the novel. TR-I and TR-II both begin with al-Sayyid's coming home at night, with Amīna waiting up for him. This repetition—like most of the others—is, of course, designed to stress the difference rather than the similarity. By repeating the identical setting, the reader is doubly aware of the change that has occurred in the meantime. Structurally, however, the reiteration serves the purpose of symmetry and rhythm. Another example can be found in the last chapters of TR-II and TR-III. In both of these chapters, Yāsīn is expecting a new birth in his own branch of the family (the first time as a father and the second time as a grandfather). At the same time there is an impending death in the big family (in TR-II 'Ā'isha's husband and sons; in TR-III, Amīna).

Language and Dialogue

The language of the Trilogy, like other aspects of the novel, follows no unified pattern, and changes in the course of the work. In the first volume it is akin to that of the Cairene novels discussed above. In the second, and especially the third volumes, it is moving towards a poetic language which we shall encounter in the author's works of the sixties.

Yet there is little doubt that in spite of these differences—or, probably because of them—the language amounts to a quiet revolution in the author's concept and use of the linguistic medium. The use of words is now more creative, the dialogue more natural, and finally the author makes greater use of his own metaphor, that "unique expression of a writer's individual vision."[1]

The question of Maḥfūẓ's vocabulary (or, for that matter, of any other Arabic writer) has not yet been tackled. There is little doubt, however, that the richness of the language of the Trilogy surpasses that of all his earlier works put together. The new lexical items that we find here are derived from both the literary and the spoken languages. There is a great variety of words conveying items of *realia*.[2] On the other hand, there is a tangible decrease in repetitious and hackneyed expressions, especially in the second and third volumes.

The dialogue, though still based on "translating" dialect into

[1] Murry, p. 12.

[2] For a list of such words (but only those of foreign origin) Charles Issawi's article "European Loan-Words in Arabic Writing : A Case Study in Modernization" in *M.E. Studies*, III, No. 2, Jan. 1967, pp. 110-33).

fuṣḥā, is now closer to the Cairene language, conveying much of its spirit and rhythm. This is achieved firstly by the increased number of non-literary items interspersed in it[1], or by literary words with a non-literary semantic content.[2] Secondly, by introducing more syntactical patterns which are typical of the spoken language.[3] There are also a few cases where short discourses are recorded in outright *ʿāmiyya*.[4]

Yet at times a feeling of artificiality still prevails, especially when tragic or agitated feelings are expressed by means of a neat *fuṣḥā*.[5]

On the whole, however, there is a greater closeness to spoken idiom, not only in matters of dialogue. The large selection of lines from popular songs, scattered all over the work is, in most cases, in the local dialect.[6] This contributes further to the relief from the rigidities of the formal language. Moreover, one often comes across expressions in the midst of the narrative portions of the book which betray their colloquial origin.[7]

Also, we occasionally come across a clever employment of tension between the two levels of language to express differences in mentality and education or to create humorous contrasts.[8]

---

1 E.g. a) الزياط (I, 557); b) لا تأخذني فى دوكة (II, 117); c) القفش (III, 53); d) رجل مزنوق (III, 90).

2 E.g. a) انت دائر ابن دائر (II, 148); b) بيتها شغال ليل نهار (III, 52); c) فتركها على الحديدة (III, 56).

3 E.g. a) الناس تكبر تعقل ونحن نكبر نتهور (I, 234); b) لم كفى الله الشر؟ ، ناو تعمل حادثة؟ (II, 300); c) وعكة وتمضي (II, 449); d) وجهك شاحب من المشي ، كلهاكم يوم وتصبحين من زباين الدكتور (III, 206).

4 E.g. a) لحدهناعال (I, 343); b) فالحال من بعضه (II, 49); c) من بعد تلتاشر سنة. (II, 87—this is apparently a quotation from a popular song).

5 An author employing *ʿāmmiyya* in his dialogue would have been able to make ʿA'isha express her feelings at the death of her last surviving child, better than by saying (TR-III, p. 188) : — ما هذا يا ربي؟ ، ماهذا الذى تفعله؟ ، لماذا؟ ، لماذا؟ أريد أن أفهم.

6 Fragments or full lines of such songs are to be found in TR-I, pp. 16, 109, 116, 292-3, 295, 299, 361, 579; TR-II, pp. 54, 218, 306, 354, 434, 437, 451-2; TR-III, pp. 70-1, 132, 167, 172, 348.

7 E.g. a) ألم يكن بوسعه أن يعدل به عن رأيه من وراء وراء (I, 274—not in dialogue); b) ذنبه على جنبه (II, 188).

8 One such case can be found in the remarkable scene between Kamāl and his father'

Lastly the language of the author acquires a more idiosyncratic touch. He makes as little use as possible of the commonplace images and instead tries to forge his own metaphor. This is especially evident in a great number of original similes. Sometimes, it is true, these similes are too elaborate to sound uncontrived.[1] Yet the great majority of them convey a sharp observation and original viewpoint.[2] Often the components of a simile are in complete harmony with the context, situation or character described.[3]

The images for these similes are, generally speaking, drawn from personal observation of daily life and natural phenomena.[4]

Some images come from the world of health, or rather ill-health. (One has to remember that the author has, throughout his life, been of unsound health.)[5]

---

on the morrow of Kamāl's finishing his secondary school (TR-II, Ch. 4). When Kamāl explains that his preference for the teachers' college stems from his aspiration for *tha-qāfat al-fikr* ('study of thought'), the father is unable to understand this expression, and connects the word *fikr*—half-seriously—with a popular song in which it is used in a different sense ([*el-fikri tāh*] = "my thoughts have gone astray").

[1] e.g. TR-I, p. 510 : فعاد يترقب حتفه بين لحظة وأخرى كأنه غريق توهم في تخبطه أنه يرى تمساحا يتوثب لمهاجمته ثم تبين له أن ما رأى أعشاب طافية ولكن فرحته للنجاة من الخطر الوهمي لم تكد تتنفس حتى اختنقت تحت ضغط الخطر الحقيقي المحيط به.

[2] E.g. : تحرك في بطء شديد تحرك حبوب البن في فوهة الطاحونة (I, 419)

[3] Al-Sayyid's thirsty probing of Zubayda's body is described as follows : (al-Sayyid, it will be remembered, is a foodstuff merchant !) : فجرى بصره على جسمها في عجلة ونهم كما يجري الفأر على جوال أرز ليجد لنفسه منفذا (I, 104),

[4] Examples : a) مثله كمثل القطة تبدو، حين يحمل صغارها، وكأنها تلتهمها (I, 330),

b) وراح يدفع الطمأنينة في نفسه كما يدفع سدادا غليظا في فوهة ضيقة (II, 333),

c) وخفق قلبه وجرى دمه حارا كحشرة هيجها القيظ (III, 100).

[5] Examples : a) لان الحب كالصحة، يهون في الوصال ويعز عند الفراق (I, 363);

b) أهواء عميقة مكبوته كالدواء الجديد يستأثر بأفكار المرضى بداء قديم استعصى علاجه بالرغم من استعماله لاول مرة (I, 377);

c) حزن ثقيل غليظ شاع في صدره كما يشيع الغثيان (I, 402).

Another source of images is the world of music,[1] a subject with which the author had had a brief flirtation during his university years.[2]

No less remarkable are those similes which refer to science, technology, and modern communication.[3] These metaphors, possibly more than anything else, show how different the language of the Trilogy is from that of the prose of old Arabic literature, the metaphors of which are drawn from a non-congenial world. Maḥfūẓ's language is, in a word, striving to become one which befits a modern urban writer.

---

d) حسبي فهمي : انه يلح عليّ كوجع الاسنان (I, 550); e) هذا الشعور الرطيب جدير بالتذوق ، كالفرجة السعيدة على أثر وجع ضرس وضربانه (II, 280).

[1] Examples: a) يقول بلسانه « اللهم التوبة » على حين يقتصر قلبه على طلب الغفران والعفو والرحمة كأنها آلتان موسيقيتان تعزفان معا في أوركسترا واحد فتصدر عنها نغمتان مختلفتان (I, 473); b) القلب القلق كالوتر المختل (I, 550—note the alliteration); c) كانت بهزة رأسها وابتسامتها كالالة الموسيقية المصاحبة للمغني اذا غيرت عزفها تمهيدا لدخول المغني فى طبقة جديدة من النغم (II, 136).

[2] See Ch. II of this book (p. 42).

[3] Examples: a) فانكتم حديثها الباطنى تحت مظهر من الرضى والادب كما تنكتم الامواج الصوتية فى جهاز الا ستقبال بالمذياع باغلاق مفتاحه (I, 360); b) ذكر اسم الله فكان كالقطب المغطس ، جذب اليه شواردهم وجمع افكارهم التي شتتها اليأس (I, 403); c) كمثل السيارة التى تتوقف محركاتها عن الدفع فيخرس أزيزها ولكنها تسير بقوة القصور الذاتي في سكون شامل (II,1 07); d) خفق قلبه خفقة عنيفة كسقطة طيارة منطلقة في فراغ هوائي (II, 285).

CHAPTER FIVE

THE SAD MILLENARIAN

Awlād Ḥāratinā—General

A wide gulf separates the Trilogy and its predecessors from *Awlād Ḥāratinā*, 1959 (referred to as AWL). The early works were realistic novels *par excellence,* although a rudimentary symbolism crops up here and there. AWL on the other hand is an allegory. The early Cairene novels of Maḥfūẓ are concerned with the lives of contemporary people. AWL is concerned with anything but individual characters of our day.

Neither is AWL a historical novel in any sense of the word. Historical novels aim at reconstructing the intimate lives of people of whom we know little, and, above all, representing them as living human beings, often relating events of the past to those of the present. AWL, however, depicts its historical (or legendary) personalities more or less following the outlines of the sacred books, the interpretations of their deeds being sometimes different. Moreover, people of the past are not represented in their own historical settings or even under their original names. They are transplanted into that world which Maḥfūẓ knows best, namely that part of Cairo in which most of his "social" novels are set.

Furthermore, both the literary style and method of characterization in AWL are totally different from those we have encountered earlier.

The idea of writing an allegory on the history of religion apparently came to the author from a friend of his who is a scientist or, at least, scientifically-minded; for in the introductory remarks, written as an overture in the same symbolic vein as the whole work, the author, in the guise of a *Ḥāra*-scribe explains as follows :

> It is thanks to one of 'Arafa's friends that I have recorded the stories of our *Ḥāra*. One day he said to me, "You are one of the few men who know how to write, so why not write down the stories of our *Ḥāra*? They are always told without any sort of order and are subject to the whims and partisanship of the narrators. Truly, it would be a good thing to set them down truthfully in their totality so that good use may be made of them, and I shall supply you with whatever information you require and explain the mysteries to you".

> At once, I put this idea into effect; in the first place because it seemed a good idea and secondly because of my affection for the man who suggested it.[1]

Translated into simple language, this passage seems to mean that his friend urged him to write a spiritual history of the world in the hope of its being a more objective one than that offered by the sacred books or the works of theologians and historians. But can that be taken at its face value? Can we assume that Maḥfūẓ was led to believe that he was the best man to rewrite or re-interpret the history of such a complex subject with objectivity and coherence? More important : could he possibly have believed that the art of fiction is the best means of achieving such an aim? This is an unlikely proposition. Indeed, as we shall see, the description of the world, past and present, is far from being all-embracing nor does it claim to be so. The episodes from the past are highly selective and, to all intents and purposes, are only a background to the last section of the book which concerns the present and future. In fact the questions which the work is out to tackle are the very same questions which tormented Kamāl in the Trilogy, namely : what is the meaning of life, belief, happiness? Why is there so much misery in our world? Is evil man-made, or part and parcel of life as such?

But why, one must ask, did the author bother to take us on a long journey through the history of the human race (or rather, the western flank of it, for the *Ḥāra* can hardly be said to include the Far East)? Why parade Adam, Moses, Jesus, Muhammad, before reaching the modern "scientific" stage. The answer may be found in TR-III. When Aḥmad S̲h̲awkat first visits the journalist 'Adlī Karīm, the latter observes that "science should today replace the priesthood and religion of the ancient world."[2] He goes on to instruct his young admirer as follows : "You ought to be as fired with enthusiasm as the devout man with his religion. Remember however, that every

---

[1] AWL, p. 7 : والى أحد اصحاب عرفة يرجع الفضل في تسجيل حكايات حارتنا على يدي ، اذ قال لي يوماً : « انك من القلة التي تعرف الكتابة ، فلماذا لاتكتب حكايات حارتنا؟ .. انها تروى بغير نظام ، وتخضع لاهواء الرواة وتحزباتهم ، ومن المفيد ان تسجل بامانة في وحدة متكاملة ليحسن الانتفاع بها ، وسوف أمدك بما لا تعلم من الاخبار والاسرار ». ونشطت الى تنفيذ الفكرة ، اقتناعا بوجاهتها من ناحية ، وحبا فيمن اقترحها من ناحية أخرى.

[2] TR-III, p. 109 : ينبغي ان يحل العلم محل الكهانة والدين في العالم القديم

era has its own prophets; the prophets of our times are the scientists."[1] But while the young Shawkat is capable of accepting such a statement with few scruples, Kamāl (and indeed Maḥfūẓ) can hardly do so. Thus comes AWL to examine the statement by first portraying the three prophets of old, then the scientist.

AWL then is a philosophical tale in its purest form. Yet there are no cut and dried conclusions which it is out to prove. The converse is true. The gist of the book is an enquiry, a search for an answer. As is the case in all the author's other works, no definitive answer emerges. As the work ends, the struggle is still as fierce as ever, the questions as disturbing.

Nevertheless there are certain points of departure in the work which can be summed up as follows :

1. The majority of the human race have always lived in destitution, because their rulers have taken for themselves the wealth of the earth, a wealth which was meant to be shared equally by all God's children. Tyranny and poverty have since the dawn of history been two sides of the same coin. Consequently the world has become impure, full of evil, lust, hatred and wars.

2. The three great prophets came, in reality, to save us from these evils. The first prophet (Jabal = Moses) delivered his people and obtained justice for them. The second (Rifā'a = Jesus) was not concerned with power or property. His sole object was to purge the soul of the people from evil. He preached love and gave his life for it. The third (Qāsim = Muhammad) was also a prophet of mercy and love, but he saw that it can be achieved only by violent means. His mission was confined, not only to his own people but to peoples of all races and colours.

However, the successes of these prophets are short-lived. Their goodwill and victories are squandered. No sooner did they disappear from the scene than their teachings were distorted and the old pattern of tyranny-cum-destitution was resumed.

3. Science (the magician 'Arafa = scientist) is capable of bringing about the downfall of evil. Science is able to produce weapons which can potentially be used to destroy unjust political and social orders, and can provide a better and richer life for all. Unfortunately it is used not for the benefit of humanity, but to serve the ends of tyranny.

---

[1] TR-III, p. 109 : ... لتكن لك حماسة اهل الدين ولكن ينبغي أن تذكر أن لكل عصر انبياءه وأن انبياء هذا العصر هم العلماء.
See also TR-II, p. 375.

Further, it secures a monopoly of power. The super-power, aided by science-made weapons, suppresses the whole of the human race. Thus, instead of bettering the lot of man, science has changed nightmares into realities.

4. Religion, it is true, has throughout the ages been at the service of wicked rulers, but man needs a belief. He does not live by bread alone. Science, which unwittingly brought about the death of God, again served humanity ill. Indeed the killing of God was possibly to the benefit of the tyrants of the earth because faith often gave simple people hope and courage.

5. Science, despite its setbacks, is the hope of our race. Possibly an elusive hope but the last remaining one. If he is ever to succeed, the scientist has to be both humanist and militant, and to lead his people as did the prophets. The risks are great, but so are the hopes. If science and justice ever win the battle and the energies of man are liberated, we shall all become scientists endeavouring to discover the secrets of nature and possibly, to put an end to death. The existential question might be solved. Belief itself might one day be revived.

So much for the abstractions of AWL. By what means did the author contrive to make them concrete? And has his story any literary value as such?

The ideas are brought to life through the characters of "modern" Cairo. The story begins when Jabalāwī, the Master of the Big House, expels two of his sons (Adham = Adam; Idrīs = Satan), for different reasons. Their seed multiplies and their houses form the *Ḥāra* ('living quarters'). The *Ḥāra* is divided into alleys (*aḥyā'*, sing, *ḥayy*), each inhabited by one branch of Jabalāwī's descendants and dominated by a *futuwwa* (pl. *futuwwāt* 'strong-arm man'). Jabal, Rifā'a and Qāsim arise in these alleys in separate generations. The period of time separating each message is not specified, but it is not longer than one or two generations in each case.[1]

The events throughout the work are intended to be plausible. There are no supernatural incidents. The protagonists, including the three who were entrusted with messages by Jabalāwī, are ordinary men who rise to help their fellows. There is nothing miraculous about their encounters with Jabalāwī or with his messengers, encounters

---

[1] In Qāsim's days we meet a woman who had seen Rifā'a in person (AWL, pp. 409-10); similarly in 'Arafa's time there are some who remember Qāsim's days (p. 466).

which set them off on their separate ways. The battles they win or lose are also plausible in the context of the *Ḥāra*. Jabalāwī himself is simply one of the domineering patriarchs of old Cairo, in some ways resembling the Master in *Bayn al-Qaṣrayn*.

One element which is difficult to accept as realistic is the long life of Jabalāwī. He survives at least five generations and dies only when the sceptical 'Arafa raids his house. Yet this point too is not altogether supernatural. 'Awāṭif, on one occasion, mentions a resident of Sūq al-Muqaṭṭam, who is said to be one hundred and fifty years old.[1]

Another element which may strike us as unrealistic is the fact that the *Ḥāra* is too autonomous and too parochial to be a part of a metropolis. This would be true if the stories took place in the Cairo of today, but the setting of AWL is apparently that of the nineteenth century—no mention is made of electricity, trams, telephones, or the like. In those days, the administration was far less centralized, a modern police force non-existent, and the *futuwwāt* all-powerful.

In being outwardly realistic AWL is different from pure allegories, which cannot be comprehended unless the reader finds the "key" by which he can translate every character or event in terms of a different reality. Such stories usually have a formal pointer to their non-realistic nature (in *Pilgrim's Progress*, the names of the characters; in *Animal Farm*, the man-like behaviour of the beasts). AWL in contrast has few if any such outright indications.

On the other hand, AWL is not a lyrical-symbolic novel. In novels like Mann's *Der Zauberberg* or Camus' *La Peste*, for instance, the symbols are never simple and no key can be found which will satisfy all readers or interpret all occurrences. Such novels make enjoyable reading even for those readers who overlook this "inner layer". In AWL the simple story is of little, if any, importance. In fact the symbols are of a one-to-one quality, and any reasonably intelligent reader with a superficial knowledge of Biblical and Koranic stories cannot fail to discern the prototypes of each of the main characters of the first four sections. The names of the characters, though not artificial as in Bunyan's tale, are intended to facilitate the identification of their bearers.[2]

---

[1] AWL, p. 483.

[2] See Appx. II. The name Qāsim is exceptional in that it bears neither phonetical nor "thematic" resemblance to the original (i.e., Muhammad). The only possible link between that name and the prophet of Mecca is that the latter had a son named Qāsim,

The question now arises as to how far the ideas embodied in the work benefited from its allegorical or semi-allegorical form. In other words, what extra dimension is added when the historic-philosophical concept is conveyed through character and action. The author himself believes that this method offers a profounder understanding of the subject. On one occasion he draws a comparison between his work and *Gulliver's Travels*. He suggests that AWL is "the converse of what Swift has done in his well-known journey. He criticized reality by means of a legend [sic], while I am criticizing the legend through reality."[1]

The legends, indeed, are retold in terms of a reality much closer to the modern Arabic reader than that of the sacred books. The special flavour of Cairo with the typically *baladī* names of places, people, and things; their specific problems, entertainments, jokes—all these are part of a reality which Maḥfūẓ knows very well.

But is such a realistic coating in itself sufficient to make AWL a novel as are his earlier works? For if Maḥfūẓ was to succeed in criticizing the legend by transferring it into a familiar realistic setting, he would have had to make the characters individual and convincing, so that the thoughts and actions of the underlying prototypes would be better comprehended. Is there any human depth to the characters of AWL?

Characters

The answer tends to be negative. The great majority of the characters are black-and-white. The *nāẓirs* and *futuwwāt* are, without exception, absolute monsters, lacking any trace of human feeling. The masses of the *Ḥāra* are faceless, mostly passive and cowardly. Above all, the main protagonists of the five different sections are only portrayed in quick-moving sketches. The main bulk of each section is occupied by endless events, battles, and adventures. The love stories (one in each section) are conventional and the women often unnatural. Yāsimīna's betrayal of Rifā'a is not altogether convincing.[2] Similarly unfortunate is 'Awāṭif's sudden desertion of 'Arafa and her stubborn refusal to have anything more to do with

who died in infancy. It may well be that Maḥfūẓ preferred to make this name less transparent as a measure of prudence in the event of unfavourable reactions from orthodox circles (cf. Ch. II, pp. 100f. *supra*).

[1] *Ḥiwār* III (Mar.-Apr. 1963), p. 72.

[2] AWL, Chs. 59-60.

him.[1] When a feminine character is relatively successful, it is not because of the richness of her individual traits, but precisely because she is a *type* (Umayma is a successful vignette of the submissive-but-sly wife who entices her husband, Adham, into committing an evil deed.)[2]

Qāsim

To return to the main characters let us have a closer look at one of them—Qāsim. This character is as good a "test case" as any. His section is the widest among the five constituting the book (about one quarter of the whole work). His biography, as it emerges from AWL, closely follows upon that of the accepted *Sīra*, and the author evinces a greater knowledge of Muhammad's life than that of the other prophets. Koranic verses are occasionally echoed in this section.[3]

The story is told in quick fragmentary scenes : a glimpse at the orphan's childhood, then at his acquaintance with the non-conformist Rifā'ite, Yaḥyā, who teaches him many things about Jabal and Rifā'a. In the next few chapters we witness his ingenuity in mediating between rival alleys, a feat which wins him general admiration and especially that of the rich but elderly widow, Qamar, who consents to marry him. Before long he is entrusted with a message from Jabalāwī through a messenger. Then comes the inevitable clash with the *futuwwāt*. An abortive attempt at suing the authorities over the *waqf* ends in Qāsim's resolving on an all-out war against the ruling clique. His followers leave the *Ḥāra* to form a semi-military base in the nearby mountain. His faithful wife dies and he joins his followers, narrowly thwarting a plot against his life. Qāsim's men grow bolder and in time descend to attack the *futuwwāt*. The latter strike back with a mob from the *Ḥāra*. They would have overcome the numerically inferior rebels were it not for a tactical error, and for Qāsim's shrewdness. After this defect the *futuwwāt* prepare a siege of the mountain. But before doing so one of their leaders is mysteriously killed (possibly by the Qāsimites). This incident sets the *futuwwāt* at each other's throats. Qāsim now comes down from his

[1] AWL, Chs. 109; 112.

[2] AWL, Ch. 7.

[3] Compare, for instance Qāsim's advice to his followers (AWL, p. 371) : تجنبوا الظهور بين الناس وأذتم سكارى to the Koranic dictum (Koran, 4/43) : لاتقربوا القرآن وأنتم سكارى.

stronghold and destroys his divided enemies. He becomes the just ruler of the whole *Ḥāra*.

The facts then, correspond, *mutatis mutandis*, with those of Muhammad's career, differing only in minor details.[1] Yet a special Maḥfūẓian interpretation of Muhammad's *Risāla* emerges. Muhammad has come to deliver all human beings alike from a wicked social and political order. He owes much to Moses and Jesus, but he was far more of a revolutionary and an "internationalist." To do Maḥfūẓ justice, it must be stressed that he is not out to preach Islam or to compare it favourably with other religions. His main theme is that there is an escalation in the humanity, militancy and comprehensiveness of the consequent socio-religious upheavals, which find their expression in religious terms. Furthermore, it is to be noticed that Qāsim's revolution, like those of the earlier prophets, was virtually nullified by his successors in office. Finally, the possible solution hinted at by Maḥfūẓ here, as in the Trilogy, is not to be attained by reviving the *Risāla*, but through the militant and socially orientated scientist who does not eschew the spiritual aspects of life.

It is not the object of this inquiry to establish the degree of originality of the author's interpretation of the specific missions of the prophets. What interests us here is the question whether the medium that Maḥfūẓ has chosen to convey his vision, namely that of an allegorical novel, adds an extra dimension to his ideas. Does Qāsim, in other words, contribute to our understanding of the character and mission of Muhammad?

The greater part of the section devoted to Qāsim is, as has been pointed out, occupied by external action—and very rapid action at that. The street battles, not those of the spirit, are given the greater prominence. The spiritual development of Qāsim is delineated, it is true, with remarkable skill; but this part recedes into the background while the noise of battle resounds. Similarly Qāsim's determination to liberate the whole *Ḥāra*, as distinct from his own alley, is only briefly explained (truly enough, the order to that effect comes from Jabalāwī, but the latter only chooses, as a rule, to entrust his specific

[1] One notable difference between the teachings of Muhammad and that of Qāsim is in the fact that the latter established a complete equality between men and women in matters of *waqf* income distribution. This is, of course, not in keeping with such unequivocal Koranic injunctions as that of Sūra 4, verse 11 :

يوصيكم الله في اولادكم للذكر مثل حظ الانثيين

missions to those of his descendants who are ripe for such missions in the first place).

In general, then, there is little in Qāsim to illuminate Muhammad's *character* with a special Maḥfūẓian light. Yet one cannot deny the author his mastery of sharp and focused characterization at times. To mention an example from Qāsim's section : an important turning point in the personality of the latter, and consequently in his career as a whole, is the scene at the *nāẓir*'s house (Ch. 77). Qāsim tried to attain the rights of the *Ḥāra*'s people by peaceful means, namely by suing the *nāẓir* over the *waqf*. He and his friends contacted a *sharī'a* lawyer who agreed to take up the case. The next day Qāsim is summoned, to his great amazement, to the *nāẓir*'s house. On entering the *nāẓir*'s chamber, he finds none other than the lawyer who, it turns out, had never contemplated setting himself against the overlord. He only pretended to do so in order to warn the *nāẓir* in good time. Qāsim now realizes that he has placed himself in great danger and that

> ... his secret was out; that the despicable lawyer had committed a breach of trust; that he was trapped. The desperation in his heart was mixed with anger. He realized that neither shrewdness nor guile would save him. So he decided on defiance. He could not retreat, therefore he had to go forward or, at the very least, he had to stand firm. In days to come he was to remeber this situation in which he found himself. It set the date of the birth of a new man whose existence he had not imagined to be possible.[1]

This dramatic change in his personality is a very crucial point. It is to dominate his subsequent action and to change the course of his life from one of mild rebellion to one of genuine revolution, a change which brings about his final victory. If such scenes as this were to have formed the backbone of the characterization in AWL, the author's aspiration to achieve a profounder understanding of the legend through a realistic medium might have been realized. As it is, such scenes are only a trickle while the bulk of the work is that of the outward manifestations of the conflict.

The same brief characterization is evident in the other main figures, Jabal is portrayed with even greater haste, while Rifā'a acquires a ridiculous rather than a saintly air.

'Arafa, the protagonist of the last section, is less an individual than the others, and his actions less convincing. The reason for the

[1] AWL, p. 376.

shallowness of this last section seems to be in the fact that whereas Jabal, Rifāʻa, and Qāsim have ready-made prototypes, ʻArafa is an altogether synthetic creation. In other words the earlier three are a "criticism of the legend," but the magician is a total abstraction representing recent historical events and processes.

Even allowing for the allegorical nature of the work, the actions and words of ʻArafa and the other characters in section V, are often insipid and childish. ʻArafa's incursion into the house of Jabalāwī[1] and later into that of the chief *futuwwa*,[2] his subsequent battle with the *futuwwa*'s henchmen and use of his jars of explosives to destroy them[3]—are scenes more reminiscent of an adolescent adventure story than the story of a struggle on behalf of the human soul. Of course, the author might have intentionally wanted to imply that ʻArafa's individualism was Quixotic and thus a source of his failure and subsequent destruction. Yet the picture that emerges lacks the realistic touch.

The abundant dialogue in the book adds little to the understanding of the inner selves of these people. It is used, above all, for conveying stark ideas and rarely the interaction between these ideas and the human beings they affect. This is especially acute in the case of ʻArafa, but also applies, to a lesser degree, to other characters.

Structure

The end at which Maḥfūẓ aimed—namely blending a novel and an allegory—has not therefore been successfully attained. Consequently we have to accept AWL as basically a system of symbols representing a certain interpretation of events, past and present. The human beings appearing in the surface story are not fundamentally different from the beasts of fables such as those of Aesop or, for that matter, of Orwell's *Animal Farm*.

A work with such a heavy burden of abstract ideas and with so many different stories and people is prone to be chaotic unless a very subtle design underlies its structure. Here the great experience of the novelist comes to his aid. Symmetry and parallelism are again brought into play and the clearly diffused material is kept under control.

1 AWL, Chs. 101-2.

2 AWL, Ch. 104.

3 AWL, pp. 505-6.

We have seen that the whole story is supposedly told by the scribe of Ḥārat al-Jabalāwī. Except for the introductory chapter, where the scribe tells us a little about himself,[1] he never again appears in the course of the novel. His function is supposed to be simply to record the stories which are current in the *Ḥāra*, possibly incorporating certain information that his friend has promised to provide for him.[2] Nevertheless every now and then, especially in the period between one cycle of events and another, our scribe comments on them, thus providing the link between the different sections. These recurring remarks are dominated by a major theme : that life had not really changed, even though at certain moments people thought it had.[3] The cumulative effect of the repetition of this theme leads the reader to anticipate a climax. Thus when the final section comes, it meshes with the earlier stories, although its hero, ʿArafa, is different from the other heroes in that he receives no message from Jabalāwī.

Another link which holds the work together is the *s͟hāʿirs*. These singers and reciters are, firstly, an intrinsic part of the action acting their own roles in the stories of the *Ḥāra*. Secondly, as symbols, they stand for the historians and theologians and possibly men-of-letters at large. They are often rebuked by our scribe for their sycophantic and subservient postures and are harshly criticized for falsifying the story of the *Ḥāra* (i.e., History) in accordance with the wishes of the rulers.[4] Thirdly these *s͟hāʿirs* fulfil a structural function. Their stories, which are occasionally quoted in the course of the work, serve as a sort of refrain. They sit in the cafés of their respective alleys (a café apparently denotes a church or a similar religious centre) and every evening recall to their hashish-drugged listeners the tales of Jabalāwī and his sons.[5] Their occasional appearance on the surface of AWL is highly beneficial to the sense of continuity. Moreover, the author is wise enough to have a *s͟hāʿir* in the later chapters repeat the words

---

[1] AWL, p. 7-8.

[2] AWL, p. 7; See *supra*, pp. 137-8.

[3] See AWL, pp. 115-7; 209-10; 305; 309; 443; 447-9; 552.

[4] See e.g., AWL, pp. 117 : أما شعراء المقاهي المنتشرة في حارتنا فلا يروون الا عهود البطولات متجنبين الجهر بما يحرج مراكز السادة ، ويتغنون بمزايا الناظر والفتوات ، بعدل لا نحظى به ورحمة لا نجدها وشهامة لا نلقاها وزهد لا نراه ونزاهة لا نسمع عنها.
See also AWL pp. 187; 226.

[5] These stories can be found in AWL, pp. 131-2; 225-6; 290-1; 322-3; 344; 459-60.

of the narrative in the earlier chapters, verbatim, thus lending authenticity to the idea that the whole book was compiled by the scribe of the *Ḥāra* from popular versions.[1]

The stories of the reciters serve yet another end : besides their "rhythmical" value, they echo or foreshadow events occurring in the present. In Ch. 66 (section IV) the young Qāsim, prior to his revelation, is being provoked at the local café by the *futuwwa* of his alley. He is mortified at not being able to answer him back. At that moment the *sh̲āʿir* of the café is heard relating that part of Adham's story where the latter, on his deathbed, is visited by Jabalāwī.[2] Now the offence given to Qāsim by the *futuwwa* has, on the face of it, little in common with the story of Adham's death. When the whole story of Qāsim is told, however, we shall see that there is indeed a triangular link between Qāsim, the *futuwwa* and that visit of Jabalāwī to his son, for it was on that visit that he promised that the *waqf* income would be given to his progeny (although this part of the story was not in fact admitted by the *sh̲āʿir*).[3] Indeed this encounter of Qāsim with the *futuwwa* is only the beginning of a series of others, more violent and more meaningful. Eventually he is to destroy all the abominable *futuwwāt*, to replace the *nāẓir* who embezzled the wealth, and to distribute the *waqf* income justly.

Such pregnant scenes are not confined in AWL to cases in which the story of the *sh̲āʿirs* coalesces with a simple event to give it a more profound meaning. In fact, Maḥfūẓ has by now learned to employ a method that can be described as "coincidental symbolism," whereby he not only succeeds in foreshadowing the forthcoming events but, in a very economical and acute manner, reflects the mood of the character. This method is to become a major feature in his short novels.

In the lop-sided characterization that prevails in AWL, however, the employment of such symbolism does not yield its full fruit. Nevertheless it would be beneficial to mention one or two examples in the present work.

Rifāʿa, on returning with his parents from exile, goes to the café of the new alley. As he sits there drinking he sees a cat carrying a mouse between its teeth. This scene nauseates him and he removes

---

1 The *sh̲āʿir*'s story on pp. 290-1, for instance, has the same wording as that of p. 55, wherein the story was originally related by the author (or the scribe); similarly the words of the *sh̲āʿir*'s story on p. 344 are virtually those of p. 103; etc.

2 AWL, pp. 322-3.

3 Cf. AWL, pp. 110-11.

the cup from his mouth in disgust. At that same moment his eyes settle on the *futuwwa* of the alley, Khunfus, spitting.[1] This is again an ominous pointer to the events which are in store for the harmless young man. He is to find nothing but sorrow in the new *Ḥāra*, and he is to be persecuted and eventually annihilated by Khunfus and the other *futuwwāt*, as was the mouse by the cat.

Similarly Qāsim, brooding in the open spaces over the sad lives of the people of his quarter, catches sight of a fast moving scorpion. Instantly, he raises his staff and kills it. He eyes the dead scorpion with disgust, then goes away.[2] His violent act, of course, reflects his mood of anger and despair, but it also foreshadows events which are to come : before long Qāsim sets out to destroy the oppressors of the *Ḥāra*, as he did the scorpion, with quick decisive assaults.

The local songs or song-fragments scattered all over AWL[3] are also made to convey a symbolic message to the reader. Their function is no longer that of an ornament, as in the Trilogy. In AWL a line from a song (always in local dialect) is often used to convey a hidden meaning which is later clarified by unfolding events. When twin boys are born to Adham, the voice of Idrīs is heard singing a song lamenting bad luck.[4] The words of the song, one later discovers, are quite prophetic as regards the end of the brothers : Hammām is to be killed by Qadrī in a scuffle and the latter is to run away, never to be seen again by his parents.

The successful use of the folk song can best be illustrated in the case of the nonsensical song which Rifā'a hears from the lips of the children of the alley :[5]

ياولاد حارتنا — توت توت
انتو نصاره — ولا يهود
تاكلو ايه — نا كل عجوة
تشربوا ايه — نشرب قهوة

[1] AWL, p. 225.

[2] AWL, pp. 345-6.

[3] E.g., AWL, pp. 51, 68, 110, 132, 181, 225, 227, 257, 331, 338, 339-40, 367, 406, 415, 469, 471, 530.

[4] AWL, p. 68 : البخت والقسمة فين يادي الزمان قلي

[5] AWL, p. 225. A literal translation of this song is as follows :

Children of our alley	—	Tut, Tut.
Are you Christians	—	or Jews ?
What is your food ?	—	pressed dates.
What is your drink ?	—	coffee.

The first words of this song, of course, have been adopted as the title of the work itself (*awlād ḥāratinā*). Moreover the second line mentions Christians and Jews, two religions whose history is allegorized in AWL. Islām is also referred to, though only implicitly (those who are neither Christians nor Jews). In fact the very timing of this song in the novel is remarkable : Rifā'a (alias Jesus) who is a Jabalite (i.e. a Jew) is about to desert his own alley for another. The first line of this song, incidentally, is quoted in an earlier novel of Maḥfūẓ, but only as an illustration of the atmosphere in a certain district of contemporary Cairo.[1]

As opposed to these elements which contribute to both the profundity of vision and coherence of structure, many points can be found in AWL where the form is not altogether satisfactorily moulded. Events follow upon each other at a frantic pace, with people dashing in and out of the arena in an incessant stream, and we are hardly given a breathing space to digest their actions and consider their inter-relationships. There are scores of secondary characters who could be eliminated without damaging the fabric of the narrative.

Furthermore, while repetition sometimes contributes to a better focus and rhythm, on other occasions it creates boredom and sometimes confusion. Indeed AWL is very repetitious, mostly to the detriment of the work. The basic idea itself is one of outwardly similar events being repeated. The chief protagonist of sections II, III, IV and V react basically to the same injustice and confront the same social and political institutions. The battles between them and the wicked strongmen of the *Ḥāra* consume a substantial part of AWL. Maḥfūẓ's old fondness for describing violent scenes and pitched battles, which was so conspicuous in his Pharaonic novels (especially in KIF) reappears. No fewer than twenty-two battles and scuffles can be counted in AWL.[2] It seems as if the author felt that an emphasis on hustle and bustle might infuse life-blood into the abstractions of the work. In fact the violent scenes hardly enhance the vivacity of the story, and their main effect is possibly to obscure the spiritual aspects. Furthermore, the surfeit of violence seems to misdirect the reader

---

1 See KHAN, p. 23.

2 AWL, Ch. 4 (p. 28); 16 (85-6); 19 (95-6); 28 (133-5); 29 (136-9); 40 (195-7); 43 (206-8); 56 (276-8); 60 (292-5); 63 (303-4); 67 (324-8); 79 (383-4); 83 (403-4); 86 (418-20); 88 (425-33); 90 (349-40); 97 (475); 98 (478); 101 (493); 104 (504-6); 107 (519-20); 113 (545-7).

from the true purpose of the work and reduce the effect of the more subtle encounters.

Language and Dialogue

On the face of it the language of this novel differs considerably from that of the earlier ones. The very nature of the work implies a different use of words; for not only persons and acts stand for something else, but also words themselves acquire new value in keeping with the world created by the allegory.

In certain cases the language of allegory is used in AWL in a refined and poetic manner. When Jabal meets Jabalāwī in the desert one night, the latter says to his descendant : "You cannot see me as long as it is dark."[1] Here the language refers to more than the plain fact that Jabal has not actually seen Jabalāwī, or that nobody, in fact, knows what he looks like. It also has a subtle poetic reference to the fact that we should not be able to see the unseen and discover the ultimate secrets of the universe so long as the night of tyranny and depravity envelopes us. This, of course, is the major theme of AWL as a whole.

Unfortunately such a pregnant language is not typical of AWL. In fact the words in the novel have very little mystical-poetical depth. If anything, the language is less connotative than certain portions of the Trilogy.

Even such key words in the language of Maḥfūẓ as those denoting "secret" or "riddle" forfeit a great deal of their mystical charge. Now they often stand for *definite* objects or qualities. Thus when 'Arafa tells his disciples that they "should learn the secrets in order to rid the sick of their evil spirits"[2], the word *asrār* ('secrets') has little wealth of undertones. The secrets are those of exorcism (*zār*), and on the allegorical level the reference is apparently to the healing powers of Jesus. Even when the scribe, in his introduction, says of Jabalāwī that he is "a riddle indeed,"[3] these words (*lughz min al-alghāz*) are simply intended to warn us not to take the stories of Jabalāwī at their face value.

What makes the language so prosaic, then, is the fact that the

---

[1] AWL, p. 178 : لن تستطيع رؤيتي ما دام الظلام

[2] AWL, p. 269 : آن لكم ... أن تتعلموا الأسرار لتتخلصوا المرضى من العفاريت.

[3] AWL, p. 5 : وجدّنا هذا لغز من الالغاز

words are used as a part of the allegorical mechanism. Their symbolism becomes shallower, and they tend to stand for abstract ideas, and are thus often devoid of feeling. When feeling enters into the picture or, in other words, when the author is expressing his own emotions, the language suddenly acquires a richer quality. Such cases as the occasional expression of disgust for the material, and of a craving for the spiritual;[1] or the great passion for discovering the secrets of the Big House.[2]

Dialogue, as has already been indicated, is plentiful in AWL; so much so in fact, that one often feels that one is reading a play, not a novel. Though not always geared to reflect the characters, the dialogue is nonetheless very lively. It betrays, more than ever before, the patterns and syntax of the original spoken idiom.[3] This last fact may

---

[1] For example : a typical expression of such feelings is to be found in the following reflections of Adham while still in the Big House (AWL, p. 19) : الحديقة وسكانها المغردون، والماء، والسماء، ونفسي النشوى، هذه هي الحياة الحقة. كأنني أجدّ في البحث عن شيء. ما هذا الشيء؟ الناي احيانا يكاد يجيب. ولكن السؤال يظل بلا جواب. لو تكلمت هذه العصفورة بلغتي لشفت قلبي باليقين. وللنجوم الزاهرة حديث كذلك أما تحصيل الايجار فنشاز بين الانغام.

[2] The scribe, for instance, tells us of his infatuation with the stories of Jabalāwī and his passion for the old man and his House as follows (AWL, p. 6.) : وكنت وما زلت أجد الحديث عنه [الجبلاوي] شائقا لا يمل. وكم دفعني ذلك الى الطواف ببيته الكبير لعلي افوز بنظرة منه ولكن دون جدوى. وكم وقفت امام بابه الضخم ارنو الى التمساح المحنط المركب أعلاه، وكم جلست فى صحراء المقطم غير بعيد من سوره الكبير فلا ارى الا رءوس اشجار التوت والجميز والنخيل تكتنف البيت، ونوافذ مغلقة لا تنم على أي اثر لحياة.

[3] Examples : a) فلأصبر عليها قليلا، اما ينصلح حالها او فلتذهب في الفداهية. (AWL, p. 33);

b) يسلم فمك يا عتريس، كلامك كالبرتقال السكرى (AWL, p. 119);

c) غوري يا تمرحنة، أنت فت سن الزواج من خمسين سنة فلم تحبين مجالس الرجال. (AWL, p. 119);

d) الواحد حيران، لا عند الاولاد راحة ولا عند الفتوات راحة ولا عند الناظر راحة. (AWL, p. 121);

e) وحياتك عيشتنا تقرف الصراصير (AWL, p. 125);

account for the amazing drop in the number of "introductory remarks" which he used so excessively in his earlier works.[1]

Words from the *'āmmiyya* now permeate the written language of the author with an unprecendented frequency. Similarly the language is richer than ever with metaphors and similes, and much less affected than ever,[2] and more often do we meet a metaphor neatly suited to the person in question or to the circumstances.[3] Apart from the use of outright similes the language shows a richer and more personal turn of phrase.

To sum up, AWL is an audacious departure from the author's familiar style. However, it loses much of its literary value because of the imbalance between the form and the content. The resort to allegory does not really lend greater profundity to the ideas. The

---

f) يا جبلاوي ، تعال شف حالنا ، تركتنا تحتنا تحت رحمة من لا رحمة لهم. (AWL, p. 126);

g) حاسب ان تنزلق البطاطة فنموت جوعا (AWL, p. 312);

h) حاسب يا معلم جلطة ، عيب قولك اسياد الحارة! (AWL, p. 326);

i) يقولون حارة الجبلاوي حارة الفتوات المجدع (AWL, p. 343);

j) سحرك اصله الخير كله (AWL, p. 521).

The last example is quoted as in the original version of *al-Ahrām*. In the Beirut editiont he word أصله becomes أصل. This is obviously a misprint, for the use of the word *aṣl* as a "prop word" appears frequently in this and other works of Maḥfūẓ. Cf. *supra*, p. 99, fn. 4; also أصله لم يكن على يقين من انك ابنه (AWL, p. 239).

1 Cf. *supra* Ch. III, p. 98, fn. 4.

2 Examples: a) واكفهر الوجه الكبير حتى حاكى لونه النيل في احتدام فيضانه. (AWL, p. 16);

b) ترسل تنهدة عميقة مثل ختام أغنية حزينة (AWL, p. 67);

c) بصوت كخشخشةالاوراق الجافة (AWL, p. 409);

d) فهبطت النبابيت كرؤس المصلين (AWL, p. 481).

3 Examples: a) وسمع البلقيطي يتثاءب بصوت مرتفع متماوج كالحية الراقصة (AWL, p. 164—the man in question being a snake-charmer.)

b) فهتف شافعى وهو يشعر كأن المنشار ينشر صدره (AWL, p. 248—the man in question being a carpenter.)

c) قال حسونة الفران انه اختفى كأن نيران الفرن التهمته (AWL, pp. 390-1, the man in question being a baker.) cf. *supra*, p. 135, fn. 3.

revolt against plain realism which was smouldering for quite a while in Maḥfūẓ's works, together with his well-known passion for the mysteries of life, combine to precipitate an amazing turn in the author's career. Yet the first product of this new style is too abstract and too prosaic to satisfy the demands of so ambitious an edifice as that which the author aimed at erecting.

Nevertheless this novel (if novel it is) is essential to anyone who seeks to discover the way Maḥfūẓ sees our world as a whole and, moreover, the world in which he could like to live. The outlook, as it emerges from AWL, is highly gloomy. In fact never before in his works has the author been so sad. Here on the whole we are presented with a history of a world that has always been harsh to its people and never, since Adham's expulsion from the Big House (= the Garden of Eden), has his posterity been able to enjoy a moment of bliss. Truly enough, the reason for our misery lies essentially in the prevalence of unjust social and political orders. An all-out social revolution whereby science and wealth can be put to the service of the people of the *Ḥāra* is the only possible way of breaking loose. As things are, however, there is but slight hope for such a dream to be realized. We live in a Godless world, and the reins are as tightly-held in the hands of the ruthless super-power (or powers) as they have ever been. The revolt of science was buried alive. There is a glimmer of hope, though; the people are now waiting for a dauntless science-conscious revolutionary to emerge and overthrow the tyrants. The very last words of AWL strike a sanguine note :

> But people endured injustice steadfastly and with patience. They held on to hope, and whenever they were persecuted they would say : "Oppression must come to an end as day must follow night. Verily we shall witness in our *Ḥāra* the death of tyranny and the coming of light and wonders."[1]

Such great expectations, however, are not altogether justified by the actual turn of events. We are not at all sure that Ḥanash, 'Arafa's brother, has found the lost note-book wherein are written the secrets of magic, as was rumoured. What is more, the young people who disappear from the *Ḥāra* are only said to have joined Ḥanash. Bearing

[1] AWL, p. 552 : لكن الناس تحملوا البغي في جلد ، ولاذوا بالصبر واستمسكوا بالامل وكانوا كلما أضر بهم العسف قالوا : لا بد للظلم من آخر ، ولليل من نهار ، ولنرين في حارتنا مصرع الطغيان ومشرق النور والعجائب.

in mind the gloomy history of the *Ḥāra*, and the unshakeable grip of the *nāẓir*, one can even detect tinges of irony behind these last words of the novel. In a way the people of the *Ḥāra* have little more reason to rejoice than the beasts of *Animal Farm* who, in spite of their frustrations,

> never gave up hope ... And when they heard the gun booming and saw the green flag fluttering at the masthead, their hearts swelled with imperishable pride and talk always turned to the old heroic days ... None of the old dreams has been abandoned.[1]

Indeed, the people of the *Ḥāra* whom Maḥfūẓ describes seem to stand no greater chance of seeing the millennium.

---

[1] G. Orwell, *Animal Farm*, Ch. 10.

CHAPTER SIX

INTO THE LABYRINTH

The Short Novels—General

> The days passed and brought with them many illnesses from which I was able, without too much trouble, and at a cost I could afford, to find a cure; until I became afflicted with that illness for which no one possesses a remedy. Every way out was closed and I was encircled by despair.

These words from a short story published by Maḥfūẓ in 1961[1] adequately provide us with the dominant mood, and at the same time they point to the focal themes, of the five short novels which the author published between 1961-1966.[2]

The feeling of despair, doom and siege is at all times at the forefront of these works. Admittedly none of Maḥfūẓ's works, as we have seen, is free from pessimism. But whereas in the early Cairene novels the catastrophe comes towards the end of the story and as the culmination of the plot, in these short novels despair is the *starting point*. Furthermore, while in the early novels the root of the tragedy lie in social conditions, the works of the sixties give prominence to tragedy of a different kind—spiritual or existential. The malady is much more insidious, more consuming than the social one. The roads are closed and there is no remedy to be found.

In the novels of the forties, in other words, the protagonists are crushed by external factors, while in the short novels in question they are, more often than not, seeking their own destruction. They are out to tackle questions which are unanswerable or to fight against forces which, unlike social structures, are indestructible. The overambitious young man or the passive victim of circumstances now give way to a morose quixotic figure, mostly in his thirties or early forties, who could have possibly led a decent life if he so wished, but a sharp inner crisis brings about his alienation and fall.

---

[1] DUN. p. 158: وجرت الايام فصادفتني أدواء كثيرة ، وكنت أجد لكل داء دواءه بلا عناء وبنفقات في حدود الامكان ، حتى أصابني الداء الذي لا دواء له عند أحد ، وسدت في وجهي السبل وطوقني اليأس ...

[2] For *Mīrāmār*, a novel published in 1967, see Postscript.

On the face of it, one of these novels, *al-Ṭarīq*, does not conform to these generalizations. But as we shall presently see, it is in its own way an acute expression of the very same crisis.

It should be stressed that the works vary in the density of their "spiritual" texture, some having more social and psychological elements than others. But the general trend, as far as the author is concerned, is that of a deepening spiritual malaise. The meticulous concern with external reality gradually gives way to an ever-growing introspection.

The first two of these novels, *al-Liṣṣ wal-kilāb*, 1961 (LISS), and *al-Summān al-kharīf*, 1962 (SUM), are clearly set in the social and political realities of present day Egypt. In the former, the protagonist, Sa'īd, is a thief just released from prison. Having been betrayed by the people closest to him, he is intent on punishing the traitors. He comes to believe that his mission of revenge is symbolic, and it is in fact aimed at all traitors and bullies. His struggle, however, ends in his destruction.

'Īsā, the protagonist of SUM, his promising career in ruins following the 1952 revolution, refuses to compromise with the new realities. He cuts himself off from the mainstream of society, thereby destroying himself as a person.

Both of these novels, then, provide a down-to-earth setting and motivation. Yet the interest in the external circumstances is reduced to a minimum, while the more intimate aspects of the crisis are given prominence. Furthermore, both of these stories, especially the first one, have a strong air of mysticism about them. Reference is repeatedly made to the search for certainty and the craving for an otherworldly repose.

The next novel, *al-Ṭarīq*, 1964 (TARIQ), does not start with a spiritual crisis. Ṣābir, its hero, sets out to look for his lost father because his mother has urged him to do so on her deathbed, and also because he hoped that his father might save him from impending poverty. In the course of his search he becomes entangled with two women, one of whom goads him to kill her aged husband. Eventually he kills both husband and wife, and it is only after he is sentenced to death for these crimes that he finds a clue to the identity of his lost father.

The outline of TARIQ might not strike one as esoteric, but the novel has many indications of being a double-layered story; in other words, the lost father who is sought by Ṣābir is more than a flesh-and-blood one. He is, to all appearances, another version of that great ancestor who, in AWL, was also unreachable by his children. Hence the events which start Ṣābir on his quest for his father can be interpreted as having a deeper meaning. His crisis, then, is no less a spiritual one.

In the two novels that follow, *al-Shaḥḥādh*, 1965 (SHAH), and *Tharthara fawq al-Nīl*, 1966 (THAR), there is no attempt to disguise the spiritual ordeal. They are straightforward portrayals of people searching for the secrets of life or attempting to explore the ultimate riddle.

SHAH is, in fact, a direct study of the process of rejection of the realities of life and society, and the drift into the mystical labyrinth. 'Umar, its hero, is a successful lawyer and a happy father who for no conceivable reason (conceivable, that is, to other people) loses interest in everything surrounding him and sets out to elicit the "secret of secrets of life" first through sex, and then through mystical literature. Finally, he deserts his home to seek a life of mystical hallucinations in seclusion.

Anīs, the chief character in THAR, is similarly immersed in his visions, albeit by means of hashish. He has long since detached himself from society to live in a boathouse, never to be separated from his fantasies, even during office hours. A great part of THAR portrays his moods and hallucinations. Apart from the few quick-moving incidents occurring at the end of the book, there is no action except for the daily hashish sessions of Anīs and his friends.

The drift away from stark realities towards mysticism is, then, the most prominent feature of this group of novels. There is a great change in the thematical stress as compared to the author's earlier works. The change, moreover, is not only in subject matter, but also in the structure, style and treatment of the characters. Yet before embarking upon a discussion of these very aspects which cause our novels to be different, it would be useful to dwell upon certain features which are common to this group and the rest of Maḥfūẓ's works.

The social theme, for one thing, is not altogether absent. This is especially true of LISS where the hero's poverty in his youth is recalled tersely but clearly, especially that scene in which his ailing mother was taken, bleeding, to a private hospital, but was turned away on account of her poverty.[1] It is this poverty that first made him steal. Moreover, he comes to see his "profession" as one of social protest,

[1] LISS, pp. 113-4.

directed against the rich. In the same novel we encounter the prostitute Nūr, another victim of an unjust social order.

In the other four novels most of the characters are less bedevilled by need. Yet in each of these works, the theme of social protest makes an occasional appearance. In TARIQ Ṣābir remarks to his lawyer, when the latter informs him that his lost father is a millionaire, "More important, the law of the land has no power over him." To this the lawyer replies, "At any rate you were aware [when committing the murders] that you are poor and subject to the laws of the land."[1]

The subject of current politics, at times closely related to the latter, is often raised. As in the early novels and in the Trilogy, there is a sharp awareness of the political scene, domestic and international. References of that nature are especially frequent in SHAH and THAR. Furthermore, one novel, SUM, has as its main character a career politician (rather, ex-politician), and that book comes as close as any to being a straightforward political novel.

Another theme which is present in many of these novels is the old preoccupation with the validity of science and knowledge. The search often starts after the character has despaired of scientific or rational solutions. The first chapter of SHAH takes place in the doctor's clinic. 'Umar has come to consult him about his depressive mood. He explains that he has come to find out whether this mood of his has an organic cause. To this the doctor remarks, "Wouldn't it be wonderful if our great problems could be solved by a pill-after-meal or a spoonful-before-bed!"[2]

The question of the limits of science; the claims of science on the one hand, and philosophy, art and death on the other hand—occupy, in fact, a great part of the conversations between 'Umar and other characters of that novel.[3] The same kind of question is touched upon in other novels as well, at times in a straightforward manner and at others esoterically. In TARIQ, for instance, Ṣābir, on arriving in Cairo to look for his father, starts with a doctor—this time a heart specialist—bearing the same name as his father. He too, like 'Umar, is disappointed : the man has never heard of his father.[4]

---

[1] TAR, p. 180.

[2] SHAH, p. 9 : ما أجمل أن تحل مشاكلنا الخطيرة بحبة بعد الاكل أو ملعقة قبل النوم.

[3] SHAH, pp. 37, 45-7, 94-9, 159-65.

[4] TARIQ, pp. 36-8. The doctor as a symbol of science or the scientific solution can also be found elsewhere in Maḥfūẓ's works. In "Za'balāwī" (see *supra* p. 57; *infra*

Fate is as cruel in these stories as ever; the Mockery of Fate as shattering. In LISS, Sa'īd, whose bullets in the past never missed their targets, now manages to hit only innocent people. Ṣābir in TARIQ receives Ilhām's selfless offer of help[1] only after he has committed his murder and has thus become irredeemably entangled with Karīma. Later he discovers the identity of his father only after having been sentenced to death. 'Īsā, in SUM, plans to marry Salwā in August, but the *coup d'état* which occurs on the twenty-third of July shatters his life.

Finally, the scene of action is the self-same Cairo;[2] and the houseboat of THAR is also nothing new.[3] Also present are the Ṣūfī, the beggar, the harlot, and similar characters.

Yet these and other elements in the short novels, reminiscent as they are of Maḥfūẓ's earlier works, have to be seen in their right perspective. Their function, arrangement, interplay and order of prominence, in other words, their aesthetic treatment, is unmistakably different from anything we have seen earlier.

Characters

The most salient difference between the short novels and the earlier works is that whereas Maḥfūẓ has in the past preferred a multi-character novel, he now concentrates on a single character. This is connected, to a certain extent, with the fact that the novels of the sixties are much shorter (BID, for instance, with four or five main characters, is three to four times longer than any of the one-character novels.) But the length does not necessarily depend on the number of characters or vice versa : SAR is roughly of the same length as BID, yet it is basically a one-character story. Moreover, the change manifests itself not only in the number of characters but in the manner of their representation as well. The characters are now mostly depicted from within. The author has given up a long-standing convenience —that of the omniscient author, and has resorted to a subtler techni-

p. 172), the protagonist-narrator is searching for a saintly man hoping that he can cure his illness after the doctors have failed to do so. In his investigation, he encounters certain people who maintain that Za'balāwī is a quack and advise the sick man to consult the doctors. To this he reacts with the thought, "as if I had not done so already" (كأنني لم أفعل DUN, p. 161).

1 TARIQ, Ch. 14.

2 In TARIQ and SUM there are, however, a few scenes which occur in Alexandria.

3 Cf. TR-II.

que. The point of view through which the events are seen is mainly that of the protagonist. The language is also that of the protagonist, and the rhythm that of his inner reactions.

In SAR, it is true, the novelist has also abandoned his omniscient vantage point by resorting to *Ich-Erzählung*. However, there is a great difference in the method employed in the short novels and that of SAR. In that early novel we find none of the twentieth century quest for the immediate experience, none of the blending of past and present, of "he," "you," and "I." The events in that novel, like the great majority of first person narratives in world literature, are related *a posteriori* and in the order of their occurrence. In contrast, the short novels in question are very much in keeping with the modern style and techniques.

The aspects just mentioned, namely the arrangement of characters in the novel and the narrative technique employed are, in the main, a matter of structure and as such they will be touched upon again. Yet these points have a palpable effect on the very nature of the characters.

For one thing, the new techniques signify a certain change in the concept of the characters on the part of the author. There is a clear shift of stress away from explicatory psychology. This is not to say that the interest in psychology has subsided. As we shall see, these novels display as keen an interest in mental processes as any. In fact the short novels, showing as they do the protagonist from within, are now constantly in touch with such processes. Yet the old ambition to explain *why* a character behaved the way he did, is now on the decline. It is gradually replaced by the question of *how* the character reacts in given situations. The author is less concerned with marshalling human experience and giving it logical and chronological coherence. Instead, the particles of the experience become valid independent units, interconnected to each other not by overt causality, but rather by invisible inner association.

Two points have to be made. Firstly in resorting to these twentieth century techniques, Maḥfūẓ never carries them too far. His writing is as lucid as ever. This is true even of such a "hallucinatory" novel as THAR. There is little apparent experimentation to be found, but there is a gradual progress towards a mode of narration which can be described as self-reflexive.[1]

[1] This term, as well as a few others used in this chapter, are borrowed from Joseph

Secondly, not all these novels are emancipated from quasi-clinical psychology. SUM (the second of the series) and SHAH (the fourth) are strongly reminiscent of case-studies in spite of their lyrical and mystical appearance. In LISS, TARIQ and THAR, the psychology is neatly counter-balanced by a forceful, life-like flux.

1. *Men*

Sa'īd — The character of Sa'īd Mahrān, the hero of LISS, comes as a refreshing surprise. His background is anything but commonplace. He is a thief, but an intellectual one, a quality which can hardly be typical of thieves—even those of Cairo. Though in the past he had also been engaged in an underground revolutionary movement (the precise nature of which is undisclosed though clearly of a Marxist brand), in the course of the novel he is not engaged in any such activities. He has a very definite self-imposed "mission" to accomplish : to settle his accounts with the traitors. He is also fighting treachery and he sees all traitors, those *kilāb* ('dogs') that bedevil the life of simple people, as his enemies.

He is single-minded, even obsessed, yet he is not a simple or one-sided character. In the short period in which we meet him in the novel (it spans no more than a few weeks) we get a vivid picture of his colourful personality, his idiosyncratic way of thinking, his severe internal crisis, his vacillation between violence and asceticism, hatred and love. Admittedly, rich and many-sided characters have been protrayed by Maḥfūẓ in the past, yet the author always remained aloof and his attitude smacked of a cold neutrality. This is true even of such characters as al-Sayyid (TR), and Aḥmad 'Ākif (KHAN). Sa'īd, on the other hand, is a character to whom the author is partial and hence so is the reader. This fact probably stems to a certain extent from the technique whereby everything is seen through the eyes of the character. Better still, we *live* through the hero and face with him the situations with which he is confronted. Even the past is not conveyed by well-ordered briefings, but by his own fragmentary recollections and visions. This technique obviously penetrates into the human experience in greater depth, but at the same time renders the reader incapable of making an objective judgement of the hero's deeds. In the case of Sa'īd, we do not know, for instance, the truth of his allegations against his former wife and assistant. We accept

---

Frank's now famous article, "Spatial Form in Modern Literature," ***Sewanee Review,*** **LIII (1945), pp. 221-40; 433-56.**

his own interpretation of the events because we have no other source of information, and also because our identification with Sa'īd makes a detached stance difficult to achieve. We are given fragments of the complete story, and are hypnotized into accepting it as the whole truth.

But fragmentary as it is, Sa'īd's portrait does not lack coherence, his acts are not devoid of internal logic. The reverse is true. His development is well-arranged and amounts to a very plausible characterization. Sa'īd is a man betrayed, and we can certainly understand his passion for bloody revenge against Nabawiyya (his former wife) and 'Ilīsh (who has now married her). No less plausible is his later determination to punish Ra'ūf (his erstwhile ideological guide), whose betrayal, to Sa'īd's way of thinking, is further aggravated by the fact that he is a renegade who has abandoned his own teachings. Sa'īd's reaction to Ra'ūf's betrayal is to try to steal some of his precious belongings (which appealed to his thief's instinct as well as to his immediate poverty) and thus to practice his "profession" against its very philosopher. Later, when Ra'ūf's newspaper incites the public against him, the journalist becomes Sa'īd's main enemy, so much so that the original traitors, Nabawiyya and 'Ilīsh, become of only secondary importance in his mind. During his long hours of lonely contemplation, he develops the conception that his case is of general significance; that this persecutors are oppressors of hope and light, or to use his own words, "Whoever kills me, is a killer of millions. I am [their] dream and hope; I am the cowards' sacrifice."[1] To kill Ra'ūf is to kill the symbol of treachery, to punish all the traitors on the earth.[2]

His transformation from a private avenger to an avenger on behalf of the "millions" is traced with great skill. Sa'īd is not a static formula, but a developing character.

Sa'īd's attitude to Nūr is yet another example which demonstrates the fullness of his characterization. At first she is but an accomplice in stealing a car, who later offers him shelter. He is indifferent to her, being possessed by his vengeful thoughts. At one point he even compares her to the unfaithful Nabawiyya.[3] But in time and through her

---

1 LISS, p. 148: ان من يقتلني انما يقتل الملايين ، أنا الحلم والامل وفدية الجبناء ...

2 LISS, p. 136: ... أن رءوف هو رمز الخيانة التي ينضوي تحتها عليش ونبوية وجميع الخونة فى الارض.

3 LISS, p. 105: ولن ينسى في النهاية انها امرأة كما أن نبوية امرأة

unselfish love, he is unconsciously *changed* into a more affectionate person. By the time she disappears "he silently confesses that he loved her and that he would willingly sacrifice himself in order to have her safely back."[1] True, the timing of the confession might tempt one to question the sincerity of his love, whether it is anything more than the selfish "love" for the shelter and food that Nūr provided. But his later poetical and anguished imaginary conversations with her leave no doubt as to the sincerity of his feelings.

The new technique, then, while not denying the author the possibility of psychological penetration, allows him to live through Sa'īd's own experience. Thus we identify ourselves with Sa'īd even though some of his reactions might strike us as haughty or even unbalanced. A detached observer might find him afflicted with paranoia; another might dub him a megalomaniac. Indeed he himself reflects at one point that "amongst people he is magnified into a giant; [it is there that] he is friendly, superior, heroic."[2] On another occasion he thinks himself to be "truly great."[3] Often he fails to see his limitations. On leaving jail he asks Ra'ūf (though half-seriously) to employ him as a journalist, but as Ra'ūf rightly points out, he is not qualified and is turned down. Later he addresses Ra'ūf in his imagination as follows : "Had you let me work as a journalist in your paper, you scoundrel, then I would have published the memoirs of our common past and your false light would have been dimmed."[4] In these words we hear as much the voice of his conceit as that of his pathetic naïveté.

Psychology is well-concealed. Sa'īd's continual soliloquy is so designed as to convey unobtrusively the background and psychological information. But there is more to it than a mere informative vehicle. His inner thoughts are represented as the flow of life itself. The themes that obsessed Sa'īd come out in the midst of other thoughts that pass through his mind.

---

[1] LISS, p. 158 : وأغمض عينيه في الظلام واعترف اعترافا صامتا بأنه يحبها ، وأنه لا يتردد في بذل النفس ليستردها سالمة.

[2] LISS, p. 154 : وهو بين الناس يتضخم كالعملاق ويمارس المودة والرياسة والبطولة.

[3] LISS, p. 149 : ... فقضى بأنه عظيم بكل معنى الكلمة، عظمة هائلة

[4] LISS, p. 115 : لو قبلت أن أعمل محررا في جريدتك يا وغد لنشرت فيها ذكرياتنا المشتركة ولخسفت نورك الكاذب.

Psychology becomes less conspicuous also because of the ever-prevailing lyricism. Sa'īd's past, and especially the love scenes with Nabawiyya, are brought into the story in the form of short, dramatic flash-backs, which save them from appearing to be just extra material designed to throw light on the origins of the hero's present mental state.

Psychology is also counter-balanced by mysticism, which is present in practically all the novels dealt with in this chapter, but is best employed in LISS. The character of 'Alī al-Junaydī, the Ṣūfī shaykh, with his incessant esoteric utterances is a very important element in the novel. His calm unworldliness is contrasted to the tumult of Sa'īd's feeling. Above all, the beautiful mystic-laden scenes in the shaykh's house put Sa'īd's plight on a level which transcends any preoccupation with mental processes. It is through the Ṣūfī chapters that Sa'īd's predicament acquires an existential dimension and that his acts acquire a metaphysical significance. After killing an innocent man whom he mistook for 'Ilīsh, Sa'īd reflects as follows : "I, the killer, cannot understand a thing. Neither can shaykh 'Alī al-Junaydī. I had wanted to uncover a part of the mystery, but I brought to the surface a mystery far more inscrutable."[1]

In other words, Sa'īd comes to perceive his act as having some hidden meaning. The word *lughz* (here translated as mystery) is often used in conjunction with death. It is employed in this sense in reference to the death of Sa'īd's father,[2] and also in conjunction with the graveyard (*al-qarāfa*) just behind Nūr's house.[3] In the whole of Sa'īd's story, then, prominence is given to a feeling or mood, not to a psycho-social analysis. The feeling is that of helplessness, of futility in the face of overwhelming puzzles. This might answer the question as to why the author has, chosen as his hero a lonely and besieged thief. In fact, a real thief, very similar to Sa'īd, did haunt Cairo a short while before LISS was written. The story of LISS coincides in more than one detail with the true story, but deviates in others.[4] Maḥfūẓ,

---

[1] LISS, p. 90 : وأنا القاتل لا أفهم شيئا ولا الشيخ علي الجنيدي نفسه يستطيع أن يفهم. أردت أن أحل جانبا من اللغز فكشفت عن لغز أغمض.

[2] LISS, p. 113 : اختفى الرجل على نحو لم يفهمه الغلام ، وبدا الشيخ علي الجنيدي نفسه عاجزا أمام اللغز.

[3] LISS, p. 125 : وكل راقد في القرافة تحت النافذة يؤيدني. ولاترك تفسير اللغز للشيخ علي الجنيدي.

[4] For a detailed comparison between Maḥfūẓ's thief and that of real life, see Fāṭima Mūsā, *Bayn adabayn*, Cairo 1965, pp. 131-6.

in other words, was not interested in retelling a story which occurred in reality. What he did was to use the story of the real fugitive as a framework for expressing his own mood of siege and suffocation.

'Īsā — How successful the portrait of Sa'īd is, becomes more pronounced when we consider 'Īsā, the protagonist of the author's next novel, SUM. On the face of it 'Īsā's story, like that of Sa'īd's, is conveyed from within, that is, through a string of internal monologues and as seen through the eyes of the character. Furthermore, there are certain component elements of a psychological nature which are common to both characters : they both feel betrayed and alienate themselves from the outer world.

Yet these points of similarity need not blur the real difference in their characterization. 'Īsā, in spite of the lyrical narrative style, brings us back, in fact, to the era of "case-studies." The author presents us with an image of a *type*, one of those who in the early years of the Nasserite revolution were estranged from the new regime, even though its achievements were a realization of an old dream of theirs.

'Īsā, having been a prominent Wafdist official, feels that the revolution has shattered his life and ambitions. Like other Wafdists, he is jealous of the new regime which is in fact implementing those ideals for which the Wafd party stood, but which it never dared put into practice. When the British army finally evacuates Egypt and when the Suez Canal is nationalized, he feels at once elated and bitter. However, when Egypt is attacked in 1956, 'Īsā comes out of his shell for a while and feels that "the wall separating him from the revolution is being demolished with unbelievable speed."[1] Yet no sooner does danger pass than he returns to his former posture.

'Īsā is so much of a political animal that the change of regime leaves no compartment of his life untouched. His engagement to Salwā is annulled because her father, the friend of the deposed King, wanted to find a way to the new rulers. This leaves him deeply scarred, especially as the girl later marries his cousin, a supporter of the new regime. During his withdrawal to Alexandria, he shelters a homeless prostitute Rīrī. In hysterical fear, he throws her out when she discloses that she is bearing his child. He then marries a widow, rich, but

[1] SUM, p. 155 : وخيل اليه أن الحاجز القائم بينه وبين الثورة يذوب بسرعة لم تخطر له ببال من قبل.

barren and much older than himself, in order to secure "a life-long insurance."[1] Yet he soon finds that a life without action, without posterity, is unbearable. He indulges in reckless gambling, which culminates in a serious quarrel with his wife. Then, accidentally, he comes across Rīrī and her daughter, undoubtedly his own. Without hesitation he decides to put an end to his past and join his "natural family". But Rīrī, now married, refuses to have anything to do with him.

'Īsā's story could have made an interesting novel, and his vicissitudes—material for an impressive characterization. Unfortunately, the outcome is disappointing. The character is not brought out with sufficient force and penetration. The fabric of the story is thin : in the course of the short novel (less than 25,000 words) we follow 'Īsā's fate through five stormy years (between 1952-1957). The episodes are patchy, in much the same manner as in AWL. Although the whole story revolves around 'Īsā, there are such wide gaps of time between the different episodes, that the feeling of a compact human experience is lost. One feels that the story, as it is presented, is only a first draft for a novel and not the completed novel. Thus despite the fact that the story is ostensibly related through 'Īsā's consciousness, it lacks the genuine touch of intimacy. 'Īsā's introspections are too objective (rather, biased against him) to be his own. Too many of 'Īsā's actions strike us as ugly and heartless (for example : his attitude to Rīrī, to his mother, and to his wife). If we were really seeing these things from 'Īsā's point of view, we would have viewed them more favourably. His behaviour in the case of Rīrī,[2] viewed from a subjective view point, might have been looked upon as an act of self-defence, not of apparent cowardice or hysteria. Worse still, too many references are made to 'Īsā in a most unflattering manner. There is a recurrent mention of his accepting bribes in the past from provincial dignitaries.[3] He is described more than once as "unclean," and he thinks of himself as the "old patriot who, in spite of his tarnished past, has suffered much for Egypt's good."[4] It might be natural for him to be haunted by these faults which brought about his downfall, yet a man would never speak of his own faults in these terms. It is the author speaking.

[1] SUM, p. 137 : يمكن أن يعتبرها نوعا من التأمين مدى الحياة
[2] SUM, Chs. 16-17.
[3] SUM, pp. 57, 61, 71, 93, 95, 130, 144, 169.
[4] SUM, p. 144 : الوطني القديم الذي تعذب بالرغم من تلوثه من أجل مصر

Even modern narrative techniques are mobilized to demonstrate his moral corruption. The Proustian style of "involuntary memory," or the device referred to in the last chapter as "coincidental symbolism" are employed to cast a doubt on 'Īsā's image by insinuation. When he is summoned to a committee investigating the integrity of civil servants, he suddenly remembers an incident in his boyhood when he sheltered from the rain under a rubbish cart;[1] again, when he speaks to Salwā's father about corruption, it flashes through his mind that in his childhood he had stolen a bar of chocolate from that same man.[2] These instances and others are clearly innuendoes : they are designed to make us aware that 'Īsā is not really a victim. We should not identify ourselves with his cause without reservations.

The externalized psychology is another aspect which contributes to 'Īsā being two-dimensional. Outright items of professional jargon are used. The term "split-personality" is twice evoked to describe 'Īsā's mental state.[3] There is a repeated assertion (at least four times)[4] that while his mind accepts the new regime, his heart refuses to do so.

The Ṣūfī element is present in this as well as in practically all the other short novels. Yet in SUM it is rather rationalized. Samīr, 'Īsā's old friend who has also lost his post, resorts to Ṣūfī literature. He utters certain words which smack of mysticism ("my word bears a greater significance."[5]) But he has little bearing on the atmosphere of the story, and more important, little contact with 'Īsā's own thinking. Samīr's mysticism, which he practices alongside commerce, is represented as yet another option open to the alienated "men of the past" (the others resorted to hypocrisy or emigrated from Egypt).

It is to be stressed, however, that SUM is not without its fascinating incursions into the minds and manners of certain members of the *ancien régime*. Nor is the character of 'Īsā himself devoid of insight. In spite of the unpleasant traits mentioned above, and in spite of the externalized psychology employed in SUM, we often feel in sympathy with 'Īsā. This is, however, because we feel that the man suffered too much for his past mistakes while his friends, who were equally corrupt, escaped unscathed. What is more, the only represen-

---

[1] SUM, p. 51.

[2] SUM, p. 25.

[3] SUM, p. 126 : انقسام الشخصية ; p. 143 : شطري شخصيته المنقسمة

[4] SUM, pp. 95, 122, 126, 143.

[5] SUM, p. 149 : كلمتي تحمل معنى أعمق

tative of the new regime, Ḥasan, has nothing about him to make him lovable. When he offers to help ʿĪsā we suspect that it is not without an ulterior motive (ʿĪsā is sure that he wants to bait him into marrying his sister). We even grow to dislike him because he marries ʿĪsā's former fiancée, the daughter of the opportunistic judge who treated ʿĪsā so inconsiderately.

Yet there is a great shallowness in the character of ʿĪsā because of the author's lukewarm and ambiguous attitude to him, and because this character, unlike the hero of LISS, fails to express anything which has a significance beyond the plain narrative.

Ṣābir — The characterization of Ṣābir, the hero of TARIQ is the very opposite of ʿĪsā. This is true as regards both the spontaneity and vividness of the portrait, and the intensity of human experience which is embodied in it.

Ṣābir is the handsome but spoiled son of a bawd. He obeys his mother's dying wish that he should leave Alexandria and look for his lost father. Unlike the brothers in the well-known folk tale, whose father made them cultivate their land after his death by telling them of an imaginary treasure which was hidden in it, Ṣābir, having accepted his mother's challenge, finds himself in ever-growing difficulties. He comes to commit a double murder and is sentenced to death.

Ṣābir is as idiosyncratic a character as any which Maḥfūẓ has ever created. His story is *really* told through his own consciousness. We thus grow so involved in his unrewarding search that we accept everything he does, even his murders, with sympathy. His story is related in such a way that there is nothing to call forth our moral judgement. Furthermore, in spite of the revealing peep that we are afforded into his innermost thoughts and reactions, there is none of the clinical "typology" with which ʿĪsā is delineated. Similarly, Ṣābir's social background and past experience, which are supplied by flashbacks, constitute no straightforward commentary on his present actions.

Incidentally, TARIQ is not devoid of psychological or sociological terminology. In the last chapter of the novel, after Ṣābir has been detained, we read with him the press commentary of his case. Among other things, one newspaper publishes an analysis by a social worker examining the social roots of his tragedy. A religious leader points out that the gist of the matter is the loss of faith. A professor of psychology comments as follows :

> Ṣābir suffered from a mother-love complex. Two points are essential to explain his criminal outbursts. Firstly, he loved Karīma because he found in her a substitute for his mother. [Secondly], because he subconsciously insisted on avenging his mother; he thus killed the hotel owner, a symbol of authority; he also hoped to expropriate his fortune just as the government had confiscated his mother's fortune.[1]

Surely such commentaries are not brought in by the author simply to enlighten the reader as to the nature of Ṣābir's motivations. The reverse can also be true : the diagnosis is quoted with tongue in cheek. The commentaries coming as they do towards the end of the novel, i.e., after we have been witness to the actual events, demonstrate just how inadequate psychology is in dealing with human relationships, how superficial when it tries to pigeonhole the complexities of life. In other words, the author is out to ridicule the application of psychology to spheres which he now considers to be beyond its reach. TARIQ, particularly its last chapter, is in a way a parody of the very method of characterization which Maḥfūẓ himself had adopted in certain works, notably SAR.[2]

Judging by appearances, there are certain similarities in the psychological facets of TARIQ and SAR. In both novels the hero is torn between two women and two types of relationships : platonic and sensual. Secondly, in both novels he sets out on a mission of discovery, but is distracted from his course by a woman. Yet these very points of similarity can serve to prove how different the two novels are. Ṣābir's entanglement with Karīma and Ilhām has more to it than a study of sexual complexes or split personality. The situations in TARIQ are infinitely more involved, the attitudes more ambiguous. Ṣābir's relationship with Karīma cannot be summed up simply. His attraction to her is not solely of a sensual nature. She is a woman carved from the same marble as he, posing a greater challenge to his manhood, and he finds himself on safer ground when dealing with her than with Ilhām.

Between Ṣābir and Karīma there is an invisible clash of wills.

---

1 TAR, p. 170 : وقال أستاذ علم نفس أن صابر مصاب بعقدة حب الام وأنه يمكن تفسير اندفاعه الاجرامي بأمرين مهمين ، فهو اولا وجد في كريمة بديلا عن إمه فأحبها ، وأن لاشعوره أصر على الانتقام لامه فقتل صاحب الفندق كرمز للسلطة وطمع في مصادرة أمواله كما صادرت الحكومة اموال أمه.

2 See *supra*, pp. 100ff.

A short while before committing his first murder, planned by Karīma, Ṣābir

> ... patted her cheek in a compassionate and masterful manner, while swimming against a wave that was sweeping him into the depths of subjugation. She is everything. She is love. She is those very hopes that set him to search for his lost father.[1]

Moreover, Karīma is an enigma which he feels unable to leave unsolved. As it is, he never discovers, nor does the reader, whether she was the same girl with whom he had had a liaison in Alexandria years ago; neither do we find out whether she was really in league with her former husband, as al-Sāwī insinuated; in other words, whether she used Ṣābīr as a ploy for her own ends or whether she wanted to get rid of her husband only because she loved Ṣābir. These as well as the other uncertainties about Karīma, serve to underline the fact that life is never simple, and they exemplify the author's more sophisticated way of viewing human relationships.

More important, the core of Ṣābir's story is not his relationship with the two women. He is, above all, a man in search of his father and, through him, of "dignity and peace." He is a Telemachus, one of a long line of such characters who have repeatedly appeared in world literature since its earliest days. Thus even if one sees in his agony of choice between the two women a reflection of a certain psychological theory, this part of his story will acquire less prominence than it did in SAR.

The character of Ṣābir, though depicting a real human predicament has also, to all appearances, a hidden, deeper meaning. In fact it tends to be yet another formulation of the eternal quest for the ultimate secrets, and a very sharp formulation at that. The character of the lost father has more than one point reminiscent of the Creator. His name is Sayyid Sayyid al-Raḥīmī (Lord-Lord-Compassionate), a name not unfamiliar in Egypt, yet combined with all the mysteries that surround its bearer, it can hardly be taken to belong to one of our race. Towards the end of the book, Ṣābir learns many interesting facts about his father. It transpires that he is an exceptionally rich and important person. The laws of the land do not touch him, as he

[1] TAR., p. 77: وربت على خدها بحنان وسيادة وهو يسبح بعزم ضد موجة تشده نحو أعماق الخضوع. هي كل شيء. الحب ، والآمال التي بعثته يجري وراء الاب الضائع.

moves from one country to another, and from continent to continent, never resting in one place. He has no occupation but "love." He has never known bad luck. He has no brothers or sisters, though he seems to have children everywhere. Furthermore, al-Raḥīmī's fortune comes from his father who had accumulated it through trading in spirits (*tijārat al-mashrūbāt al-rūḥiyya*).[1] These attributes are too evocative and too ambiguous. They are reminiscent—not without a tinge of irony—of the Almighty.

The spiritual undertones of Ṣābir's search can be further illustrated if we compare TARIQ to certain short stories which were written by Maḥfūẓ in the same period and included in *Dunyā Allāh* (1963). One of these stories, "Zaʿbalāwī,"[2] a quotation from which opens this chapter, seems to describe precisely the same situation. The protagonist of the short story is also engaged in a search. He is looking for a saintly man called Zaʿbalāwī, and leaves no stone unturned to find him. Among those whom he asks about the man are the shaykhs of the quarters.[3] Like Ṣābir, he is assured time and again that the man he is after is alive (*ḥayy*).[4] Also like Ṣābir, he just misses his target.

In that short story the symbolic theme is much more transparent and one can hardly misinterpret the author's intentions. The striking similarity of situations, atmosphere, and language between it and TARIQ gives us a precious clue towards understanding the deeper meanings of Ṣābir's search.[5]

---

[1] TARIQ, p. 180. The same pun occurs, and in a less ambiguous manner, in a short story "Mawʿid" written by Maḥfūẓ in this period. The following conversation takes place between two characters in that story (DUN, p. 87):

— ماذا عن رجل يشرب الخمر ويقرأ كتب الارواح؟

— الخمر أيضا مشروب روحي ، هكذا يسمونها.

[2] See : S. Somekh, "*Zaʿbalawī*; Author, Theme and technique," *Journal of Arabic Literature*," Vol. I (1970), pp. 24-35.

[3] DUN ("Zaʿbalāwī"), pp. 161-2; TARIQ, p. 19.

[4] This epithet, *ḥayy*, is of course, one of God's most common attributes, and is strongly reminiscent of the language of Muslim mystics. In the Ṣūfī *dhikr* sessions this word is repeatedly uttered when mentioning the Almighty (see Lane, pp. 459-60).

[5] Like many double-layered works of art, TARIQ is open to more than one interpretation, provided that these interpretations are in keeping with the artist's philosophy and aspirations, as put forth in the bulk of his work. Thus one can accept, though not without reservations, such an interpretation as that offered by a young Egyptian critic, Ṣabrī Ḥāfiẓ. In his article in a Lebanese monthly, *al-Ādāb* (June, 1964 pp. 18-21, 56-63) he argues that the message of TARIQ is "that a great silence surrounds us, and that there is an immense starvation for freedom." (p. 19). However, at times one feels that

Ṣābir's, then, is a double-layered story, the two layers dwelling side by side, enriching each other. It is because of his profound characterization that the "inner" meaning of his search becomes deeper than that of an outright allegory; and it is because of the symbolic undertones of the search that Ṣābir's "outer" story acquires a further dimension.

'*Umar* — How deeply Maḥfūẓ's novels of the sixties are obsessed with the great search can be seen when considering the character of 'Umar al-Ḥamzāwī, the protagonist of SHAH. If the object of the search in TARIQ was not explicitly stated, and the words *sirr* and *lughz* were used in an ambiguous manner, 'Umar leaves us in no doubt that he is looking for the secret of life and for a way to God.

'Umar resembles, in more than one particular, Jean-Baptiste Clemence, the protagonist of Camus' *La Chute.* Both men are respectable lawyers who decide to desert society; but while Camus' hero ends in becoming a talkative "judge penitent," 'Umar takes to ever-growing withdrawal which ends in hallucinatory mysticism. 'Umar is the most vigorous representative of those "tragic visionaries" whose crisis is not caused by fate, destitution or similar "exterior" factors. Nor is his fall precipitated by any obvious flaw in his character. At one point he suddenly perceives the futility of his life and indeed of all human life. He is no longer able to accept that man's life should be spent in the pursuit of the material. He loses interest in the evanescent triumphs of mundane reality and craves a "moment of total emancipation."[1]

The story of 'Umar's "fall" starts when he remarks to a client of his, involved in a land dispute, that though the case can be won today, the land might be confiscated by government decree tomorrow.

---

some critics, discussing this and other of Maḥfūẓ's short novels, have strayed too far in their search for hidden meanings. Fu'ād Dawwāra, in his review of TARIQ (*al-Majalla,* July 1964, pp. 143-56) suggests a system of references which, to say the least, is astonishing. The father, according to Dawwāra, is none else than the nineteenh century Muslim reformist Jamāl al-Dīn al-Afghānī. His dealing with wine is "a clear reference to spreading revolutionary ideas" (p. 147). The secondary characters are also interpreted. Karīma stands for political opportunism, while her murdered husband represents the collapsing capitalism, and her first husband—imperialism. Ilhām, on the other hand, represents the modern liberal ideas!

[1] SHAH, p. 174: وتاقت نفسه الى لحظة الانتصار المأمولة ، لحظة التحرر الكامل.

To this the client retorts, "What is important is that we win the case. After all, isn't one living one's life knowing too well that God will reclaim it?"[1]

The middle-aged lawyer is taken aback by his client's logic. Subsequently he becomes estranged from everything reminding him of the present. He recalls the days of his youth—days of poetry and naïve idealism. All that is now gone. Life is stagnant. A strange pining for a kind of "movement" or "intoxication" overwhelms him. He seizes on anything that will arouse him from his lethargy. For a while he imagines that this "movement" can be achieved through sex. This leads him to several adventures with women; until he finally deserts his home to live with Warda, a night-club dancer. Yet before long, these excitements lose their hold on him, and he engages in an anguished search of certitude. On one of his nocturnal meditations in the Muqqaṭam desert (the self-same site where Jabalāwī used to meet his favoured son in AWL), 'Umar at last seizes a moment of beatific vision. "This is ecstasy," he exclaims' "this is certitude involving no reasoning or logic ... The breath of the unknown, the whisperings of the secret ... Isn't this worth deserting everything?!"[2] Now 'Umar is finally ensnared by these visions. Nothing and nobody can shake him from his unworldliness, from his pursuit of similar moments. He is not even affected by the birth of a son, nor by the release from prison of a friend who has sacrificed twenty years of his life to save him. He becomes a complete stranger to his friends and finally decides to shun human society and live in seclusion. His hallucinations, however, do not yield the contact with the ultimate secrets that he seeks. Finally, reality intrudes upon his solitude bringing him back to society, bleeding but hazily remembering a line of poetry, "If you really want me, why have you deserted me?"[3]

The question is to be asked again: Is the character of 'Umar an "inquiry" into a certain mental process, namely the drift into mysticism, or is it a genuine reflection, through art, of a spiritual malaise? In other words, is SHAH an exercise in which the psychology of

---

[1] SHAH, p. 51: المهم أن نكسب القضية ، ألسنا نعيش حياتنا ونحن نعلم أن الله سيأخذها؟

[2] SHAH, p. 134: هذه هي النشوة ... اليقين بلا جدل ولا منطق .. أنفاس المجهول وهمسات السر .. الا يستحق أن ينبذ كل شيء من أجله؟

[3] SHAH, p 191: ان تكن تريدني حقا فلم هجرتني؟

mystical experience is tackled or is it an attempt at poetic expression of a mystical mood?

To be fair to the author, one must admit that his is a very difficult undertaking. It is next to impossible, even for mystics themselves, to express a mystical moment—let alone one who has not practised mysticism. "The subject of it," writes William James, "immediately says that it defies expression, that no adequate report of it can be given in words."[1] This is one of those subjects which can best be touched upon symbolically. Maḥfūẓ, however, takes in SHAH a rather too rational look at mysticism. The story of ʿUmar has a certain clinical touch. The first chapter of the novel describes his visit to a doctor to complain about his strange mental state. The doctor describes ʿUmar's condition as being a "bourgeois ailment." Then through a long series of stages he gradually drifts into utter passivity. After a stage of hopelessness, he finally makes a transient "contact" while meditating. All this reminds one of certain textbooks on the psychology of religion.

There is also too much rationalism in the delineation of ʿUmar. He engages in a series of intellectual discussions with his friends, his wife, and even the cabaret-girls he befriends. The well-known fondness of Maḥfūẓ to juxtapose the hero with "representatives" of different solutions, reappears. ʿUmar's friend Muṣṭafā is a "passive" believer in science. In the past he was an artist, but he is now an "entertainer"; yet he argues that we can "find in science the beauty of poetry, the ecstasy of religion and the ambition of philosophy."[2]

ʿU<u>th</u>mān, his other friend, is an "active" believer in science. He is a communist who has no time for idle meditations, and who asserts that the human heart is nothing but a pump. To him, it is tantamount to superstition to think that the heart is a means to thought. "You cannot reach" he tells ʿUmar, "any truth worth its name except through intellect, science and action."[3]

On the whole, there is an abundance of external action and relatively little introspection. The author, it seems, was aware of this point and to compensate for the excess of action he crams the last chapter of the novel with a multitude of nightmarish visions. Yet this very

---

[1] James, *The Varieties*, p 380.

[2] SHAH, p. 24: ستجد في العلم لذة الشعر ونشوة الدين وطموح الفلسفة

[3] SHAH, p. 162: ولن تبلغ أي حقيقة جديرة بهذا الاسم الا بالعقل والعلم والعمل.

"corrective" is to the detriment of the symmetry of the novel and creates the feeling of too sudden a change. What is more, this visionary lapse is terminated by another flurry of brisk action. On the whole one tends to agree with Dr. 'Abd al-Qādir al-Quṭṭ, an Egyptian critic, who believes that there is here a discrepancy between the ambitious spiritual theme and the form through which it has been realized.[1]

Yet the character of 'Umar at times succeeds in capturing our fancy. This is especially true in the scenes where he is confronted with his poetically-minded daughter, Bu<u>th</u>ayna, whose mystical verses spark off in him a longing for the sublime and for the naiveté of youth.[2]

Anīs — With Anīs, protagonist of THAR, the preoccupation with mental processes is again on the decline. Instead, we find a more subtle incursion into the inner world of a man who has also deserted the society of men.

Anīs has long since passed the initial stages of alienation. He is far deeper in the labyrinth than 'Umar. His eyes, as his superior comments, "look inward, not outward as is the case with other people."[3] Unlike 'Umar, he is not seeking after movement or excitement. Nothing that happens in our world can stimulate him to come out of his trance.

> In fact there is no movement. A circular movement round a still axis; a circular movement titillating with the Absurd; a circular movement which inevitably brings about vertigo.[4]

All that we know of Anīs—now in his early forties—is that he comes from a village; that he was married in his early youth but has lost both his wife and infant daughter under tragic circumstances; that, though he had studied medicine, he never obtained a degree.[5] At present, he is a minor government employee spending his nights

---

1 *al-Ahrām*, 3 July, 1965.

2 SHAH, pp. 36-47; 83-4; 93-8; 136-41.

3 THAR, p. 10: عيناك تنظران الى الداخل لا الى الخارج كبقية خلق الله ..

4 THAR, p. 10: لا حركة ألبتة في الحقيقة. حركة دائرية حول محور جامد. حركة دائرية تتسلى بالعبث. حركة دائرية ثمرتها الحتمية الدوار.

5 THAR, pp. 60, 67.

smoking hashish, never sober in daytime. So much so, in fact, that when he is asked by his superior to prepare a certain report, he presents a file of blank pages—his pen having run out of ink![1]

Anīs is not a mystic, if that word denotes a religious seeker. Nevertheless he is an addict of mystical literature, and he is searching for the "Absolute." The time in which he is living is cosmic, not historic, and his visions of the past, present, and future intermingle. He meets simultaneously such creatures as pre-historic man, Cleopatra, Omar Khayyam, and men of other planets.

His only friends are a middle-aged group of men and women who come each night to participate in hashish sessions in a Nile houseboat. However, his relationship with them is not really of a social nature; for while they occupy themselves with chatter or sex, Anīs is engulfed in his stupor, rarely uttering a word. The only bond he sees between them and himself is Death,[2] in other words, the desire to escape from the world of man.

What makes Anīs a fascinating character is that there is no attempt on the author's part to make his visions, demeanour and words, plausible—plausible that is, according to our standards. His is a self-contained universe with its own logic.

When in the first chapter, his superior, on receiving the blank report, inquires, "Now tell me, Mr. Anīs, how could such a thing happen?"—Anīs remains silent, but deep in his thoughts he echoes that question and poses another. "Yes, how? How did life creep for the very first time in water mosses between stone cracks in the ocean's depth?"[3]

At first we tend to regard such seemingly incongruous reactions as not more than the nonsense of a hashish addict. Yet we soon come to see a greater depth and relevance in such reflections which amount to a substantial part of THAR. After all, even the hazy associations of a drug-addict are not without their inner logic. At times a greater insight into reality is achieved through the breakdown of the outer layer of cause and effect. Anīs' fantasies are, in effect, a commentary on life, and the very cleavage between him and reality calls forth a new perception of that reality. His "reaction" quoted above, joins

---

1 THAR, pp. 7-10.

2 THAR, p. 50: هل أخبرتها بأن الذي يجمعنا ها هنا هو الموت؟

3 THAR, p. 9: خبرني يا سيد أنيس كيف أمكن أن يحدث ذلك ؟ أجل كيف. كيف دبت الحياة لاول مرة في طحالب فجوات الصخور بأعماق المحيط.

with many others throughout the book to produce an acute feeling of the human tragedy, a revolt against the stifling human bondage, a disgust with the stresses and strains of society. When he goes back to pre-history, in reaction to the question "how could this happen?" he is hiding from the constrictions of his society in the unlimited boundaries of "cosmic time."

The last scene of the novel provides us with another such example. The scene occurs after all Anīs' friends, including Sammāra, have behaved in a shameful manner concerning the car accident in which they were involved. While he is still relatively lucid, he engages in a conversation with Sammāra, which has all the appearances of conforming to common logic. Then the drug takes effect and he suddenly retreats into prehistory and produces another of his harsh and dismal commentaries on human society.

> The source of all troubles is the dexterity of a monkey ... he learned how to walk on his feet thus releasing his hands ... He descended from the monkey paradise on the treetops to the ground of the jungle ... He was told : "Come back to the trees or else the wild beasts will prey on you" ... So he held a tree branch in the one hand and a stone in the other and proceeded cautiously onto an endless road.[1]

Anīs' actions, as well as his inner reactions, are motivated by a complicated machinery. He speaks when nobody expects him to do so and keeps silent when asked the simplest of questions. Equally unpredictably he acts or refrains from action. Thus we have no right to ask, as does one critic,[2] why of all people he was the one to take a genuinely conscientious stand about the car accident. The author was indeed very wise in not giving clear-cut answers, and in maintaining the ambiguities which surround Anīs' actions and words. Above all, the author was right in not giving way to the temptation of studying the psychology of a drug addict.

2. *Women*

The five men discussed above are, in fact, the only full characters

---

[1] THAR, p. 201 : أصل المتاعب مهارة قرد ... تعلم كيف يسير على قدمين فحرر يديه... وهبط من جنة القرود فوق الاشجار الى أرض الغابة ... وقالوا له عد الى الاشجار والا أطبقت عليك الوحوش ... فقبض على غصن شجرة بيد وعلى حجر بيد وتقدم في حذر وهو يمد بصره الى طريق لا نهاية له.

[2] Dr. al-Quṭṭ in *al-Ādāb*, Beirut, Oct. 1966, p. 13.

in the short novels. Other characters are never seen from within, although some of them are very skilful vignettes, such as the Ṣūfī shaykh in LISS and ʿAmm ʿAbduh, the Imam and pimp in THAR. On the whole, however, there is nothing in the minor male characters in these works which amounts to a new feature in the author's art.

A different picture emerges when one considers the women of the short novels. Admittedly their role, too, is secondary, and they are also portrayed from an external point of view. Yet they are at times brought out with such skill and insight that a new quality of characterization emerges. No discussion of the characters of the short novels would be complete without making mention of a least some of these women.

The most outstanding group are, again, the prostitutes, Nūr in LISS and Rīrī in SUM being the most noteworthy. If we compare these two to women in the early Cairene novels, we shall instantly discover that we are dealing with two different sets of characters. For one thing, Nūr and Rīrī come from the villages, not, as in the early novels, from the slums of Cairo. For another, we know very little about the history of their fall. The "how" question, which loomed behind Iḥsān, Ḥamīda, and Nafīsa, has now totally disappeared. Finally, and most important, Rīrī, and Nūr, in spite of their brief appearance, are among the most natural, most lovable of Maḥfūẓ's feminine characters. The simplicity and warmth with which Nūr behaves and speaks immediately captures our imagination. When at one point she comes home after having been beaten up by youngsters who refuse to pay her,[1] we have the feeling of a Dostoevskian "holy prostitute." When she disappears, we mourn her fate not only because by losing her Saʿīd has lost his last hope of escape, but also because we have become so attached to her in her own right.

Another type of woman who appears in the short novels is a young and educated one, who strives to become fully emancipated. It will be remembered that at least one such woman has made an appearance in the author's earlier work, namely Sawsan in TR-III. But while that character was both ice-cold and uninspiring, her equivalents in the short novels are warm and convincing human beings.

At first sight, Ilhām of TARIQ looks like any other office girl in Cairo. She is timid, prudently friendly and naïvely curious. We tend

---

[1] LISS, p. 117f.

to agree with Ṣābir when he describes her as "that big child."[1] On falling in love, however, she changes and becomes, in a most natural manner, a daring woman. We are moved with Ṣābir when at their first visit to a cinema together, and after holding her hand in the dark, "he wanted to withdraw his hand, but she clasped his fingers. He, in turn, held her hand, gratified."[2]

We admire her the more for her loyalty to Ṣābir even when he becomes evasive and depressed. We are again moved by her audacious gesture when—after Ṣābir tells her the truth about his mother and himself in the hope that she would desert him—she calls him next day, and in a quivering voice says, "Ṣābir, I wanted ... I want ... to tell you that everything you told me yesterday makes no difference to me."[3]

Bu<u>th</u>ayna, 'Umar's daughter in SHAH is by far the liveliest character in that book. She is both refreshingly unsophisticated, though educated, and unmistakably Egyptian in spite of her "modern" outlook.

Finally, Sammāra Bahjat, who in THAR is second in importance only to Anīs himself, is in a way a "corrective" to Sawsan. She too is a Leftist journalist and before actually appearing in the houseboat, is described by someone as "frighteningly serious."[4] Yet when we get to know her, we are surprised to find a warm, intelligent woman who refuses to repeat memorized cliches because she does "not like to fail like those tendentious plays."[5] At times, it is true, she behaves in too exemplary a manner, yet her attitude to the actor Rajab, especially as expressed in her diary[6] reveals the more human aspects of her personality. She is, in fact, interested in the "corrupt" actor though she wishes to convince others—and indeed herself—to the contrary. Her irresolute behaviour after the car accident, also shows

---

1 TARIQ, p. 41 : آه ، هذه الطفلة الكبيرة

2 TARIQ, p. 95 : وأراد أن يسحب يده ولكنها شدت على أصابعه فشد على راحتها ممتنا.

3 TARIQ, p. 150 : صابر .. أردت .. أريد ... أريد أن أقول أن كل ما قلت لي أمس لا يهمني.

4 THAR, p. 46 : اذا حكمنا عليها بما تكتب فهي جادة لدرجة الرعب

5 THAR, p. 59 : لا أريد أن أردد الاكليشيهات المحفوظة ولا أحب أن أسقط كالتمثيليات الهادفة!

6 THAR, pp. 109-16 (esp. pp. 114-5).

her as a fallible human being. It would be difficult to imagine the doctrinaire Sawsan (in TR-III) behaving in such a "bourgeois" manner.

Structure

In discussing the characters of the short novels, many references were made to the structural aspects of these works.

We have seen that on relinquishing the role of the objective author, the novelist gains at times a greater measure of intimacy. We have also seen that, when he so wishes, the author of the self-reflexive novel can find ways and means of introducing extrinsic information or commentary. But this ,it seems, is to the detriment of characterization. The lyrical novel gains by our, and the author's, identification with it. Its techniques, notably the medley of persons and tenses, means greater subjectivity and far less omniscience. Thus, it is only natural that in LISS we are unable to discover what happened to Nūr; or, in TARIQ—the real motives of Karīma. By the same token, it is better that we are acquainted only with fragments—rather hazy fragments—of the past experience of Sa'īd in LISS and Anīs in THAR.

If we are to live through the consciousness of the character, it would be unnatural for the "recovered past" to come out clearly and in chronological order. A tightly-woven texture is likely to suppress the semblance of immediate experience and to damage the lyricism of the work.

This brings us to the question of the overall structure of these novels. The mastery of arrangement which marked many of the author's works in the past, especially BID and the Trilogy, is displayed in the short novels to even greater effect. The length of these short novels ranges between twenty and thirty thousand words, and indeed it would be inconceivable that a well-developed plot would be contained in such a narrow space without a great command of structure. However, one feels that certain techniques, that were appropriate to the old narrative form, are now cumbersome in the self-reflexive novels.

It has been noted that many of the novels of the forties are marked at both ends with dramatic occurrences, helping the author to enclose the action in well defined boundaries. In the novels of the sixties the application of such structural rigidity is not as useful.

True, the quick-moving first chapters, especially in LISS, are highly economical. They introduce us without delay to the heart of the matter. Yet at times a vigorous opening creates an impression of externalized action, an impression which is in contrast with the nature of the work. This is especially true of SUM and SHAH.

The endings of these short novels are even more brisk. Four of them end with acts of violence. In LISS, Sa'īd is killed by the police; in TARIQ, Ṣābir strangles Karīma and is himself sentenced to death; in SHAH, 'Umar is awakened from his fantasies by a police bullet; in THAR, Rajab's car kills a pedestrian, an accident which, the following day, brings about a hysterical commotion. In the case of SUM, there is no act of violence, but the last chapters are crowded with unexpected events : Rīrī and her daughter appear on the scene again; 'Īsā, now penitent, is rejected; finally a past acquaintance, a real *deus ex machina*, is conjured up to shake 'Īsā out of his alienation.

In short Maḥfūẓ is not an author who can write an open-ended novel as did, for example, Virginia Woolf. If we cast a glance at the last chapters of these novels, another fact, closely related to the latter, emerges. The rhythm of the action is suddenly accelerated. The slow, contemplative movement gives way to a dizzying one.

To a certain extent, however, the disharmony in TARIQ and THAR is in keeping with the nature of these novels. In the first it mingles with the nightmarish atmosphere of the narrative, and in the second —the catastrophe is somehow of a piece with Anīs' apocalyptic visions. In these two novels, as well as in LISS, it is noted, that the time-span is short (a few weeks in each) and the compactness of the experience involved allows for a sudden turn of events, in other words, for a dramatic irony.

In SUM and SHAH the vigorous ending can hardly be accepted as a natural climax. The long time-span of these two works makes these condensed endings foreign to the tempo of the rest of the work. For if such a culmination is to form an integral part of the work, even by way of contrast, the experience should be a compact one. In SHAH, however, a year and half separates the main events of 'Umar's story from the last scene.[1] In SUM, the author altogether fails to convey the sense of time through the action itself, and it is only by the occasional mention of political events that we come to realize, to our surprise, that between chapters 19 and 22, for instance, a number of years have elapsed. Thus when the final occurrences take place, they seem too remote to stem from or reflect upon the centre of the action.

[1] SHAH, p. 185.

I shall, in the next few pages, look briefly at the new techniques that can be found in LISS, TARIQ, and THAR, in other words, those novels which seem to me superior from a structural point of view.

al-Liṣṣ wal-kilāb

The success of LISS does not stem from its borrowing new techniques such as the stream of consciousness. What is remarkable in the technique of this novel is the degree of freedom that the author displays in adapting them to further his own individual voice and style. No less laudable is the economy and the unobtrusiveness with which these innovations are introduced.

The mood that underlies the novel is, as has been pointed out, the feeling of siege and suffocation. The very first words of the book strike this note. "Once again he breathes the air of freedom, but there is a suffocating dust and an unbearable heat in the air."[1] We are soon to find that the "air of freedom" is indeed polluted and stifling. A series of frustrations awaits Sa'īd. His daughter does not recognize him; the authorities are protecting the traitors; his attempts to kill "the dogs" end in utter failure; the police ring is closing around him; finally Nūr, his "guardian angel", disappears and his end comes soon after.

The trend of the plot is that of mounting despair, of ever-diminishing hope. On the other hand, the story of the past which is conveyed through the stream of consciousness, is that of great hopes, of love, and of idealism. In this way the past recollections become more than a device to convey the background information.

The contrast between past and present is not a static one. The visions of the past become more shining and idyllic as the present reality becomes grimmer. Thus, it is no coincidence that the most heavenly recollections of the past[2] occur after he discovers that he has killed an innocent man and that his enemy has disappeared. He is now sought by the police as a killer and is virtually a prisoner of Nūr's house which faces, symbolically enough, the graveyard.

In using the stream of consciousness, Maḥfūẓ does so with great moderation. The reader is never confused and rarely does he need to re-read a paragraph.

---

[1] LISS, p. 7: مرة أخرى يتنفس نسمة الحرية ، ولكن في الجو غبار خانق وحر لا يطاق.

[2] LISS, pp. 98-104.

Symbols and leitmotifs are also employed sparingly. The name of Sa'īd's daughter, Sana', often recurs both as a rhythmical item, punctuating his frenzied thoughts, and symbolically, meaning "light," and "radiance."[1] The name of Nūr (again denoting "light") enhances the feeling that she is the light shining in his darkness. It is often used in the same breath as the word *ẓalām* ('dark').[2] At times the word *nūr* is used simultaneously in its literal sense and as the name Nūr.[3]

Sa'īd's dream[4] reflects the realities as in a concave mirror, but also conveys with greater force the brutality of these realities.

al-Ṭarīq

The structure and techniques to be found in TARIQ are basically the same as in LISS : a short duration of plot, few characters, an immediate experience transmitted through a flux. The use of the stream of consciousness, however, grows bolder and the language more economical. The role of the leitmotifs, such as the blind beggar who chants his pious songs by the hotel, is greater. The "montage technique" is frequently called into use to further the compactness and the lyrical immediacy of the plot. Often two separate scenes are connected by the conjunction *wa* to stress their continuity.[5]

---

1 Examples : a) LISS, p. 8 : وسناء اذا خطرت في النفس انجاب عنها الحر والغبار والبغضاء والكدر.
b) LISS, p. 98 : وجفولك يا سناء مؤلم كمنظر القبر
c) LISS, p. 159 : وسناء — كذلك — قد تجد نفسها يوما بلاقلب يهتم بها.

2 Examples : a) LISS, p. 91 : يا له من ظلام ... متى تعود نور وهل تعود بمفردها؟
b) LISS, p. 105 : ... ولا تسأل متى تعود نور وعليك أن تكابد الظلمة والصمت والوحدة.
c) LISS, p. 115 : الام أطيق أن ابقى في الظلام حتى تعود نور قبيل الفجر؟

3 Examples : a) LISS, p. 64 : هي كما ترى نور ونور
b) LISS, p. 117 : رأى النور في نافذة نور ...

4 LISS, pp. 81-3.

5 E.g., TARIQ, p. 22 : فبصق في موقد كبير ينفث بخور الهند These words conclude a scene in which Ṣābir, still in Alexandria, discusses his future with a friend

A device which bears an affinity to the montage technique is that of introducing press reactions. Ṣābir learns a great deal from the newspapers' comments on his case—and so does the reader. This is of course, a device much used by novelists. In fact, Maḥfūẓ himself has used it in LISS.[1] Yet in TARIQ, there is more to it than mere device, as we have already seen.[2] The irony with which these comments are quoted and arranged amounts to a new approach.

The dream is also resorted to, but with a greater subtlety. Unlike Sa'īd's dream, which is introduced by the words "he dreamt that ...," Ṣābir's dream comes abruptly. At first the reader follows the events of that dream without being able to ascertain whether it was not really yet another meeting between Ṣābir and a man bearing his father's name. Thus in the middle of the scene, a strange turn of events takes place when Ilhām comes in and Ṣābir realizes that the man is not only his father, but hers too. The dream, it is true, is terminated by the words "and he woke up."[3] Yet its very similarity in several details to the real story of Ṣābir underlines the nightmare in which he lives. The veneer of the detective story apparent in TARIQ thus acquires a Kafkaesque flavour.

In passing, it should be added that TARIQ is in fact the first attempt by the author to work up a detective plot. A large part of the book—beginning with Ṣābir's killing of Karīma's husband—is written in the best fashion of mystery stories. Certainly the "whodunit" atmosphere in the novel is not intended for its own sake. But the skill with which this part of the book is conducted, especially Ṣābir's conversations with al-Sāwī[4] leads one to believe that Egypt could have had its foremost detective writer in Maḥfūẓ.

Tharthara fawq al-Nīl

THAR, the last work to be discussed here, is the most daring as far as narrative techniques are concerned. The stream of consciousness is more complicated here : it has become fragmentary and less chronologically arranged, but at the same time more meaningful. The internal

of his mother. They are immediately followed by the words وتعلق بصره بالاسكندرية والقطار يرج الارض مبتعدا which save the author from having to relate the things that happened between the two scenes.

[1] LISS, pp. 86, 123 and esp. p. 145-6.

[2] *Supra.*, pp. 169-70.

[3] TARIQ, p. 69.

[4] TARIQ, pp. 139-44; 152-60.

monologue often mingles with the dialogue.[1] The background description gives way to what Maḥfūẓ himself calls "modernistic decor."[2]

The action, for its greater part, is arranged in a quasi-theatrical manner. There are seven "scenes" which occur in the same setting (the houseboat), comprising one or two chapters each, and following the same pattern. Each of these "scenes" starts when Anīs' friends arrive for their evening hashish session and ends several hours later, when they leave Anīs to his fantasies.[3]

Another new technique is that of stopping the action to introduce a diary. This is, of course, a technique which has often been employed by novelists, but it is a new feature in Maḥfūẓ's works. Sammāra's diary ("A Plan for a Play," Ch. 10) fulfills more than one function. It describes the hashish group from an outsider's point of view, but it also offers a peep into Sammāra's own character. On the face of it, the diary is a presentation of a constructive and optimistic view, in total contrast to the nihilistic atmosphere of the houseboat. Sammāra's own declaration of loyalty to science and reason[4] is an antithesis to Anīs' escapism. However, there is here, as in the press quotations in TARIQ, an air of incredulity. On the one hand, her idealism sounds refreshing, on the other—naïve and immature. The author's erstwhile neutrality is now replaced by a sceptical ambiguity.

The use of symbols is also subtle and sometimes fraught with sarcastic ambivalence. Thus 'Amm 'Abduh, the houseboat attendant, is a giant who bears certain features reminiscent of Jabalāwī or Za'balāwī. Yet he is at once holy and profane, wise and obtuse.

The variety of techniques incorporated in THAR indicate that Maḥfūẓ is anxious to break altogether with the old modes of writing. He is in search of new techniques befitting his new themes and sensations. In THAR, it is true, no techniques are introduced which have not appeared years ago in the writings of European and American authors. Yet their arrangement and interplay point to a greater experimentation on Maḥfūẓ's part. So much so in fact, that we should

---

[1] E.g. THAR, p. 72. ... كان [المعري] أعمى فلم ير سمارة وهي معاصرة له.
— زوجي يسعى للصلح.
— لا سمح الله ...
.. أعمى فلم ير. انقطع الخيط وتبدد شيء بهيج.

[2] *al-Kātib* (Cairo), Feb. 1964, p. 23.

[3] THAR, Chs. 3-4; 5-6; 7; 8; 9; 11; 13.

[4] THAR, p. 110.

not be surprised if in the future he will come out with techniques which are unmistakably his own. There is no reason not to believe him when in a recent article he writes :

> It might well be that I shall hit upon a subject to which no form is suitable, save for that of the *maqāma*. I shall then not hesitate to write my novel in that form.[1]

Language and Dialogue

If there is a steady move towards new ventures in matters of characterization and structure, the language undergoes an even swifter change. This is, of course, not a sudden development. We have seen that the Trilogy, for all its detailed descriptions, has the rudiments of rich connotative language. We have also seen that the language in AWL, though lacking in lyricism, is remarkable for the terseness and briskness of its dialogue.

The novels of the sixties herald a new quality, which combines the terse with the connotative. Gone is the urge to portray everything in plain words and to report conversations in full. The new language is infinitely more concise and evocative.

The language of the self-reflexive fiction is, of necessity, fraught with feeling. Thus when Sa'īd in LISS thinks on the one hand of his enemies and on the other of his beloved daughter, he cannot reflect on his predicament in a detached manner. The pace underlying this novel is that set by his turbid, agitated thoughts.[2] The sentences are short and their sequence is not necessarily logical. The rhythm is at times made more emphatic by the repetition of certain words and sounds.[3]

---

[1] *al-Fikr al-mu'āṣir*, Dec. 1966, p. 112 : ... ومن الممكن جدا أن أهتدي الى موضوع لا يصلح له شكلا الا المقامة. عندئذ سأكتب روايتي بطريقة المقامة دون أن أبالي بشيء.

[2] E.g., LISS, p. 9 : ومن خلال هذا الكدر المنتشر لا يبسم الا وجهك يا سناء ، وعما قريب سأخبرك مدى حظي من لقياك ، عندما أقطع هذا الشارع ذا البواكي العابسة ، طريق الملاهي البائدة ، الصاعد الى غير رفعة ، أشهد أني أكرهك ... والقدم تعبر من آن لان نقرة مستقرة في الطوار كالمكيدة وضجيج عجلات الترام يكركر كالسب ، ونداءات شتى تختلط كأنها تنبعث من نفايات الخضر ، أشهد أني أكرهك.

[3] In the example quoted in the last footnote, the expression أشهد أني أكرهك is repeated. Note too, the alliterative يكركر كالسب which blends with أكرهك الكدر and كالمكيدة

Other elements, such as rhyming prose, are at times brought into play to produce a greater poetical effect.[1]

Such poetic language, of course, does not occur all the time, neither is it evident in all the novels in question. The language of SUM, for instance, is often neither emotive nor suggestive.[2] On the whole, however, the days of naïve language are past. Words acquire a greater depth,[3] and poetical ambiguites are on the increase.[4] The employment of lexical and grammatical items is marked here by considerable freedom.[5] Words are transplanted fearlessly from one semantic field to another.[6]

---

[1] Note the rhyme in the following (LISS, p. 8) : ... ولعلكما تترقبان في حذر، ولن أقع في الفخ ، ولكنني سأنقض في الوقت المناسب كالقدر. وسناء اذا خطرت في النفس انجاب عنها الحر والغبار والبغضاء والكدر. وسطع الحنان فيها كالنقاء غب المطر. ماذا تعرف الصغيرة عن أبيها؟ .. لا شيء ، كالطريق والمارة والجو المنصهر.

[2] ʿĪsā, who like Saʿid, is a shattered man, is on the face of it, portrayed from within. Yet there is nothing in his internal monologue that resembles that of LISS. In his most distressing moment (when jilted by Salwā) he reflects as follows (SUM, pp. 72-3) : ولعله من حسن الحظ أنه تلقى ضربة القلب وهو فريسة لضربة السياسة فلم تستأثر به وحدها. وجعل ضيقه بكل شيء يستفحل حتى لم يترك في النفس متسعا لاي قيمة. كيف توهم نفسك بأنك تريد عملا كما توهم الاخرين؟ العمل هو آخر ما تريد.

[3] Not only such words as *kilāb, nūr*, are used symbolically in LISS, but also *ghubar* ('dust'), *ḥarr* ('heat'), express both the concrete and the abstract. The following are some examples : a) ... ولكن في الجو غبار خانق وحر لا يطاق (LISS, p. 7).
b) وسناء اذا خطرت في النفس انجاب عنها الحر والغبار والبغضاء والكدر (LISS, p. 8)—note the alliterations!
c) وستصوت نبوية حتى تملاء الدنيا غبارا (LISS, p. 77).

[4] When Saʿid addresses the imaginary jurors in the cemetery, he notices that : وقاضي اليسار يغمز لك بعينه فأبشر (LISS, p. 148, 'and the judge on the left winks at you—cheer up, then!')

The word *yasār* has at least three meanings in Arabic : 1-ease; 2-wealth; 3-left. The last meaning, which is the one most likely to be intended here, can itself mean the judge sitting on the left, or the judge of the Left (i.e., the Leftist moral judgement).

[5] This applies, of course, to the medly of tenses and persons which is a major feature in the language of all five novels in question. It also applies to the amazing use of the conjunction *wa* (e.g., SHAH, p. 125; THAR, p. 166).

[6] Note the frequent use of grammatical terms in the dialogue. The following are only a few of these cases :

The creative simile, whose increase in use have noted in the last two chapters, is still in evidence, but is now without much of the earlier contrivance. There is a stronger awareness of plastic imagery,[1] and words from the field of music[2] play an even greater role than they did before. Frequently the simile gives way to a compressed metaphor.[3]

There are few background descriptions. When outer reality is portrayed it is not, as before, an attempt at describing a stationary scene, but is often a unique impressionistic attempt to catch the fleeting moment.[4] Dialogue now takes the place of much of the descrip-

---

a) « لو » حرف لوعة يطمح بحماقة الى توهم القدرة على تغيير التاريخ (SUM. p. 88);
b) بطل او مجرم ، هي من أسماء الاضداد (SHAH. p. 154);
c) انك اذا استعملت الحب يوما كمبتدأ في جملة مفيدة فستنسى حتما الخبر الى الابد! (THAR, p. 22).

The employment of grammatical terminology—which is also used by logicians—is an apparent comment, by way of paradox, on the breakdown of logic in modern life; a theme which is central in these novels.

[1] Examples: a) فابتسمت عن طاقم لاح بريقه كياسمينة في حديقة اقتلعت أشجارها (SUM. p. 20).
b) ولكن كيف اقتلعت وردة من نفسه كأنها زهرة صناعية؟ (SHAH, p. 119).
c) يضفي على الظلمة ضياء مسطولا كعين البنفسج الناعسة (THAR, p. 85).

[2] Examples: a) وندت عن حسناء ضحكة بارعة كلحن جنسي (SUM, p. 72).
b) فقالت سناء بنبرة كرنين الوتر الرفيع من القانون اذا مسّته يد العازف خطأ; (THAR, p. 87).
cf. *supra*, p. 136, fn. 1.

[3] Examples: a) رشقته بنظرة مخملية (SUM, p. 62);
b) تألق الفرح أخضر في عينيها (SHAH, p. 39);
c) نظرة شوكية (THAR, p. 7);
d) الافكار الفسفورية (THAR, p. 102).

[4] E.g., LISS, p. 60: وكأن القهوة جزيرة في محيط أو طيارة في سماء. وفي أسفل الهضبة التي تقوم عليها القهوة تحركت السجائر — كالنجوم — في أيدي الجالسين في الظلمة من رواد الهواء الطلق ، وعند الافق الغربي لاحت أنوار العباسية بعيدة جدا يشعر بعدها بمدى توغل القهوة في الصحراء.

tion. Internal monologue intermingles with copious but terse dialogue to produce a dynamic effect.

Although the dialogue is still basically in *fuṣḥā* it comes closer than ever to the language of real life. One is tempted to assume that this is so because many of the themes of the short novels are abstract, and because not a few of their characters are intellectuals. This might well be so, yet uneducated characters speak equally naturally in this same *fuṣḥā* which is now as well suited to uneducated Nūr in LISS as to the intellectual Anīs in TARIQ or 'Umar in SHAH. The dialogue has at last rid itself of bookishness and acquired both plasticity and transparency. Maḥfūẓ, by his loyalty to the *fuṣḥā*, has achieved that which must surely be reckoned as one of his major feats.

POSTSCRIPT

Since 1966, the date of the last novel discussed in the proceeding chapter, Maḥfūẓ has come out with five new books, only one of which, *Mīrāmār*, is a novel proper [1]. However, there are elements in all the books which are striking in their novelty as regards theme, technique and language. In the following remarks I shall first discuss the novel briefly, then touch upon certain new elements in the four collections of short stories which appeared between 1967-1971.

Mīrāmār

This is a depressing book, which surpasses in its gloom any of the novels of the sixties in that its suffocating atmosphere is not mitigated by the intermittent humorous situations which are to be found in Maḥfūẓ's earlier works. Treachery, malice and avarice have the upper hand, and violence is ever-present. Its verdict on the Egyptian socio-political scene of the mid-sixties is unprecedented in its harshness. Many Egyptian and Arabic critics have detected in *Mīrāmār* (henceforth MIR), a prophetic voice warning Egypt, on the eve of the Six Day War, of the catastrophe that was in the offing [2].

Indeed MIR constitutes a close and straightforward look at the political scene. One of its protagonists is an active member of the ruling party — and he is by no means a positive character. We also meet here a Royalist, a Wafdist, a Communist, etc., even though they are not necessarily typical representatives of these trends and ideologies, but rather idiosyncratic types. There is also a young village girl, simple but strong-willed, betrayed by some and encouraged by

---

[1] In 1972 yet another book of Maḥfūẓ appeared — *al-Marāyā* ("The Mirrors"). In the colophons, this book is described as a "novel", but some readers will find it difficult to accept this definition. It is, in fact, a succession of fifty-five chapters, each describing a different character which the narrator has met during his lifetime. The names of these characters are fictitious, but there is little doubt that most of these chapters portray real people, some of whom are easily identifiable. Although many of these characters are interlinked and the narrator is present in practically all the situations, there is, however, no central line of action. Neither is the narrator a protagonist in the real sense, for in most of the scenes he is a passive observer. *Al-Marāyā* is as close as any of the author's works to autobiographical reminiscences. However, the work deserves a close scrutiny.

[2] E.g., G͟hālī Shukrī, *al-Muntamī* (second edition, 1969), pp. 433ff.; Karam S͟halabī, in *al-Jumhūriyya* (Baghdad), 8 June 1972.

others, who seems to represent the Egyptian people in its search for a better life.

Unlike Maḥfūẓ's other short novels, MIR is crowded with people and events. This and the unconventional form of the work make its plot difficult to summarize:

The story takes place in the mid-sixties, in a small pension in Alexandria called "Mīrāmār" where we meet the following characters:

* Marianna, the owner, a Greek woman of about sixty whose business is no longer as flourishing as it used to be in the past.

* 'Āmir Wajdī, a retired journalist in his eighties who, after long years of patriotic struggle, finds himself alienated and despised. He has come to Alexandria to spend the rest of his days in the pension. His past is rich in revolt and heresy, but he now seems to find solace in Koranic verses.

* Sarḥān al-Buḥayrī, about thirty, employed as an accountant in an industrial concern, is an active member of the ruling party. He speaks highly of socialism, but his heart is set on achieving riches and an easy life.

* Manṣūr Bāhī, a young broadcaster of twenty-five. A convinced Communist who, under pressure from his elder brother, a police officer, deserts his comrades. He has an affair with Durriyya, wife of his imprisoned comrade, but jilts her after persuading her to leave her husband. He is obsessed with the idea of treachery which torments his soul incessantly.

* Ḥusnī 'Allām, a young hedonist from a feudal family; he has come to Alexandria to spend his money recklessly, "before the deluge".

* Ṭulba Marzūq, a former official of the royal regime. His property has been confiscated and he is bitter and malicious. He is, at all times, on watch against agents of the regime, dreaming of a miraculous return of the old days.

* Zahra, a young village girl who has run away to Alexandria because she was being forced to marry an old man. She was employed as a chamber-maid in "Mīrāmār". Her beauty charms all the residents and, in fact, she is the centre of attention in this book.

It transpires that Sarḥān al-Buḥayrī has come to stay in "Mīrāmār" because of his attraction for Zahra, mistaking her for an easy prey. She falls in love with him, but refuses to surrender to his advances and, in time, Sarḥān actually seems to fall in love with her. His love, however, is not strong enough to counter-balance his ambitions and snobbism. When he despairs of getting Zahra without marriage, he turns to a teacher living nearby, who was teaching Zahra to read. Sarḥān's marriage to the teacher seems imminent, but Zahra interferes and frustrates the engagement.

Shortly afterwards Sarḥan is found dead and Manṣūr Bāhī confesses that, having found him unconscious, he beat him to death for betraying Zahra. The police investigation, however, reveals that Sarḥān, in fact, had committed suicide. It later turns out that he killed himself when his plan to smuggle merchandise was foiled. Manṣūr, therefore, hit him after he was already dead, thinking that he was in a drunken stupor. In the wake of these events, Marianna decides to fire Zahra from her work in the pension.

The novel is written in the form of personal testimonies "delivered" by four of "Mīrāmār's" boarders. It is divided into four sections written in the first person, the speakers being ʿĀmir, Ḥusnī, Manṣūr and Sarḥān respectively. A fifth section, far shorter, brings back ʿĀmir's voice.

The first four sections tell virtually the same story, describing the short period in which the foretold events occur in the pension, and ending in Sarḥān's death on New Year's eve. In the concluding section, the story is carried on one or two days further, bringing in Manṣūr's "confession" and finally the unravelling of the mystery.

In its structure MIR is reminiscent, to a certain extent, of a well-known Alexandrine Quartet, namely that of Lawrence Durrell [1]. Both Maḥfūẓ and Durrell attempt to focus on the same set of events from several angles, with a final section moving forward in time. There is also a similarity in the setting of these two novels, and even the difference in the social milieus which constituted their respective backgrounds is significant. For while Durrell tells the story of the European community in Alexandria up to the mid-fifties, Maḥfūẓ is concerned with the Egyptian society of that city of the sixties. However, there is a character linking, as it were, Durrell's milieu to that of Maḥfūẓ — namely, the person of Madame Marianna, mourning as she is the past in which foreigners constituted the hub of Alexandrine society.

To return to the structure of MIR, there is little doubt that its form is less pretentious, less intricate, than Durrell's Quartet. It lacks all the niceties of form that Durrell has so adroitly accomplished. There is no recourse whatever in MIR to such literary devices as letters, diaries, manuscripts, or an author writing about an author writing about an author etc. Neither is the new form exploited by Maḥfūẓ to convey the feeling of the relativity of human perception in a way similar to the Japanese fable *Rashomon*. In MIR every successive chapter reveals to the reader new facts about the plot, not necessarily because each "confessor" sees things differently, but simply because the narrator in each successive section enlightens us with facts which his predecessor was not in a position to witness, thus contributing additional pieces to the jig-saw puzzle.

In any case, it is clear that MIR introduces a new technique so far unexplored by our author. Furthermore, it brings Maḥfūẓ back to

[1] MIR, however, is not the first attempt in Egyptian literature to write a novel in this form. It was preceeded in 1962 by Fatḥī Ghānim's Quartet, *al-Rajul alladhī faqada ẓillahu* ("The Man Who Lost His Shadow"). There is an abridged English translation of this novel (*The Man Who Lost His Shadow*, trans. Desmond Stewart, London, 1966).

the first person narration — a style which he employed only in his early works (SAR, 1949), although it is now employed in a totally different manner. Lastly, MIR constitutes a departure from the single protagonist novel, but without falling back on the technique of the omniscent author.

Throughout MIR, Maḥfūẓ tries to give each of the four narrators his own distinctive tone and style, often employing recurring expressions and leitmotives. This is noticeable in the first section ("'Āmir"), e.g. in the occasional quotations of Koranic verse. In section three ("Manṣūr"), the catchword is "betrayal", "treachery", (*khiyāna*). The employment of such features is less successful in section two ("Ḥusnī") and section four ("Sarḥān"), although in the former section the expression "farakīkū la talumnī" ("Don't blame me, damn it!") occurs several times and is apparently intended to characterize Ḥusnī's outlook, his obsession with a carefree life.

The characterization that emerges from this experiment is uneven. 'Āmir comes through as a warm, convincing character. He is the only character the author treats with sympathy. Manṣūr, the tormented Communist, is an interesting character though not sufficiently coherent. Sarḥān and Ḥusnī are only superficially portrayed, and all the other characters are amazingly pale. Ṭulba and Marianna are nothing but caricatures coming from a hostile pen. Zahra, the lovable chamber-maid, is seem only through other people's eyes; we have no direct expression of her feelings and views. Certain critics [1] find this last point puzzling, considering that she is the real representative of Egypt, the only "positive" character. But this fact should not surprise anyone who is familar with Maḥfūẓ's latest works. In his novels of the sixties, there is no great interest in the inner selves of "positive" characters (cf. SUM, SHAH, THAR).

The style of MIR, though essentially poetic, by no means reaches the peaks achieved in such works as TARIQ or THAR. The most arresting pieces are those describing the Alexandrine autumn, the seasonal weather changes, which clearly reflect the events of the novels and the moods of the characters. However, whatever poetry there is in this book is dimmed, here as in AWL, by the excess of violence, or rather by the endless petty scuffles between Sarḥān, Ḥusnī and Manṣūr. These scuffles look childish and tasteless especially since most of them are described more than once (in some cases, three or four times) in the different sections of MIR.

---

[1] E.g. al-'Ālim, *Ta'ammulāt*, p. 132.

It is very likely that the surfeit of violence and malice are an end in themselves, conveying a definite message to the reader. However in the context of the new form that Maḥfūẓ undertakes in MIR this excess is clearly detrimental.

To sum up, MIR is different in content from the novels discussed in the last chapter, in that its author is less interested in the spiritual aspects of life, in mysticism, in the search for the meaning of life. The introverted, alienated hero is here relegated to the fringe, while politically-minded people and current issues take precedence.

It is difficult to say whether Maḥfūẓ's art has benefited from the new form. In fact, Maḥfūẓ has not used it again, and the works that he wrote after MIR might indicate that he was not fully satisfied with the results of this experiment.

It is clear that the great success MIR enjoyed in the Arab world (both as a novel, as well as a film and play) arise mainly from the nature of the political and social issues it raises, as well as from its author's fame.

Other Recent Works

After *Mīrāmār*, Maḥfūẓ seems to have withdrawn, at least temporarily, from the realm of the novel, opting for shorter literary forms. This is by no means an indication that there has been a decrease in the author's output and fertility. In the period between 1968-1971, no less than four new volumes of his stories appeared. A scrutiny of these volumes reveals yet another "rhythmical change" in both content and style. The new content, i.e., the new issues raised in these stories, is a matter for an extensive study, not the least because they reflect the author's attitudes towards the crucial political issues of present-day Egypt.

The most striking feature in these volumes is, undoubtedly, the constant drive towards the literature of the absurd, and consequently the breakdown of causality.

Admittedly, in the first of these volumes, *K̲hammārat al-qiṭṭ al-aswad* ("The Red Cat Tavern"), which appeared in 1968, we still witness basically the same atmosphere and techniques as in the author's works of the early sixties, but in several stories we detect a sudden divorce from formal logic, and there is a frequent confusion between reality and nightmare [1].

[1] E.g., in the stories "Firdaus" (*K̲hammārat* ... pp. 98ff.); "K̲hammārat al-qiṭṭ al-aswad" (*ibid.*, pp. 156ff.); "al-Masṭūl wal-qunbula" (*ibid.*, pp. 218ff.).

In the following volume, *Taḥt al-miẓalla* ("Under the Awning") 1969, there is a pronounced shift towards the absurd. A nightmarish world is portrayed, whose inhabitants can hardly understand the events taking place around them. The title-story of this book is an excellent example :

> On a rainy day, a group of people, waiting at a bus-stop, witness a set of incidents which look like scenes from a horror film, in which sexual acts are committed in public and people are slain. Indeed, at first they believe that it is a filming, but when they discover that real people are being murdered, they complain to a policeman standing idly by. The latter, instead of arresting the murderers, draws his pistol, killing all the innocent bystanders.

Another surprise which this volume presents to Maḥfūẓ's readers is the group of five short plays, the first attempt at drama in the author's career, also constructed along the same baffling lines.

Naturally, dialogue is the basic vehicle in the plays, but dialogue is also a major feature in the new short stories as a whole. In most of them there is no external description of the characters, no recording of their inner throughts, and, in many cases, the protagonists are nameless or bear "thematic" names (e.g. ʿAbd Allāh, denoting "Man").

The last two volumes appeared in 1971. They are *Ḥikāya bilā bidāya walā nihāya* ("A Story Without Beginning or End"), and *Shahr al-ʿasal* ("Honeymoon"). Here the elements described above, notably the abundance of dialogue, are totally dominant. Many of the stories embodied in these volumes can hardly be described as such. They are, rather, concatenations of short scenes, bearing clear allegorical connotations. One cannot escape the feeling that, although outwardly they have little or no reference to political issues, they are, in fact, a poignant commentary on current politics.

Violence now reaches unprecedented dimensions. There is hardly a story without several scenes of terror. In some cases, the number of people who die in the course of a single story is astounding [1].

At times the reader is under the impression that there is an apotheosis of the act of violence. One of the characters in "ʿAnbar Lūlū" [2] remarks on one occasion : "Murder itself has become mysterious, even though it is the most obvious thing on earth". To this another character, a young lady, retorts : "Mysterious or not — isn't it wonder-

[1] E.g., the title story in *Shahr al-ʿasal* (pp. 3ff.), "al-ʿĀlam al-'ākhar" (*ibid.*, pp. 35ff.); *Khammarat* ..., the stories "al-Majnūna" (pp. 142ff.); "al-Ṣada" (pp. 18ff.).

[2] *Ḥikāya*, pp. 246ff.

ful to have this man visit the front and the refugee camps, and then climb to the top of Cairo Tower to shoot in all directions? [1]"!

But in contrast to MIR, violence in these short stories is much more in tune with their lyrical style. The very fact that the stories are often written in the form of abstract fables renders the violent scenes less realistic, and at the same time more pregnant with meaning. It would seem that Maḥfūẓ has succeeded in these stories in finding the proper form in which the excess of violence could be conveyed artistically. His incessant experiments have enabled him to solve yet another difficult artistic problem. There is little doubt that these volumes of short stories, notably the latest two, are amongst the best works to come from the author's pen.

* * *

Maḥfūẓ is still writing. In fact it was only in 1972 that he has been able to devote all of his time to literature. To foresee the surprises which this ever-developing writer has in store for us would be an impossible task. Indeed it is too early at this stage to essay a definitive assessment of his work. This book, therefore, can be nothing but a tentative appraisal. What is certain, however, is that Maḥfūẓ has given modern Arabic literature its first fully-fledged novelist; and that in him, Egypt contributes a fresh new voice to world literature.

---

1 *Ibid.*, p. 279.

APPENDIX I

EDITIONS AND DATES

There is some difficulty in establishing the dates of Maḥfūẓ's books. For one thing, none of the current imprints, published chiefly by Maktabat Miṣr in recent years, records its precise printing date. In each of these copies, however, a colophon is affixed listing all of Maḥfūẓ's works which had appeared to date, together with the dates of the first and subsequent printings of the books. I have compared their colophons and found that often there are considerable discrepancies in them. I have assumed, however, that the latest date appearing in a particular colophon represents the printing date of the book to which it is affixed. In the list of abbreviations (see Bibliography A) I have given these dates (in the last column) in square brackets.

No less a difficulty arises in establishing the dates of the first publication of some novels, especially the early ones. I have found, too, that on this point the colophons are unreliable. Needless to say, these dates are of importance for understanding the author's literary career and the development of his art.

The confusion is especially evident as regards the dates of KHAN and QAH, the author's first two novels on modern Cairo. All the colophons agree that QAH appeared in 1945 and KHAN in 1946. These dates are accepted without comment by Maḥfūẓ's critics. Maḥfūẓ himself describes QAH as his first realistic novel to be published.[1]

A scrutiny of some Arabic periodicals of the time produces different conclusions. KHAN was definitely published in 1945, for in that year there appeared in *al-Risāla* three different reviews of the novel.[2] On the other hand, there is no mention of QAH before the late months of 1946.[3] Furthermore, the critic Sayyid Quṭb, who followed Maḥfūẓ's works closely, clearly indicates that QAH appeared *after* KHAN.[4]

As to other early works of Maḥfūẓ, we are fortunate in having the exact dates of RAD (July 1943) and KIF (Aug. 1944).[5]

Turning to ZUQ, SAR, BID — the colophons give us the dates as 1947, 1948, 1949 respectively. The reviews (supposing they appeared shortly after the novels themselves) do not always coincide with dates given in the colophons. The first review of ZUQ appeared in Jan. 1948[6] and it can be assumed that the novel had appeared late in 1947 or early 1948. But the reviews of SAR appear only in the

---

1 Dawwāra, p. 280.

2 *al-Risāla*, 15 Oct.; 3 and 17 Dec. 1945.

3 *al-Kātib al Miṣrī*, Sept. 1946; *al-Adīb*, Sept. 1946; *al-Risāla*, 7 Oct. and 30 Dec. 1946.

4 *al-Risāla*, 30 Dec. 1946, p. 1440 (rev. of QAH).

5 These dates can be found in the list of publications of لجنة النشر للجامعيين which is prefixed to al-Māzinī's novel *Ibrāhīm al-Kātib* (second ed., Aug. 1945).

6 *al-Risāla*, 26 Jan. 1948; cf. *al-Kātib al-Miṣrī*, Feb. 1948 : *al-Adīb*, Mar. 1948.

early months of 1950,[1] and thus it is likely to have appeared late in 1949 or early in 1950, not, as in the colophons, in 1948.

The reviews of BID appear not before the second half of 1951,[2] while the colophons register 1949.

The Trilogy and the works that followed produce no such problems, for by then the author was in the public eye.

In the following table the two alternative (or equal) dates of each of the early novels is given (asterisk denotes an unconfirmed date, which is deduced solely from the reviews) :

NOVEL	COLOPHONS	OTHER SOURCES
ABA	1939	1939
RAD	1943	1943 (July)
KIF	1944	1944 (Aug.)
KHAN	1946	1945*
QAH	1945	1946*
ZUQ	1947	1947*
SAR	1948	1949*
BID	1949	1951*

As for the collection of short stories, HAMS, it is again doubtful whether we can believe the colophons (which register 1938); there are many indications of a much later date.[3]

---

1 *al-Risāla*, 23 Jan. 1950; *al-Adīb*, Mar. 1950.

2 *al-Risāla*, 2 July 1951; 6 Aug. 1951; *al-Adīb*, Oct. 1951.

3 See *supra.*, p. 46, fn. 2.

APPENDIX II

PLOT CUTLINES OF MAḤFŪẒ'S NOVELS

'Abath al-aqdār (1939)

The action of *'Abath al-aqdār* ('The Mockery of Fate') takes place in the days of Pharaoh Khūfū (Khufwey, Cheops) of the Fourth Dynasty (approx. twenty-sixth Century B.C.). It concerns the career of Dadaf (Ra'djedef), the son of the high priest of Rē', from his birth until he mounted the throne of Egypt in his early youth.

The novel opens on the very day of Dadaf's birth. In Khūfū's palace in Memphis, an old fortune-teller predicts—to Pharaoh's dismay—that none of his sons will ascend to the throne after his death. Instead, the old man announces, the newly born son of the high priest of Rē' will be the next Pharaoh. No sooner do Pharaoh and his sons hear the ominous news than they set out for On, the high priest's homeland, intent on murdering the infant. The party arrives at the priest's house just after the mother and child, accompanied by the servant Zāyā, have left it. Pharaoh however kills the son of the maid Kātā, who was also born on that day, assuming that he was the one they sought. The high priest commits suicide, and Pharaoh's party now return to Memphis, believing that they have rid themselves of a possible contender.

Meanwhile the childless servant Zāyā kidnaps the baby, leaving the mother alone in the desert, where she is in turn kidnapped by Sinai tribesmen.

Zāyā and the infant arrive in Memphis, helped by Pharaoh himself, who finds the two lost in the desert! She discovers that her husband, who has been working as a builder on the great Pyramid, has died. Luckily, however, she attracts the attention of the Pyramid superintendent, Bishārū, who takes her to his home —first as concubine, then as wife. Thus Dadaf has the opportunity to grow up in a comfortable home.

At twelve, Dadaf chooses a military career. During his training at the Military Academy he proves himself to be a distinguished cadet. Consequently, the Prince appoints him officer in his bodyguard. At the graduation ceremony he wins first prize in all the sporting events and thus wins the favour of the Crown Prince, who is attending the ceremony with his sister Merī Sī 'Ankh.

Dadaf has already fallen in love with a peasant girl with whom he used to flirt on the banks of the Nile. On seeing Pharaoh's daughter, Merī Sī 'Ankh, he is convinced that she is none other than his "peasant girl." The Princess indignantly denies any connection with that girl, but later implicitly admits it (she masquerades as a peasant in order to enjoy an occasional break from the stiff formality of palace life).

Dadaf makes rapid progress in the Prince's court. Thanks to his extraordinary courage he saves the Prince's life in a hunting incident, and at twenty he is appointed commander of the bodyguard. Soon he is chosen by Pharaoh to command the contingent which is to drive off the marauding Sinai tribes. On the eve of the army's departure the Princess visits the young commander to confess her love.

The Sinai campaign ends in victory. Among Dadaf's many captives is an Egyptian woman of fifty who claims to have been kidnapped by the tribe twenty years earlier. Dadaf takes the woman back to Memphis, and, to his utmost bewilderment, finds that she is his real mother of whose existence he knew nothing. Meanwhile the Pharaoh consents to give his daughter to the victorious officer.

Things now move rapidly : the Crown Prince, frustrated and impatient, plots to kill his father in order to ascend the throne. Dadaf uncovers the plot and at the very last moment saves Pharaoh. The latter falls ill and, gratified by Dadaf's vigilance, summons his family and aides to announce that he is depriving his sons of the throne and, instead, is appointing Dadaf, his future son-in-law, to inherit it. Before dying, however, Pharaoh is informed of Dadaf's real identity. He now discovers how futile were his endeavours to defy Fate. He dies sadder but wiser, leaving his throne to the young hero.

Rādūbīs (1943)

The story is set in the short reign of Pharaoh Merenrēʿ II, of whom historical records have barely anything to tell except for the fact that he ruled Egypt for one year.

The young Pharaoh has just ascended the throne. He has the reputation of being a hedonist and philanderer. He is also arrogant and high-handed : no sooner has he become king than he clashes with the priests over the issue of their lands. He is intent on confiscating the inherited estates, and eschews the advice of experienced statesmen who warn him of the perils of antagonizing that formidable class.

In a little island opposite his capital lives a beautiful courtesan, Rādūbīs (Rhodopis), to whose luxurious house flocks the cream of society. On the day in which the novel opens—the Nile festival day—she sees the new Pharaoh and is fascinated by him. On the very same day it happens that an eagle lifts one of her gold-rimmed sandals and throws it at the Pharaoh's feet. Pharaoh, mystified, inquires about the owner of the sandal, and before long visits her home. At once he becomes so attached to Rādūbīs that he begins to spend most of his time with her, and to squander a good deal of the state's treasury to decorate her house. Finally he deserts his loving wife, Nitocris, and moves into her house. Rādūbīs herself changes her way of life. She becomes genuinely devoted to Pharaoh, thus frustrating her numerous lovers (among whom is Ṭāhū, commander of Pharaoh's guard and his close friend).

The priests now claim that their wealth is being confiscated only to be spent on a prostitute. The high priest Khanūm Ḥatib (who has been dismissed from the post of Prime Minister) is successfully agitating among his people against Merenreʿ. Rādūbīs advises Pharaoh to declare general mobilization in order to nip the rebellion in the bud. But since there was no pretext to justify such a call to arms, Pharaoh decided—again on Rādūbīs' advice—to ask the governor of the southern region to send a message falsely alleging that the tribes of Maʿaṣāyū (Medjayu) have rebelled against his troops. The letter arrives and Pharaoh summons the priests and notables and has the letter read before them. The high priest however foils the scheme when he informs the meeting that a delegation of the Maʿaṣāyū notables have arrived only the day before to pledge their loyalty to Pharaoh. The priest thus scores a decisive victory over Pharaoh, who is now sure that he has been betrayed. (It later turns out that the secret scheme was disclosed by the frustrated commander, Ṭāhū).

That very day is the day of the Nile festival. A full year has elapsed since the story began. The crowd which has gathered in the capital to celebrate is carried away by a militant mood. They boldly denounce Merenre' and his concubine and, instead, hail the abandoned queen Nitōcris (who has emerged as a dignified and courageous woman). The people clash with the guards and finally reach the gates of Pharaoh's palace. Pharaoh decides to act bravely; he calls a halt to the bloodshed and walks out unguarded to meet the people. His appearance takes them by surprise. Their anger is about to subside, when a ring-leader shoots an arrow at Pharaoh, seriously injuring him. The king asks his wife to transport him to Rādūbīs' home to die there. No sooner does he see his love than he dies.

Rādūbīs puts an end to her life by taking poison.

Kifāḥ Ṭība (1944)

Kifāḥ Ṭība ('Thebes' Struggle') takes place in the period when the Hyksōs ruled Egypt (approx. sixteenth century B.C.). It tells the story of the fierce battle which the Egyptian Pharaonic family—backed by the Egyptian people—waged against the intruders, culminating in the expulsion of the latter and the ascent of Aḥmas (Ahmose, Amosis) as undisputed Pharaoh of all Egypt.

The occurrences which this novel relate occupy a period of thirteen years and fall into three distinct parts.

In the first part we witness the native Pharaonic family in its distress. The Hyksōs under Abūfīs (Apophis) are the masters of Lower Egypt, while the indigenous monarchs are in command only in Upper Egypt, governing virtually as vassals of the Hyksōs chieftain. As the novel opens a messenger from Abūfīs arrives in Thebes, the southern capital, to make some humiliating demands on Sīkinra' (Sekenere'), the ruler of Upper Egypt. The demands are not only humiliating : they are tantamount to complete surrender of independence. Sīkinra' and his people decide to defy the Hyksōs ruler and reject his conditions, realizing that in so doing they are risking a war with the Hyksōs; a war for which they are ill prepared.

Abūfīs was, it appears, ready for war and his army moves south without delay. The southern army fights gallantly, especially in naval battles, but the formidable Hyksōs chariot corps soon play havoc with them, and Pahraoh himself is brutally killed in the battlefield. His family leaves Thebes, taking refuge in Nubia; the whole of the south surrenders to the invaders.

The second period opens after a lapse of ten years during which period, we soon find out, the fire of independence has not died away. The Pharaonic family has wasted no time : it has been building a clandestine army in Nubia under the leadership of Kāmūs (Kamose), son of the late Pharaoh.

Kāmūs' son, Aḥmas, disguised as a rich merchant, succeeds in penetrating the tightly closed border between Nubia and Egypt. By means of priceless presents, bribes, and deceptions he contrives to reach the governor of Thebes and subsequently the Hyksōs monarch himself, procuring for his ships a license of free passage to Egypt. This enables him to recruit patriotic Egyptians for the Pharaonic army, and transport them to Nubia. Aḥmas finds among the oppressed Egyptians a deep hatred of the foreign rulers coupled with a readiness to fight for liberty.

While carrying out his dangerous mission, Aḥmas meets the charming Aminrīdis, the daughter of the Hyksōs king. The two become attached to each other and Aḥmas is saved by her from certain death after injuring a Hyksōs officer in a duel.

In the third part of the novel, preparations for invasion are at last complete. This time Kāmūs' forces are well equipped both for land and sea battles. The army marches, taking the border garrison by surprise and storming northward. The cities of Upper Egypt fall into their hands, one after another, and many citizens of the newly liberated areas join their ranks.

In one of the battles, however, Kāmūs is killed, and Aḥmas becomes Pharaoh and supreme commander of the army. When the southern capital, Thebes, falls into their hands following a bitter battle, the Pharaonic family refuse to move into the city, vowing to do so only when the whole of Egypt is purged of the Hyksōs.

Among the Hyksōs captives taken in Thebes, Aḥmas finds none other than Aminrīdis, whom he now rescues from the wrath of the people. Aminrīdis, however, treats Aḥmas—now that she knows his true identity—with dignified contempt and refuses to have anything to do with him.

The Egyptian army continues to chase the Hyksōs northward. Abūfīs hastily retreats and is eventually enclosed in the fortified capital of the Hyksōs, Huwārīs (Avaris). Realising that there is no easy way of penetrating the fortifications, Aḥmas decides to cut off the water of the city by digging a channel to divert the Nile. The threat of thirst soon disheartens the Hyksōs, who come forward to offer to evacuate the city and leave the land of Egypt, on condition that their men be allowed to retreat safely; and also that Aminrīdis should be handed back in return for thirty thousand Egyptian captives. The Egyptians accept the conditions without delay, but before sending Aminrīdis back, Aḥmas visits her to inform her that she is free. At this point she changes and begins to return the love of the young Pharaoh. The two, however, know only too well that theirs is a hopeless love, as the proud Abūfīs will never give his daughter to his enemy.

K͟hān al-K͟halīlī (1945)

In September, 1941 following the Axis' air raids on Cairo, many people hurriedly left the Sakākīnī quarter. Aḥmad 'Ākif, a low-ranking government clerk of about forty, was one of them. He and his parents (the father, a former clerk himself, and the mother) move to a flat in K͟hān al-K͟halīlī, the well-known ancient quarter, not far from the Azhar Mosque.

In his youth Aḥmad had been an ambitious person who dreamt of a glorious career as a writer, scientist, etc., but had to give up his hopes and accept the life of a minor clerk owing to the fact that he had to become the breadwinner of the family and help his younger brother Rus͟hdī to finish his University training.

In the new quarter Aḥmad is befriended by some middle-aged neighbours who spend their evenings in a local café. He finds this company more interesting than his yellowed books. He also enjoys the happy atmosphere of the K͟hān during Ramaḍān. The greatest novelty that the new quarter brings to him is a sixteen year old schoolgirl, Nawāl, who lives next door and whom he sees from his window and in the shelter. She seems disposed to accept his advances, but Aḥmad, though rejoicing in this new and sudden hope, is as shy as a school-boy. He dreams secretly of approaching her father (who is one of the café group) to ask for her hand.

The Month of Fasting is over, and the *Fiṭr* Festival brings with it happy tidings : Rus̲h̲dī has been transferred from Asyūṭ to the capital, where he is to live permanently.

Rus̲h̲dī is in his twenties, handsome and flamboyant. He leads the life of a dandy and indulges in drinking and gambling. Being unaware of his brother's desperate attachment to Nawāl, he starts to flirt audaciously with her, almost as soon as he settles in Cairo. Naturally the girl prefers the younger and more handsome of the two. Gradually, to Aḥmad's misery and despair, love develops between the two young people.

Aḥmad reconciles himself to the new development, though unable to heal his wounded heart. Rus̲h̲dī meets Nawāl every morning on her way to school. Shortly afterwards he asks Aḥmad to approach the girl's father about getting engaged. Suddenly Rus̲h̲dī feels the symptoms of a lung disease which prove to be consumption. Rus̲h̲dī will not listen to the doctor's advice to go to a sanatorium, being reluctant to leave Nawāl and other amusements, and above all, for fear of losing his job. He refuses to discontinue either his clandestine meetings with Nawāl early in the cool mornings, or his nightly outings with his friends.

His brother, the only person to know of his condition, watches his deterioration with great horror. Within a few months Rus̲h̲dī's condition reaches a point where he cannot resist the doctor's orders. After spending a short while in a sanatorium he writes a heartbreaking letter to his brother asking him to bring him back home in order to die there.

When he is brought back he is a complete wreck. The true nature of his illness becomes common knowledge. Nawāl reluctantly gives in to her parent's wishes, and disappears from his life. His mood (and that of his family) is still further depressed when the bank's doctor informs him that he is to be dismissed as he has failed to return to work after the six months sick leave.

At home, as a result of his trying illness, Rus̲h̲dī becomes morbid and moody. He eventually decides to return to the sanatorium, but death intervenes.

The last few chapters of the novel present a distressing picture of a bereaved family, whose only hope and light has suddenly been extinguished. They decide to leave K̲h̲ān al-K̲h̲alīlī as quickly as possible.

al-Qāhira al-jadīda (1946 ?)

The scene is Cairo in the early 1930's. As the novel opens we meet three philosophy students in their last years of study.

'Alī Ṭāhā is an elegant young man from a well-to-do family. He is concerned with the social and political conditions of his people, and believes in "science rather than divine secrets; society rather than paradise; socialism rather than competition." He has a charming girl friend, Iḥsān, daughter of a poor tobacconist. 'Alī hopes to marry and, to use his own words, make Iḥsān "a wife different from those of typical Oriental households."

Ma'mūn Ruḍwān is a brilliant student, well-behaved and industrious, who passionately believes in "God in heaven and Islam on earth." He is an honest believer, and sincere friend. He is engaged to a relative whom he intends to marry as soon as he graduates.

Maḥjūb 'Abd al-Dā'im, the third friend, believes in nothing, and cares for nothing but his own interests. He is the poorest of the three—his father being a poorly paid clerk in a dairy company in al-Qanāṭir. Besides being moneyless, Maḥjūb is not particularly attractive and his emotional life is rather frustrated. He is unsuccessful with girls and contents himself with casual intercourse with a squalid cigarette-end scavenger, which costs him very little.

As the plot starts moving, Maḥjūb receives a letter calling him home : his father has fallen ill. It turns out that the father has had a stroke which has left him paralyzed and unable to continue his work. Maḥjūb now has to resort to extreme measures of austerity : he leaves the students' hostel and lives on one meal daily. He is too proud to ask for help from his friends, even when it comes to buying an essential textbook. Things prove to be even worse than expected, so much so in fact that he decides to visit a rich relative of his mother to ask for help. There he meets the relative's pretty daughter, Taḥiyya. On seeing her he refrains from asking for help and instead starts dreaming of winning her affections in the hope that through her he may find a short cut to success. He contrives to invite her to an archaeological site where, overcome by desire and conceit, he attempts to woo her in a rather crude manner. Taḥiyya runs away, terrified, and thus Maḥjūb loses any hope of help from her father.

His next step to save himself from starvation is to ask for financial help from Sālim al-Ikhshīdī, who comes from the same village as he, and who has risen to a high governmental office through betraying his one-time radical activities. Instead of actually helping him, Sālim sends him to a journalist friend through whom he can earn a meagre monthly sum by translating articles.

Graduation day comes. 'Alī gets a comfortable job in the university library; Ma'mūn receives a scholarship to study in France; but Maḥjūb, without the backing of family connections, is offered no job. The ridiculous payment for his translations would, of course, not suffice for his own keep let alone that of his parents. He is on the verge of total despair and finds no way out but again to ask al-Ikhshīdī's help. The latter decides to exploit Maḥjūb and make him a tool for his own advantage. Salīm offers him a comfortable government job on condition that Maḥjūb marries a certain girl. It soon turns out that the position is that of secretary of the general-manager Qāsim Bey (a position up to now occupied by al-Ikhshīdī himself). The woman whom he is offered in marriage is, he is told, a friend of the Bey. What is more, the Bey would be continuing his relationship with the girl after her marriage. After a brief hesitation Maḥjūb accepts the fiendish offer and very soon discovers that the girl is none but the beautiful Iḥsān, 'Alī Ṭāhā's former friend, who had in the meantime jilted him and followed her wicked parents' advice to accept the wealthy (but married) Bey's advances.

A hurried wedding is arranged, and the new couple move into a flat paid for by the Bey. Maḥjūb assumes his new post, and at home he tries to work out some *modus vivendi* with his wife. But a tense atmosphere prevails between them. They take to drink and join a group of licentious young men among whom their tension is slowly eased. However, a few weeks later some ominous news reaches the couple : the government is about to resign. This may mean the end of Qāsim

Bey, and, consequently Maḥjūb may be transferred to some negligible provincial position. Eventually the governmental upheaval takes place, but their fears prove to be unjustified : Qāsim Bey, far from being demoted, now becomes a minister in the new government. Maḥjūb—through his wife—contrives to be promoted too, and becomes the head of the minister's bureau.

But the rising career very soon comes to an abrupt end. On a Saturday evening (which is the time for Qāsim's weekly visit to Iḥsān) as Maḥjūb is about to leave the house, a strange series of incidents takes place. His father, now partially recovered, suddenly appears, and harshly rebukes his son for neglecting his parents and for not even informing them that he has married. Since the father had no way of knowing of his new address, Maḥjūb at once suspects that this is the work of Sālim al-Ikhshīdī, who is jealous of him, and furious because he has seized the job that he believed should have been his own. Before Maḥjūb can calm his father down, the Bey arrives. Very soon the door bell again rings, and in comes the wife of the Bey in a rage. A major scandal ensues in consequence of which the Bey gives up his ministerial position and Maḥjūb is transferred to the south.

Zuqāq al-Midaqq (1947)

In *Zuqāq al-Midaqq* there is no central plot in the accepted sense. It is rather the story of an alley in the al-Ḥusayn quarter in old Cairo. The period is 1943-4 and the World War has not left unchanged the life of this ancient, humble alley.

The novel presents us with a group of the alley's people, depicting a few months of their lives. Their fates intermingle and affect each other.

The main character in the book is Ḥamīda, a native beauty, illiterate, naïve, sharp-witted and insolent. Among the many people who admire her looks is 'Abbās al-Ḥulw, the poor, good-natured barber of the alley. Ḥamīda realises only too well that he is the only man in the neighbourhood who is suitable to be her future husband, but is disgusted by the prospect of poverty, toil, and filthy children. 'Abbās is prevailed upon by a friend to work in a British army camp in the desert in order to make some money. Before leaving for the camp, he persuades Ḥamīda to become his fiancée, though without much enthusiasm on her side.

As soon as 'Abbās departs, a new suitor seeks her hand. He is Salīm 'Ilwān, a rich merchant who does not live in the alley, but owns a flourishing grocery store there. Salīm is in his fifties, married and father of married children, but is now unable to suppress his excessive passion for a young female body. Ḥamīda and her foster-mother instantly accept his offer jilting the fiancé in the desert camp. Ḥamīda's expectations of a wealthy home are frustrated, however, for Salīm suffers a sudden blow to his health which renders him unfit for worldly pleasures, and his marriage plans are cancelled.

A handsome outsider, Faraj Ibrāhīm now comes into the picture and woos the naïve shrew with consummate skill. He gradually prevails upon her to desert her home and come to live with him. Ḥamīda soon finds out that her lover is a pimp who owns a "school" for training pleasure-girls to entertain the foreign soldiers; before long she becomes steeped in this art.

'Abbās returns to the alley a few months later on his first leave to find, to his dismay, that his beloved has disappeared. He realizes that she has eloped, and vows to take revenge on her seducer. By sheer accident he stumbles upon Ḥamīda herself—now lavishly made up and garishly dressed—and tries to reproach her. Ḥamīda, whose love for Faraj has by now turned to hatred, decides to take advantage of 'Abbās' scorn to punish her seducer. She promises to meet him a few days later in a certain wine shop, to show him the man who deceived her. Before the appointed date, however, 'Abbās sees her entertaining a group of drunken English soldiers in the same wine-shop. He furiously attacks her with an empty bottle, inflicting heavy wounds on her. The disappointed soldiers fall upon him and beat him to death.

Among the other characters who live in Zuqāq al-Midaqq, mention should be made of the following :

Mu'allim Kirsha—the homosexual owner of the alley's coffee house. His incessant hashish smoking, his frequent affairs with good-looking young men and his continuous squabbles with his wife and son punctuate the novel.

Zīṭa (or Zēṭa)—a resident of the gutter, whose profession it is to counterfeit disease on the bodies of poor people who wish to become beggars, so that their alleged bodily defects might soften the hearts of passers-by. Zīṭa, by virtue of his expertise, is master of the beggars of al-Ḥusayn quarter.

"Doctor" Būshī—the self-styled dentist of the alley whose treatment, though painful and often dangerous, is cheap enough for the poor people around him. It transpires, however, that he gets his artificial teeth by digging into new graves with Zīṭa's help. When the two are caught red-handed by the police a major scandal ensues.

Saniyya 'Afīfī—a well-to-do miserly widow in her fifties, who in the course of the novel succeeds in acquiring a young husband thanks to the good offices of Ḥamīda's adoptive mother.

Sayyid Ruḍwān al-Ḥusaynī—a saintly creature who bears the suffering of the alley and serves as a voluntary mediator and preacher to its people. Towards the end of the novel he sets out on pilgrimage to Mecca to ask forgiveness for the whole alley.

Shaykh Darwīsh—a former teacher who has become insane. He utters mystical sayings interspersed with English words.

al-Sarāb (1948 ?)

The story is told in the form of reminiscences of its protagonist, Kāmil Ru'ba Lāẓ.

Kāmil is the son of a wealthy Cairene family of Turkish origin. His father, an idle alcoholic, deserted his wife when Kāmil was an infant, and retired to his house to drink his life away. Kāmil lived with his mother in the house of his grandfather, a retired army officer. The boy, utterly spoiled by his deserted mother, grows up to become an unsociable introvert. At school he is an absolute failure, finishing his secondary education at the age of twenty-five, and thus frustrating his grandfather's dream of enlisting him in a military academy. He enters the law college, but has to leave two months later when he is terrified on being called upon to deliver a speech in the oratory class. Eventually a minor clerical job in the government is found for him.

Being shy and completely attached to his mother, he had no dealings whatever with the opposite sex, and found a substitute in occasional drink and constant masturbation.

He eventually falls in love with a pretty neighbour, Rabāb, a student in a teachers' college whom he chanced to see daily at the tram stop. For two years, however, he keeps silent about it. Meanwhile his compassionate grandfather dies and Kāmil is aware that his meagre salary is insufficient to maintain his mother and himself, let alone a family. But his lethargy is shaken when he hears that Rabāb is being wooed by another suitor. He approaches his father for some financial help, but is ruthlessly dismissed. Soon, however, the father dies and Kāmil inherits a handsome sum of money. He now plucks up courage to address Rabāb and ask her to marry him. Her family receive him favourably, and soon give their consent. His mother receives the news with much anxiety, but finds no way of expressing her misgivings.

Kāmil and Rabāb are married and they move, together with Kāmil's mother, into a new flat, with Rabāb resuming her post as a teacher. Yet Kāmil's happiness is incomplete. He discovers that he is unable to perform his marital functions. Months pass and the couple remain virgin. Rabāb utters no complaint, and shows much affection for her loving husband. One night Kāmil has been out drinking, and, on returning home finds his way to his wife. He finds his wife uninterested, and before long she begs him to return to their days of "pure love." Kāmil consents and soon resorts to his premarital habits. He also begins spending his nights out, leaving his wife free to go about visiting her family and relatives after her teaching hours.

One day Kāmil surprises his wife reading a mysterious letter. On inquiring about it, Rabāb instantly tears the paper up, explaining that it was an unsigned letter containing nothing but nonsense. Kāmil ostensibly accepts her explanation, but serious doubts creep into his mind. He takes leave from his office and begins to spy on his wife on her way to and from school. A few days pass, and no incriminating evidence emerges. In the meantime he meets an unattractive widow of forty, 'Ināyāt, who woos him and subsequently seduces him. He soon finds himself spending all his evenings with her. Her ugliness excites his senses and her voluptuousness gives him an extreme pleasure.

A few weeks later, Kāmil returns home at night to be told that Rabāb is staying overnight with her parents, having caught, so he is told, a severe cold. He rushes to see her and offers to call a doctor, but her mother objects. Next morning, before going to the office, he visits her again and finds her pale and unwell. At work he is unable to carry on and leaves at midday to see his wife. He finds her dead. Her mother explains that a young doctor—a relative of Rabāb—had been called, and he decided to carry out an immediate operation which resulted in her death. Kāmil, half-mad, rushes to the police, demanding an inquiry. The police step in and find that the "operation" was in fact an abortion. It becomes clear to Kāmil that he has been cuckolded, since he himself had not touched his wife for months. The investigator dupes the young doctor into confessing that he was not only responsible for the fatal abortion, but also for Rabāb's pregnancy. Kāmil returns home and there shocks his ailing mother with the whole truth. That night she dies of heart failure, but Kāmil, having left the house early in the morning, does not know of her death until the afternoon, when it is announced in the evening paper. He reacts in a wild manner, accusing himself of murdering his mother as well as his wife. Subsequently he faints and goes into a coma for three days. On awakening he realises that his past is dead and buried together with the two beloved souls that he has lost in the course of a day. He has no one left but the homely 'Ināyāt, who, surely enough soon finds her way to him.

Bidāya wa-nihāya (1950)

This is the story of the decline and fall of a middle-class family in Cairo in the mid 1930's.

The sudden death of the father, a minor government clerk, leaves his family to face a life of destitution. The mother, a strong-willed and resourceful person, takes the most austere measures to save her family from ruin, but her efforts are doomed to failure. The elder brother Ḥasan (twenty-five years old when the plot begins) is an idle and spoiled man, aspiring to a singing career. Eventually he degenerates to a life of depravity, leaves home, lives with a prostitute, and takes up drug smuggling. He however keeps in contact with the family, helping his brothers in time of urgent need.

The daughter Nafīsa (about twenty-three) loses whatever hopes she has of marrying. She is unattractive and now has to work as a dressmaker to help keep the family. Her new vocation means not only social degradation in Egyptian terms, but also stresses her depressing position, especially since she must sew bridal gowns. She accepts the advances of Salmān, a grocer in the district, and eventually surrenders to him, in the hope that he will one day marry her. But once he has seduced her, he jilts her to marry a wealthy girl. Nafīsa, overcome by despair and poverty, and responding to her strong sexual compulsions, gradually stoops to occasional prostitution.

Her younger brothers, Ḥusayn (nineteen years) and Ḥasanayn (seventeen years) are nearing the end of their secondary education. Ḥusayn, well-behaved, serious, and pious, finishes his studies, gives up the idea of higher education, and accepts a poorly paid clerical position in Ṭanṭā, away from his family, to pave the way for his younger brother. In Ṭanṭā, he meets a suitable girl, the daughter of his superior, and for a while entertains the dream of a happy married life. However, he relinquishes his dream at once when his mother hints that his marraige would deprive the rest of the family of its livelihood.

Ḥasanayn is, on the other hand, excessively ambitious, and willingly accepts the sacrifice of Ḥusayn and the others. He finishes his schooling, and attends the military academy. He is commissioned as a professional officer, and starts dreaming and planning his ascent to a higher social status. He discards his young fiancée, a neighbour of theirs (to whom he insisted on becoming engaged when times were at their worst), in the hope of marrying a rich girl. He endeavours to erase his past and asks for the hand of an important government offcial's daughter. For a short while, the tide seems to be turning in a favourable direction. Then a succession of frustrations follows : he discovers, to his dismay, that the high society is not willing to accept the brother of a seamstress and a smuggler. Ḥasan refuses his entreaties to quit his dubious way of life. Later the police come to their flat in search of Ḥasan. Ḥasanayn, struck by shame and wrath, decides to move with his family to a different and more dignified neighbourhood. But another blow comes when Ḥasan arrives at the new house, badly injured and fleeing from the law. The final blow to Ḥasanayn comes when he is called to the police station to be informed that his sister has been found in a brothel with a lover. Her brother forces her to commit suicide by drowning herself in the Nile. He ends his life in the same way.

The Trilogy (1956-7)

1. *Bayn al-Qaṣrayn*

This volume tells the story of a middle-class Cairene family before and during the 1919 revolution. The plot covers a period of eighteen months (from 10 Nov. 1917 to 8 Apr. 1919).

In his house at Bayn al-Qaṣrayn (not far from the al-Ḥusayn Mosque) the Master (*al-Sayyid*) Aḥmad ʿAbd al-Jawād, a merchant of about forty-five, rules his family with the utmost rigour.

Al-Sayyid's personality, however, has other facets of which his family know very little. For whereas his children never see him smiling, he is at the hub of a group of middle-aged merchants who spend their nights merrily together till the small hours; and whereas he imposes the severest moral restrictions on his wife and children, he himself is a great connoisseur of women and drink.

As the action commences, we witness al-Sayyid engaging in yet another amorous affair, this time with a well-known singer (*ʿālima*), Zubayda. She is not young but is regarded by al-Sayyid as his ideal of fleshy femininity. His success indeed arouses only admiration and jealousy among his firends.

Later when he has had enough of Zubayda, a new adventure fires his imagination. A neighbour dies, whose widow, Bahīja, no less plump than Zubayda, offers him her favours. Al-Sayyid, whose moral standards would not allow him to trifle with a neighbour's wife, now feels free to act since the husband is no longer among the living.

At home, where he is as harsh as a father can be, his household can avoid his wrath only by constant lying. Moreover they feel no qualms in shielding each other through deceit in the face of their father, who would not forgive the slightest deviation from the standards of behaviour which he imposes. His three sons behave like slaves in his presence. The same applies, of course, to his wife and two daughters, who are never even allowed to peep through the windows.

In the course of the novel he finds himself in a most humiliating position in which he himself—but not his family—tastes an element of poetic justice. On leaving Bahīja's house late one night, he is caught by British soldiers and brutally dragged to a pit which rebellious students have earlier dug, and made to join others until the next morning in refilling it.

Amīna, his wife, is a daughter of a shaykh. Al-Sayyid married her after divorcing his first wife who rebelled against his rigid rules. Amīna accepts her husband's excesses with loving submission; it is his right to rule his house in his own fashion. At first, though, she felt resentful and somehow jealous because her husband spent all his evenings away from home, yet as the days passed she came to accept it as yet another indisputable privilege of the Master.

Amīna is never allowed to set foot outside the door and for the last twenty years or so has seen the outside world only a few times, when her husband took her for an occasional visit to her aged mother.

One day, when al-Sayyid is away in Port Said on business, she is prevailed upon by her children to seize the opportunity to pay a visit to al-Ḥusayn's Mosque. The temptation is too strong to resist and thus, accompanied by her son, Kamāl, she hesitantly makes her way to the revered Mosque. On her return, however, she is hit by a car and is ordered to stay in bed for some time. On his return, al-Sayyid reacts gently, to her great relief. But as soon as she recovers, he orders her out of the house without delay. The woman silently obeys and goes to live with her mother. None of her grown-up children have the courage to utter a word of protest or appeal to their father. The most the boys can do is to visit her secretly in her exile. Eventually al-Sayyid calls her back, thanks to the good offices of a respectable old lady, a friend of the family, who comes to intercede with al-Sayyid. The woman's mission is two-fold; for she has also come to propose that her son marry 'Ā'i<u>sh</u>a, al-Sayyid's younger daughter.

Al-Sayyid's eldest son, Yāsīn, is in his early twenties and serves as a minor school clerk. His father divorced his mother just before his birth, and he spent his first nine years with his mother. Later, when he joined his father, he developed a profound disgust for his mother. His memories of his boyhood with her fill him with horror, for he remembers certain affairs that she had with men. Although he has left his mother forever, he follows the news of her continuous amorous adventures with the utmost abhorrence. She has lately married a young man who obviously is only after her money, and Yāsīn is upset, not only because of the disparity of their ages, but also because such a marriage might affect his inheritance of her property.

He himself is an ill-educated dandy, no less lecherous than his father. Lately he has been after a lute-girl who works with Zubayda, his father's mistress (which gives him an opportunity to discover his father's secret life). But unlike his father, Yāsīn is unable to lead a sensual life without causing scandals. His obsession with sex renders him reckless and unrestrained. Even in his father's house he will not refrain from his debauched behaviour. One night he assaults their middle-aged housemaid, Umm Ḥanafī. The startled woman screams with horror, waking al-Sayyid. Consequently his father arranges—without consulting him—a marriage between Yāsīn and Zaynab, the daughter of a close friend. The newly-married couple live in al-Sayyid's house, and Yāsīn is at first pleased at having a wife of his own. Before long, however, he reverts to the habit of spending his evenings out. The young wife finds this behaviour intolerable, but she nevertheless puts up with it for a while. Yāsīn, on his part, does not make things easier for her. One evening he tries to seduce her black maid, and is caught in the act by Zaynab. The horrified wife—who is now pregnant—runs away to her parent's house. The father's attempts to prevent a divorce fail, and Yāsīn has no choice but to grant the woman her freedom.

Towards the end of the volume, Yāsīn's mother dies leaving her son with a house in Qaṣr al-<u>Sh</u>awq.

Fahmī, Amīna's eldest son, is a law student of about eighteen. He is diligent, quiet and meditative. He secretly falls in love with their neighbour Maryam, who is a little older than himself. The girl encourages him, but Fahmī is too well-mannered to look openly at her, let alone to make any approaches. Finally he asks his mother to convey to his father his wish to marry the girl. Al-Sayyid reacts furiously : it is not for his children to fall in love. Fahmī turns to political activity engaging wholeheartedly in the patriotic movement. He is elected a member of the Students' Council and marches at the head of mass demonstrations, defying the soldiers' rifles. When his father accidentally learns of his son's activity, he is beside himself; and although he is far from opposing the Wafd movement, he tries to dissuade his son from political activity. The son openly rebels and refuses even to promise to comply with his father's wish.

Kamāl is the youngest son, about ten years old. He is to become, to a large extent, the hero of the other volumes of the Trilogy. In this book, however, he is too young to be in the centre of the story. He is resourceful, playful, and fond of stories and music. He becomes friendly, much to his family's displeasure, with the English soldiers who camp opposite their home.

The daughters Khadīja (twenty) and 'Ā'isha (sixteen) are completely opposite in appearance and disposition, for while the elder sister is unattractive, diligent, down-to-earth and somewhat malicious, 'Ā'isha is a dreamy beauty, good-natured and lazy. Both sisters are, of course, semi-literate and prisoners of their home. Khadīja has long been waiting for a husband and feels unwanted. This feeling is enhanced by the fact that many men show interest in her sister. The father, however, would not let his elder daughter down : he refuses to marry 'Ā'isha first. Eventually he is compelled to do so by Mrs. Shawkat, widow of an old friend, a woman of Turkish origin, rich and domineering. Her younger son, Khalīl, is sluggish but kind, and, thanks to his family's income, does no work whatever. 'Ā'isha is wed quietly (this being a condition laid down by al-Sayyid) and moves to the Shawkat's house in al-Sukkariyya. She is happy in her new life and soon becomes pregnant. Her delivery, however, is a difficult one, and when she finally gives birth to a daughter, Na'īma, the doctor finds that the infant's heart is weak and warns that she might not live more than twenty years.
Khadīja, in turn, is rescued by the same Mrs. Shawkat who wishes her to marry her eldest son Ibrāhīm, a widower of forty. Khadīja finds herself happily once again under the same roof as her sister.

The first volume of the Trilogy ends with a horrible catastrophe which befalls al-Sayyid's family on the very day of universal jubilation. The people's struggle, which cost many lives, triumphs : the leader of the nation, who had been detained by the British, is set free. There is general elation everywhere. On the same day Fahmī asks forgiveness from his father for disobeying him, and sets out to help arrange a peaceful procession in honour of the leader, a procession licensed by the authorities. But the cheerful marchers are suddenly shot at indiscriminately and Fahmī falls dead on the street. Three students come to al-Sayyid's shop to inform him that his son has become a national martyr.

2. *Qaṣr al-Shawq*

The period covered in this volume : Sept. 1924 - Aug. 1927.
Five years have elapsed since Fahmī's death. The house of al-Sayyid is cheerless

and sombre. The memory of the beloved son haunts the family, and Amīna, at forty, has grown into a gloomy and inflexible old woman.

Al-Sayyid has prematurely aged and his severity at home, especially towards his wife, has considerably mellowed. He has kept away from women and wine, but his friends have lately persuaded him to resume drinking. His old passion for women is consequently rekindled and he soon falls in love with Zannūba, the lute-girl who was in past years Yāsīn's mistress. He now finds out, however, that his erstwhile powers to dominate women have waned. Zannūba makes heavy demands which cost him large amounts of money. She goes so far as to demand marriage. The old debauchee feels helpless, and for a while even contemplates bowing to her demand. But he is saved by the thought of the humiliation such a marriage would bring to his family. Nevertheless his infatuation with Zannūba does not subside until he discovers that she is also having an affair with Yāsīn (he knew nothing of their earlier attachment). At that point he is attacked by bodily weakness, and is to discover that he is no longer fit for a life of pleasure. He relinquishes it all with a mixture of penitence and nostalgia.

Kamāl, at seventeen, completes his schooling and to his father's dismay enters the teachers' college. He dreams of becoming a writer, and starts publishing articles in some newspapers. A humourous situation ensues when al-Sayyid discovers that his son has written an article on Darwin's theory of evolution. He summons Kamāl to interrogate him as to who has inspired him with such blasphemous ideas, which are incompatible with the Koranic story of Creation. Kamāl evades his father's wrath by claiming that he has not committed himself to the theory.

In point of fact, Kamāl has been going through a crisis of belief. His naïve faith, which he inherited from his mother, has long been replaced by more sophisticated ideas. But now, on becoming acquainted with modern science, he feels unable to go on believing in God at all.

Another passion which torments his soul is his love for an aristocratic girl, 'Ā'ida Shaddād. She is the sister of a friend and is older than he. He fell in love with her while still a schoolboy, and is totally enchanted by her beauty and European manners. 'Ā'ida seems at a certain point to be encouraging his attachment, thus further inflaming his passion by the hope that his love is returned (faint as this hope may be, considering the disparity in their ages and social position). Finally it turns out that she had been exploiting his childish infatuation to kindle jealousy in an wealthy youth in whom she is interested, and who soon marries her.

Kamāl, frustrated, takes to drinking, although in moderation, and even visits a brothel. On one of these visits he meets his brother Yāsīn, who reveals to him the shocking facts about the father's debaucheries.

Yāsīn himself continues to bring shame and embarrassment on his family. He falls in love with Maryam, Fahmī's sweetheart who has, in the meantime, married and divorced. His insistence on marrying her brings much grief to Amīna, and Yāsīn is obliged to leave his father's house and live in his own place in Qaṣr al-Shawq. Yet again his attachment to his second wife soon dies away. He is out again looking for fresh adventures. By chance he meets Zannūba, his old friend and now his father's mistress. The two become very drunk and in a fit of wildness Yāsīn brings the lute-girl to his own house. Maryam, mortified, runs away into the night, and Yāsīn far from regretting his outrage, promptly divorces her.

Zannūba is now fully in control of Yāsīn, and having despaired of the possibility of marrying al-Sayyid, she contrives to get his son to make her his third wife. They are married secretly, and when al-Sayyid hears of Yāsīn's latest blunder he is unable to do anything beyond scolding him.

Yāsīn's son by his first wife (named Ruḍwān), was born and raised in his maternal grandparents' home. Now he is about to be seven, an age at which his father can legally claim him, but Yāsīn respects his father's wish to give up the boy and let him grow up in a respectable home.

Khadīja and 'Ā'isha, though living in the same house, have developed different kinds of relationships their mother-in-law. Khadīja, saucy and domineering, is never at peace with the old woman. Their daily wrangles culminate in an amusing scene in which al-Sayyid himself is invited by the old woman to come to their home and rebuke his insolent daughter. Khadīja has two boys, 'Abd al-Mun'im and Aḥmad.

'Ā'isha, on the other hand, is as submissive as a daughter-in-law can be, thus gaining the old woman's affections (her sister accuses her of being a vulgar flatterer). She has three children - Na'īma, the girl whose birth was mentioned earlier, and two boys. She enjoys her life of leisure and freedom, but her happiness suddenly comes to a cruel end; her husband and two sons die suddenly of typhoid and 'Ā'isha, together with her daughter, go back to live with her parents.

3. *al-Sukkariyya*

The events of this volume—the last of the Trilogy—begin eight years after the end of the second part, and cover a period of nine years (1935-1944).

In the house of al-Sayyid, the Master is an ailing old man. He sells the business and retires to his home. His friends die, one by one, and finally he himself becomes an invalid and his last years are spent in desolation. The air raids of 1941 find him unable to walk and he has thus to be carried by his family back from the shelter. He dies, humiliated, after one of these raids.

Amīna's old age is also filled with misery. Her sorrow for 'Ā'isha's plight is no less painful than the memory of her own son. There is, however, one bright spot in their lives : Na'īma, the grand-daughter is now as beautiful and lively as her mother had been. She is the darling of the family and enjoys more freedom than did the girls of the earlier generation (although her grandfather refused to allow her to go to a secondary school). She has a great fondness for music and singing, but at the same time, she is deeply religious.

Kamāl still lives with his parents. In his thirties, he is unmarried and has developed a feeling of spiritual barrenness. He finds no satisfaction in his work as a teacher of English, nor are his dreams of a literary career fulfilled. Admittedly, he is now a contributor to a literary periodical in which he publishes a monthly article on philosophy. But this activity, he feels, is far from being creative. His articles are, in the main, nothing but neutral accounts of different trends in philosophy. Any graduate of a modern university, he reflects, could write better ones.

He is introduced to Riyāḍ Qaldas, a young Copt writer who publishes short stories in the same periodical. Their friendship saves both men, to a certain extent, from intellectual isolation. But nothing will dissipate their pessimism and scepticism.

Kamāl has long since lost all touch with ʻĀ'ida or her family, but he has never forgotten his first and only love. By sheer accident he meets her younger sister, Budūr, whom he remembers as an infant, now grown up and a student at the American University in Cairo. The girl, who looks amazingly like her sister, notices Kamāl's interest in her and is not unresponsive, but Kamāl is too timid to approach her. After a while he finds out that she has married, and this welcome echo of his early youth fades from his life. ʻĀ'ida herself, as he later learns, is divorced by her first husband, marries a school inspector of English, and dies soon afterwards. Kamāl, it turns out, has attended the funeral of the inspector's wife, not realising that the dead woman was none other than ʻĀ'ida.

Yāsīn, in his forties, now has "reformed" to a certain degree, thanks to the ingenuity of his wife Zannūba. She has been both firm and understanding, allowing her husband as much freedom as would keep him under control. Zannūba herself has proved to be ambitious and cunning and in time succeeds in being accepted by Yāsīn's family, her past partially forgotten. They have a daughter in her teens, Karīma.

Ruḍwān, Yāsīn's son by his first marriage, is now a handsome young man living with his father. While in college, he indulges in politics, and quickly comes to prominence, thanks not only to his abilities, but also to his dubious connections with homosexual politicians. His position in the government makes him an eminent member of his own family. He helps his cousin to employment, and his father to promotion. He even saves Kamāl from being transferred to a provincial school.

At Kh̲adīja's house in al-Sukkariyya (which gives this volume its title) the two sons have both entered the political arena, but unlike Ruḍwān they are motivated by idealism, not by personal ambition. They belong, however, to opposite extremes of the political spectrum. Their temperaments and personal inclinations are equally diverse.

The elder brother, ʻAbd al-Munʻim is a religious person who joins the Muslim Brotherhood and devotes all his spare time to promoting the idea of neo-Islamic activism. He is handsome and has success with girls, but because of his piety, he finds it necessary to marry early in order to avoid wicked temptations. At eighteen he asks his parents to find him a wife, and Kh̲adīha has no choice but to wed him to her niece, Naʻīma. The parting between ʻĀ'is̲h̲a and her only surviving child is painful for both mother and daughter. The future, however, has greater agonies in store for ʻĀ'is̲h̲a. Hardly a year passes before Naʻīma and her unborn infant die in labour. The doctor's ominous prediction at her birth, twenty years earlier, has come true. ʻĀ'is̲h̲a is on the verge of madness and for the rest of her days becomes detached from the surrounding world, waiting for death to re-unite her with her beloved ones. ʻAbd al-Munʻim later marries Karīma, Yāsīn's daughter, in spite of his mother's objections.

Aḥmad, his younger brother, develops an early attachment to ideas of social justice and while still in secondary school becomes an enthusiastic reader of the Leftist journal, *al-Insān al-Jadīd* ("New Man"). When he joins the University he starts writing for it. An unsuccessful affair with a female student of a rich family persuades him further to eschew bourgeois values. On graduating he joins the staff of that journal, and there he falls in love with an older member of the staff, Sawsan, an active Communist. Aḥmad joins the ranks of the Revolution himself and marries Sawsan to his mother's exasperation (she loathes Sawsan's humble origin). Thus the house in al-Sukkariyya becomes a hive of two-fold radical activity. Finally both 'Abd al-Mun'im and Aḥmad are arrested, the former leaving behind a pregnant wife.

As the Trilogy ends, the two brothers are still detained. Kamāl has not found a way out of his confusion and barrenness (although towards the end he is more attuned to Aḥmad's way of thinking). In the house at al-Sukkariyya, the grandchild of Khadīja and Yāsīn is about to be born. In the house at Bayn al-Qaṣrayn, Amīna is in a coma; she is soon to depart from this world.

Awlād Ḥāratinā (1959)

Awlād Ḥāratinā is an allegorical novel in five books, each telling the story of a different generation of the descendants of a common ancestor, Jabalāwī. The main outlines of the story are drawn from certain events in the religious history of Judaism, Christianity and Islam. Some of the protagonists' names are reminiscent of the archetypes, either through phonetic similarity (thus Adham = Adam; Idrīs is apparently a reference to Iblīs, 'devil'); or through "thematic" references (Jabal, 'mountain,' perhaps a reference to Mt. Sinai, and hence to Moses; Rifā'a—the stem *rf'* = 'lift up, raise'—hence the apparent reference to Jesus'; 'Arafa—the stem *'rf* = 'know', hence science or the scientist).

I — Adham : In a great house in Cairo, on the edge of the desert, lives the patriarch Jabalāwī. One day he calls his sons before him and declares that he had decided to hand the management of the *waqf* over to Adham, his son by a black slave. Idrīs, the first-born, is grossly offended : he insults his father and is promptly expelled from the house. Shortly afterwards, a housemaid is also expelled because she is pregnant with Idrīs' baby.

Idrīs stays near the house and lives idly, bullying the poor inhabitants of the area; Adham is a good-natured man : he manages the estate successfully spending his leisure enjoying his father's beautiful garden. He falls in love with Umayma, marries her, and soon they are expecting a child. His happiness, however, comes to an abrupt end. Idrīs sneaks into the house and asks his brother to go into Jabalāwī's private room, where the *waqf* document is kept, and find out what share of the inheritance, if any, Idrīs will have. Adham is naturally unwilling to do this for his brother, but Umayma persuades him that it will be to their own advantage to know what the future has in store.

Early one morning when his father is taking a walk, Adham enters his room, but Jabalāwī returns unexpectedly and catches him in the act. Consequently he throws Adham and his wife out of the house for ever. Outside, they find the abominable Idrīs waiting to greet them with malicious glee; he has now avenged himself on the brother.

Adham builds a hut beside the Big House, hoping that some day he will be re-admitted. He works hard, patiently enduring his brother's insults. A daughter, Hind, is born to Idrīs, while Adham's wife gives birth to twin boys, Qadrī and Hammām. The twins grow up and become shepherds. Qadrī falls in love with his cousin Hind, and meets her in secret.

One day a messenger comes from the Big House and invites Hammām to an audience with his grandfather. Qadrī who, unlike his brother, is ill-natured, flies into a rage because he was not also invited, and when Hammām sets out, without enthusiasm, to the house, Qadrī and Idrīs follow him, the latter dragging his daughter Hind behind him. However, Hammām alone is admitted, and the voice of the grandfather is heard from inside the house cursing his other grandchildren for "their sin."

Jabalāwī invites Hammām to come and live in the house. He sends him to take leave of his parents. Despite their insistence that he should go, Hammām is unwilling and puts off the decision. While minding their sheep, one day, Hammām and Qadrī quarrel, and Qadrī accidentally kills his brother; he flees and joins Hind.

Adham and Umayma spend the rest of their lives in inconsolable grief, while Idrīs, unmoved by their tragedy, continues to taunt them. However, before Adham's death, Jabalāwī visits him to tell him that he is forgiven and that the income from the *waqf* will be given to his descendants.

II — Jabal : An unspecified period of time has elapsed: Jabalāwī is living as a recluse, holding himself aloof from his descendants, who now populate the whole of the surrounding area (known as *Ḥārat al-Jabalāwī*); the income from the *waqf*, which was promised to Adham's posterity, has been embezzled by the *nāẓir*, (the supervisor of the *waqf*), who employs a number of *futuwwāt* (plural of *futuwwa*, 'strong-arm man') to rule the district; the inhabitants live in destitution.

In that part of the *Ḥāra* in which the Ḥamdān clan live, the embittered inhabitants decide to send a delegation to the *nāẓir*, demanding that something be done about the misconduct of the *futuwwāt*, as well as about their own poverty. The *nāẓir* receives them angrily and denies that they have any part in the income. He then sends the *futuwwāt* to the Ḥamdān quarters to punish the rebellious clan.

In the *nāẓir*'s house lives Jabal, an adopted son, who manages the *nāẓir*'s property. Jabal's parents were Ḥamdānites, and when his people are victimised he is distressed and gradually comes to identify himself with their plight.

One day he comes across a man of Ḥamdān being harshly treated by a *futuwwa*. He intervenes, and in the subsequent fight, kills the *futuwwa* and secretly buries him.

The *nāẓir* and the *futuwwāt* suspect that their man was killed by the Ḥamdānites, and although they have no proof, they decide to punish them again with utmost brutality.

At this point Jabal leaves the *nāẓir*'s house and moves into to the Ḥamdānite alley, only to discover that the man whom he has saved from the *futuwwa* will not keep silent about the murder. Realising the danger to his life, Jabal flees to Sūq al-Muqaṭṭam. Here he meets two girls fighting their way to the water-tap.

He helps them thereby earning the gratitude of their father, Balqītī, a professional snake-charmer (*ḥāwī*). Balqītī gives him shelter and teaches him his profession, and before long Jabal becomes a skillful snake-charmer; he marries his master's daughter, Shafīqa.

A few months later Jabal comes back to the Ḥamdānite alley, bringing with him his pregnant wife. He has an urgent message for his people : Jabalāwī has appeared to him and urged him to lead his people in the fight for their rights. He approaches the *nāẓir* on their behalf, but is turned contemptuously away.

Subsequently the whole area is afflicted with a plague of snakes. The *nāẓir* implores Jabal to charm the snakes away, promising in return to respect the rights of the Ḥamdānites. Yet once the houses are cleared of the snakes, the *nāẓir* goes back on his promise. Furthermore, he sends the *futuwwāt* to exterminate the clan of Ḥamdān once and for all. However, Jabal has foreseen his treachery and is not taken by surprise : as the *futuwwāt* are entering the Ḥamdānite close, they fall into a pit and are destroyed to the last man by the angry Ḥamdānites.

The *nāẓir* is helpless, but as a last ruse he offers Jabal the position of chief *futuwwa*. Jabal, however, insists on his people's share of the income, and the *nāẓir* is left with no choice but to grant it. Now the inhabitants of the neighbouring alleys come to Jabal, petitioning him to get them their rights. Jabal however, refuses, reminding them that they were unsympathetic to the Ḥamdānites in their plight. He rules over his people to the end of his days and metes out justice which, though occasionally harsh (literally, an eye for an eye) is impartial.

III — Rifā'a : A long time has passed since the days of Jabal, and the *futuwwāt* are once again in full control of the *Ḥāra*. In Jabal's alley lives a carpenter, Mu'allim Shāfi'ī and his wife, 'Abda. In order to avoid the *futuwwa* of the alley, with whom he is on bad terms, they leave the alley to Sūq al-Muqaṭṭam, where his pregnant wife might give birth in peace.

Many years pass; the *futuwwa* who hated Shāfi'ī dies and the family returns home. Their son Rifā'a, who was born in exile, is a slim, dreamy young man. His father opens a workshop and sets about re-establishing himself in the alley. His son, however, has befriended and old woman who holds séances to exorcise devils from the sick in mind and body. He is fascinated by her "trade" (which as a rule is practised by women). His parents try to arrange a marriage for him but Rifā'a is unwilling to marry. He runs away from home, staying for a while in the desert.

Shortly after his return he alarms his father by telling him that Jabalāwī has appeared to him at night, demanding that he, his beloved son, should do something for his people. Unlike Jabal, Rifā'a is averse to violence; indeed he has no interest whatever in such wordly matters as the *waqf* income or the *futuwwāt*; his sole purpose is to save his people from their own devils (*'afārīt*; sing. *'ifrīt*).

One day there is a violent commotion in the alley : the good people of the alley, are about to lynch a young prostitute, Yāsimina, for having an affair with the chief *futuwwa*, Bayyūmī, who is a non-Jabalite. Rifā'a interferes and offers to marry the sinner. A sad wedding takes place. But Yāsimīna is hurt by the fact that her husband is interested only in saving her soul. Neither she nor any other of the Jabalites is willing to undergo Rifā'a's treatment.

Rifā'a then moves to a different alley where he has more success : he cures many of the sick and a large number of people come under his influence. Among those whom he has saved are four young men of hitherto dubious repute. They become his devoted disciples. Yāsimīna, despairing of her husband's virility, soon resumes her liaison with Bayyūmī.

Meanwhile the *futuwwāt* and the *nāẓir* have grown suspicious of Rifā'a's activities, despite repeated assurances on his side to the effect that he has no interest in the *waqf*. A *futuwwa* tries to attack him, but the bystanders, of their own accord, rally to his defence, and are about to stone the man to death when Rifā'a intervenes and saves him. This incident convinces the *futuwwāt* that they must get rid of him.

News of the impending danger to his life reaches Rifā'a, and he is persuaded by his disciples to flee. Yāsimīna is unwilling to follow him and thus to be separated from her lover; she tells Bayyūmī of Rifā'a's plan to flee and the *futuwwāt* are able to capture the party. Under cover of darkness they drag Rifā'a to the desert where they kill and bury him.

In their grief, his disciples dig up the body and carry it away secretly to the cemetery. Then they take refuge in the desert. With some reluctance they accept the advice of one of their number, named 'Alī, to take vengeance on the killers. The *futuwwāt* are soon alarmed by the fact that many of their friends are being mysteriously murdered. Yāsimīna too falls into the hands of the disciples and suffers the same fate.

There is a persistent rumour that Rifā'a's body has been removed by Jabalāwī himself and taken to the big House, and in fact neither the *futuwwāt* nor Rifā'a's parents are able to find it. Finally the disciples come face to face with the *futuwwāt* in a pitched battle and kill their leader, Bayyūmī.

The *nāẓir* summons the triumphant disciples and appoints 'Alī head-man (virtually *futuwwa*) of Rifā'a's alley. He also allows the disciples their share of the income from the *waqf*, which they distribute equally among the Rifā'ites. Thus a short while after Rifā'a's death his followers take control of the alley—a possibility which would never have occurred to him.

IV — Qāsim : Qāsim is an orphan from Ḥayy al-Jarābī' ('Jerboas' alley') which borders the alleys of both the Jabalites and the Rifā'ites. He has grown up in the house of his uncle, Zakariyyā, a poor itinerant potato-seller. At an early age he began to accompany his uncle to help him on his rounds. He has also met Yaḥyā, a former Rifā'ite who has left his people for another district; and through him Qāsim has learned much about Rifā'a, Jabal and Jabalāwī and has been fascinated by what he heard.

But Qāsim's uncle has a son, Ḥasan, and when he is old enough to help his father, Qāsim has to make way for him. He himself becomes a hired shepherd. Among those who employ him is Qamar, a rich widow of forty, who treats him with great kindness. One day when a dispute has broken out among the *futuwwāt* and it seems as if the matter will end in violence, Qāsim intervenes and manages with great ingenuity to bring peace. As a result he rises in popular esteem and Qamar hints that although he is only a poor shepherd, she would be willing to accept him as her husband. They are married and Qāsim ceases to mind sheep and instead manages his wife's property.

Yet his personal happiness does not shield him from disquieting thoughts :

he compares his own lot with that of the other inhabitants of the *Ḥāra* and is appalled by their misery. One night he fails to return home. His friends search for him and eventually find him in the house of his friend Yaḥyā, where he is sleeping after having fainted in the nearby desert. When he has recovered, he tells Qamar that while he was meditating in the desert, Qindīl, Jabalāwī's servant, came to him to tell him that Jabalāwī is aware of the plight of his descendants and that he urges Qāsim to restore justice to all his children.

Qamar accepts the story without hesitation and becomes Qāsim's first and staunchest supporter. Then his cousin Ḥasan and their friend Ṣādiq similarly come to believe. Yet his older relatives are dubious : they are apprehensive of the attitude which the *nāẓir* and *futuwwāt* might take since Qāsim is claiming that his mission is to the whole of the *Ḥāra*, a much bolder claim than that of either Jabal or Rifā'a. He further claims that his principles combine the best of those of Jabal and Rifā'a : his aim was to establish an era of mercy, which is to be achieved through violent strife. He establishes a club for young men with the overt purpose of gymnastic exercise, but in fact with the intention of recruiting and training supporters.

A drunken follower however reveals some of their secrets and the Qāsimites are afraid lest they reach the ears of the *futuwwāt*. To forestall this, they decide to take the initiative by suing the *nāẓir* himself in the *sharī'a* court for misconduct in the management of the *waqf*. They approach a lawyer, who pretends to be interested in their case, but promptly informs the *nāẓir* of the whole affair. Qāsim is summoned before the *nāẓir* who threatens him; Qāsim remains unmoved. Next, he is placed under virtual house arrest and is not allowed to meet his friends. However, the *nāẓir* does not dare to take harsher measures because of Qāsim's social standing, being Qamar's husband. While trying to visit Qāsim, one of his followers is struck to death by a *futuwwa*. During the funeral Qāsim instructs his men to leave the *Ḥāra* to some distant place where the club can be set up again. One by one they leave for the mountain where they form a community of their own. Meanwhile Qāsim, whose beloved wife has died, stays alone in the *Ḥāra*. The *futuwwāt* are exasperated by the disappearance of Qāsim's followers and attempt to kill him, but he is warned in time, and manages to escape and join his followers.

His life has been saved by Ṣādiq's sister, Badriyya, who though only twelve years old, is a resourceful and courageous girl : Qāsim is prevailed upon to marry her.

Qāsim's men feel more confident and grow bolder. News reaches them that the *futuwwa* who killed their fellow is to be married. Qāsim's men attack the wedding procession killing the *futuwwa* and routing his men.

The *futuwwāt* now lead a mob from the *Ḥāra* to Qāsim's place in the mountain. After a brief siege, the attackers divide into two parties in an attempt to outflank the rebels. For a while the issue is in the balance, but is decided when Ḥasan kills the chief of the *futuwwāt* and Qāsim succeeds in deceiving one party of the enemy into believing that the other party has been destroyed, and so causing them to retreat in haste.

The *nāẓir* now orders the *futuwwāt* to starve the Qāsimite community into surrender. However, before a siege can be imposed, Ḥajjāj, the *futuwwa* of Rifā'a's alley is mysteriously murdered. The Rifā'ites accuse the Jabalites of killing him so as to secure the post of chief *futuwwa*, now vacant, for their own man. Fighting breaks out between the two groups, but ceases when Qāsim and his men descend from their stronghold. Qāsim manages to persuade most of the people that he has no quarrel with them but only with the *futuwwāt*. The people desert their leaders, who are left to fight alone against Qāsim's men; soon they are all killed.

The *nāẓir* flees and Qāsim replaces him as ruler of all the *Ḥāra*. He redistributes the *waqf* income equally (for the first time women are given a share), and the people of the *Ḥāra* live in peace and brotherhood. Qāsim wins their affection not only by his abilities as a leader but also by his virility (he marries many times in later years).

V — *'Arafa* : An unspecified period of time has passed. To the *Ḥāra* comes a young man named 'Arafa and his younger brother Ḥanash. They settle in the basement of an old house between the alleys of Rifā'a and Qāsim. 'Arafa is a magician (*sāḥir*). It later emerges that he is the bastard son of a woman of the *Ḥāra* who was ill-treated by the *futuwwāt* and driven out of her home; the brothers have returned to the *Ḥāra* to avenge her. They work day and night in an inner chamber trying to produce by magic an explosive which would serve as a weapon against the *futuwwāt*.

Meanwhile 'Arafa falls in love with 'Awāṭif, the daughter of a poor coffee-stall owner. The girl seems to return his affection, but there is an obstacle to their union : Sanṭūrī, the *futuwwa* of the Qāsimites, is showing an ominous interest in the girl. 'Awāṭif's father, in a fit of rage, speaks out against the *futuwwāt*; he is beaten up by Sanṭūrī and dies on the following day leaving his daughter to the mercy of the *futuwwa*.

'Arafa, however, secretly marries 'Awāṭif, with the approval of the Rifā'ite *futuwwa*. Sanṭūrī flies into a rage, and violence is averted only by the intervention of the chief *futuwwa*.

'Awāṭif is alarmed when her husband tells her that he refuses to accept without question the stories about their great ancestor Jabalāwī, and that he is determined to get into the Big House, where none has set foot since the days of Adham. His mission is to find out whether there really is a secret *waqf* document, and if there is, what it contains. With the help of Ḥanash, 'Arafa tunnels under the high wall of the house and manages to get into Jabalāwī's bedroom by night. However he stumbles over an old black man who was sleeping there. In panic he strangles the man and flees the house without seeing the document.

Next day an alarming rumour spreads : Jabalāwī has died, heart-broken at the murder of his faithful servant. The whole *Ḥāra* is thrown into a tumult of grief and wrath, but is unable to find the culprit. 'Arafa himself is dumbfounded and full of remorse; he realizes, paradoxically, that it is only now, when Jabalāwī is dead, that he believes the stories told of him. Moreover he now understands the significance of Jabalāwī's life to the *Ḥāra*. He resolves to work hard at his magic so that he will be able to bring Jabalāwī back to life. He is intent, too, on destroying the *futuwwāt* once and for all, not only to avenge his mother and 'Awāṭif's father, but also for the sake of all the people; for he believes that, were the *futuwwāt* destroyed and out of the way and the *waqf* revenue justly distributed, everyone in the *Ḥāra* would be able to practice magic, and that in this way the secrets of eternal life would be revealed.

He steals into the house of the chief *futuwwa* and stabs him to death. The *futuwwā*'s henchmen pursue him, but he routs them by throwing his explosive device in their faces. He escapes, confident that no one has recognized him.

Next day, however, 'Arafa is summoned to the presence of the *nāẓir* who has discovered that he is the killer of both the *futuwwa* and Jabalāwī's servant. The *nāẓir* proposes a deal : he will not reveal 'Arafa's guilt, and in return 'Arafa must work for him and supply him with the secret weapon. With this he would be able to rule the *Ḥāra* without having to rely on the *futuwwāt*. 'Arafa accepts the offer under duress. His explosives, which were devised to save the people, now serve to strengthen the *nāẓir*'s grip on them. The *nāẓir* proceeds to destroy the *futuwwāt*, and to set up 'Arafa and his family in the house of the chief *futuwwa*. He sees to it that 'Arafa is not disturbed in his work and that he is unable to escape.

'Arafa, frustrated and depressed, takes to drink and hashish. 'Awāṭif leaves him after surprising him in the garden with a housemaid.

Late one night, when he is returning from the *nāẓir*'s house under the influence of hashish, 'Arafa meets—or so he imagines—an old woman who claims to be Jabalāwī's housemaid. She tells him that Jabalāwī, as he lay dying, asked her to go to 'Arafa and assure him that he had his blessing. 'Arafa takes heart : he resolves to escape from the *nāẓir*'s clutches. Accompanied by Ḥanash, he leaves by night, taking with him nothing but a notebook which contains the secret of his magic. Ḥanash succeeds in escaping but 'Arafa stops off at 'Awāṭif's house in an attempt to persuade her to come with him, and is caught by the *nāẓir*'s men. As he is being led away, he throws his precious notebook on a rubbish heap.

'Arafa and his wife are buried alive. The people of the *Ḥāra* do not mourn for the man, since they hold him responsible not only for Jabalāwī's death, but also for supplying the *nāẓir* with the terrible weapon. Soon, however, their attitude changes and they realise that he was striving for their own good. Later they learn that Ḥanash has secretly returned to search for the lost notebook; it is even rumoured that he has found it and that he will use 'Arafa's devices to save them all. Many young men disappear from the *Ḥāra* and it is believed that they have joined Ḥanash. The *Ḥāra* regains its hope that some day evil will be overcome.

al-Liṣṣ wal-kilāb (1961)

Like Samson, Sa'īd Mahrān, a once all-powerful thief, is betrayed and thus becomes helpless and desperate, "like any other man." He, too, is motivated by revenge, but unlike the hero of olden days, Sa'īd could not avenge himself, not even in a "let me die with the Philistines" fashion.

We first meet Sa'īd on his leaving prison after serving a four-year sentence. Without delay he sets off for the old Cairene quarter where his former wife, Nabawiyya, and his former assistant, 'Ilīsh, occupy his old home as man and wife. He is more than convinced that these two not only caused his imprisonment, but also laid hands on his money. He is determined to take back his daughter, Sanā' (now five years of age) and punish the traitors.

He discovers before long that 'Ilīsh, with the help of the authorities, has taken ample precautions against him. Sanā', on her side, does not recognise her father, and turns away from him.

Sa'īd then goes to the Ṣūfī shaykh, 'Alī al-Junaydī, his late father's spiritual guide, seeking shelter, both physical and spiritual. He is given a temporary dwelling, but the mystical utterances of the shaykh do not quench his passion, nor do they solve his worldly problems.

His last hope lies in Ra'ūf 'Ilwān, a journalist, who in the past was a staunch fighter for the rights of the poor (apparently an extreme Leftist), and who educated Sa'īd and provided moral justification for his "profession" in terms of Class Doctrine. But much to Sa'īd's despair, Ra'ūf has meanwhile backed out of his past convictions and become a respectable and rich journalist. Sa'īd, finding his old friend lukewarm and evasive, listens with disgust to his advice "to start a new life."

Ra'ūf, then, is a traitor too. In fact he is now treachery incarnate, and is to be punished as well. Sa'īd makes his first attack by attempting to break into Ra'ūf's luxurious home at night, but the latter is on guard and catches him red-handed. Only Sa'īd's penitent words stop him from calling the police.

His next attempt, this time against 'Ilīsh, is even more lamentable; he acquires a pistol, steals a car, and attacks the traitor's house, but 'Ilīsh and his wife have, in anticipation of such an assault, already left the house for an unknown, destination. Sa'īd's bullets, therefore, kill the innocent man who has occupied the flat.

Now Sa'īd is again an outlaw wanted, this time, as a murderer. The press, and especially Ra'ūf's newspaper, incite the public against him. He finds refuge with Nūr, a prostitute who in the past was in love with him and is still, luckily enough, as affectionate. At her home on the edge of the city, facing the cemetery, he contemplates and plans his next move of revenge, this time directed against Ra'ūf.

But fate again frustrates him, and his bullets kill Ra'ūf's door-keeper instead of his master.

The entire police force is now after Sa'īd. The press keeps the issue at boiling-point, with Ra'ūf's paper particularly vocal in demanding that the culprit be found and punished. Sa'īd thus becomes virtually a prisoner of Nūr's flat, totally dependent on her for his food and news.

The final blow comes to Sa'īd when Nūr suddenly disappears, leaving him desolate, hungry, and helpless. The bitter end follows when, starving, he leaves his hideout in search of food. He is trapped in the cemetery by the police dogs. He refuses to surrender and is shot dead among the graves.

al-Summān wal-kharīf (1962)

'Īsā al-Dabbāgh, a young but high-ranking civil servant, returns to Cairo from an inspection mission during the battles in the Canal zone to find Cairo in flames (i.e., the so-called "black Saturday" on 26 January 1952). Being a rising Wafdist functionary, he immediately comprehends the gravity of the incidents and, indeed, the political events which ensue bring about the downfall of his party's government. He himself is demoted to a lesser position.

'Īsā, however, takes it as yet another interlude in the varying fortunes of his party. He decides to take this opportunity to look after his private affairs. He proceeds to arrange his engagement to Salwā, daughter of a prominent judge and a king's protégé. The date of the marriage is fixed for August.

On July 23rd the officers' coup d'état takes place. The Wafd is regarded by the new rulers as part and parcel of the *ancien régime*, and its members find to their distress that they are not favoured, nor is their patriotic past remembered. A committee investigates 'Īsā and finds him guilty of favouritism and bribery. As a result he loses his job. A second and more severe blow comes when his fiancée's family sever his engagement to Salwā. Everything that 'Īsā has built is now in ruins.

His cousin Ḥasan, who rises to prominence through affiliating with the new régime, offers him a position in a state-owned firm, but 'Īsā obstinately refuses to accept it. He feels that Ḥasan is helping him because he wants him to marry his sister, to whom he is indifferent. He spends his days idly, meeting his former political friends in a café.

A few months later 'Īsā decides to leave Cairo for a while and move to Alexandria. His mother and married sisters try to dissuade him but to no avail. In Alexandria he rents a flat in a Greek quarter, finding it a further escape from the Egyptian scene. He spends his days roaming around on the beach, recollecting the past, nurturing his melancholic thoughts, drinking. One autumn night he takes home a young prostitute, Rīrī. Being homeless, the girl implores him to keep her in his flat to serve him and keep him company. 'Īsā reluctantly accepts her, and in time finds himself enjoying her company. However he ruthlessly throws her out when he discovers that she is carrying his child.

News arrives of his mother's death, which brings 'Īsā back to Cairo. Here he learns that his cousin Ḥasan is now engaged to Salwā, his former fiancée, a fact which deepens his alienation and distrust of the new régime, personified by Ḥasan.

'Īsā sells his mother's house to a rich old widow and in the course of the transaction meets her daughter, Qadriyya, who is not young, thrice divorced, and sterile. Nevertheless he decides to marry her because she will be a "life-long insurance."

The Suez Canal is nationalized. This he welcomes rationally but is at one and the same time maliciously envious. His alienation from the new régime however, is mitigated when Egypt is attacked in October 1956. His patriotic feelings are aroused and he is disgusted to find that some of his old friends, though paying lip-service to the régime, are so corrupt as to rejoice in the perilous position in which Egypt finds itself.

The short war is over, and gone is the danger; the gulf between 'Īsā and the revolution widens again. Lack of employment, lack of idealism, frustration, and lack of interest in his wife—all these make him indulge in gambling and drinking in the resort of Rās al-Barr to an extent that even his placid wife cannot endure, and she finally locks him out one night. They are re-united thanks to the good offices of friends; and in order to separate 'Īsā from his gambling company, the couple leave the resort for the beach of Alexandria.

There 'Īsā stumbles upon Rīrī and her daughter—undoubtedly his own. The young woman is no longer a homeless prostitute. She owns a beach bar, and her daughter is cared for by a servant. His enquiries show further that she is married to a good, old man who had consented to adopt the girl and to accept Rīrī as a wife. 'Īsā suddenly decides to change direction, face the truth resolutely, and accept Rīrī and their common daughter. But Rīrī responds furiously, refusing to listen to his pleas.

In the last chapter we meet 'Īsā sitting in the dark under the statue of Sa'd Zag͟hlūl, when a familiar figure approaches him. He is a young revolutionary whom

'Īsā had met in rather unpleasant circumstances; a few years earlier he was present when the youth was arrested and interrogated. The man is now in his prime, buoyant, healthy, and holding a red rose in his left hand.

Much to 'Īsā's surprise, he addresses him in a friendly manner and invites him to discuss "the world around us." He even shows sympathy for 'Īsā's downfall. Finding no response from 'Īsā, the youth takes his leave. But a sudden gust of enthusiasm overtakes 'Īsā and he rises and strides in the man's wake, hoping to catch him before he has gone too far.

al-Ṭarīq (1964)

"The whole story is like a dream; I came from Alexandria in search of my father. Strange occurrences took place which caused me to forget my original task and finally I found myself in jail." In these words Ṣābir, the hero of the novel, sums up the essence of his story.

Ṣābir is a handsome Alexandrian youth whose mother, a former doyenne of the underworld, has spent five years in prison. On her deathbed she tells her spoilt son that his father is Sayyid Sayyid al-Raḥīmī, a rich man of an aristocratic Cairene family. She urges Ṣābir to search for him in the hope that he will provide for his son. Ṣābir leaves for Cairo, where he stays in a small hotel. His search proves tiresome and frustrating, but in the meantime Ṣābir becomes involved with two women. The first, Karīma, is the young wife of the aged hotel proprietor. She secretly spends her nights with him. The second, Ilhām, a secretary in a newspaper office, is intelligent, modest and unaffected. Ṣābir quickly falls in love with her.

Weeks pass without a sign of the father. Ṣābir's money is gradually depleted and having no profession or connections in Cairo, he agrees to Karīma's plot to kill her husband and share his fortune, to which Karīma is the sole heir. The murder is carried out, and the police open an investigation. The hotel's servant is arrested as a suspect.

Karīma, now staying with her mother, fails to communicate with Ṣābir, who is penniless and desolate. The dead husband's assistant, Muḥammad al-Sāwī, kindles his spleen against Karīma by hinting at certain past intimacies between her and the arrested servant. Further he discloses some unknown facts about Karīma's past. Thus Ṣābir learns that she was married to a relative, a man of the underworld. The old man, falling in love with her, virtually bought her away from her first husband. Al-Sāwī asserts that during her monthly visits to her mother she used to meet her former husband. He also suggests that the whole murder was planned by the ex-husband.

Ṣābir, overcome by jealousy and shocked by the possibility that he is being duped, steals out of the hotel at night to see Karīma. He accuses her of treachery, but she denies the story as utter madness, and reasserts her love for him. Hurried steps are heard in the night. The police arrive. In his despair Ṣābir strangles his mistress.

In prison he discovers that al-Sāwī's story was in effect a trap arranged by the police to lure him to Karīma's house. They had suspected Ṣābir from the outset, and were looking for incriminating evidence.

Ṣābir is accused of the two murders. The case becomes a sensation and the press makes a great story of Ṣābir's past in all its details. Ilhām, does not desert him at this point. She sends a lawyer to help his desperate case. The lawyer reveals to him the true identity of his father; he is a tycoon who lives in different countries and with several women, but whose present address is unknown. It turns out that the father had visited Egypt—and even Alexandria—at precisely the time that Ṣābir set out in search of him.

As expected, the court sentences him to death, and his only hope now, a poor one though it be, is that the appeal court will consider the extenuating circumstances and change the verdict to life imprisonment.

al-Shaḥḥādh (1965)

'Umar al-Ḥamzāwī is a successful Cairene lawyer of forty-five, happily married and father of two daughters. However, sudden weariness attacks him, rendering him bored and unable to work or enjoy life. A doctor whom he consults finds nothing wrong with his health, but advises him to take leave from work and engage in exercise.

'Umar and his family spend a holiday at the beach of Alexandria at the end of which he feels physically more fit. Yet, on returning to Cairo he once again loses interest in everything. He is filled with a feeling of barrenness and lethargy, and he is unmoved even when his wife announces that she is again pregnant.

He now tries to find stimulations of a different nature; he accompanies his friend Muṣṭafā al-Mīnāwī, a popular broadcaster, to night clubs and finds a certain relief in flirting. Eventually he meets a cabaret-dancer, Warda, with whom he soon becomes infatuated. He rents a luxurious flat for her, and there spends the best part of his time. Feeling utterly happy and content, he finally deserts his family to live with her.

His love, however, soon fades away. He grows bored with Warda, and embarks upon further adventures.

The appeal of women finally vanishes and 'Umar finds more comfort in nocturnal solitude, meditations and the mystical poetry of the East. At one point, when meditating in the desert, he catches a moment of heavenly bliss, of harmony and certitude.

Zaynab, his wife, gives birth to a boy and 'Umar is prevailed upon to rejoin his family. He complies without much enthusiasm. Meanwhile an old friend of his, 'Uthmān Khalīl, is released from prison after having served a twenty-year sentence. (He had been caught in revolutionary activities to which 'Umar and Muṣṭafā were also party; they were saved from a similar fate through 'Uthmān's sacrifice.) 'Uthmān, it turns out, is still as radical as ever. He is unwilling to modify his views and accept the present Egyptian régime (the plot takes place in the nineteen-sixties) as the realization of his old dreams. Furthermore, he is baffled and dismayed by the change that has come upon his friends. Admittedly, they do not disown him, and 'Umar puts at his disposal the facilities of his own office ('Uthmān, too, being a lawyer by profession). Yet they have drifted from the ideal of socialist revolution, and have become rich, fat and cynical. Nor can he understand 'Umar's weird mystical escapades. Strangely enough he finds a common language with Buthayna, 'Umar's daughter, a school-girl of considerable maturity, who (like her father in his youth) tries her hand at poetry.

The family's reunion does not last long. As time passes 'Umar's zest for mysticism gathers force, until he finally decides to give up everything to seek absolute solitude in an unknown spot, away from the worldly hustle and bustle. He finds himself a far-off hut, surrounded by shrubs, where he spends a year and a half in meditations and wild-dreams. He arrives at a stage where fancy and reality intermingle and hallucinations take full control of him. His family and friends, who have discovered his hide-out, refrain from intruding upon his solitude.

However, one day 'Uthmān breaks into his privacy. The old revolutionary is once again in trouble. He is sought by the police, and has come to his friend seeking refuge. Moreover, 'Uthmān has an exciting piece of news; he has married Buthayna, who is now expecting a child. But these tidings fail to shake 'Umar out of his stupor. 'Uthmān despairs and is about to leave when the police surround the hut. 'Uthmān is arrested, and 'Umar is wounded by a stray bullet. The two friends are taken in a police van back to the world of men, while the delirious 'Umar is still in the grip of his feverish visions, craving for the ineffable.

Tharthara fawq al-Nīl (1966)

Cairo 1964. In a Nile houseboat (*'awwāma*) a group of middle-aged addicts gather nightly to indulge in drugs and sex. They are of a rather high social status (a popular cinema actor, a lawyer, a journalist, a writer, etc.). The member who is in charge of the *'awwāma*, however, is a minor civil servant, Anīs Zakī. He is a widower (his wife and infant daughter having died many years before) and is at any time, including office hours, under the effect of drugs. He resides in the *'awwāma*, never leaving it except for his office. He is well-read in history and mysticism and his days pass in "historical" fantasies.

A young female journalist, Sammāra Bahjat, is introduced into the *'awwāma* by one of its members. In fact she is an idealist and has no interest in drugs. The apparent reason for her frequenting the houseboat is to collect material for a projected play in which she will tackle the problem of anti-social characters.

Anīs stumbles upon Sammāra's handbag, and being in an aggressive mood, he opens it and reads her diary, in which was outlined the plan for her play. He finds her comments on the *'awwama*'s members patronizing and rather malicious. Next evening, as the party gathers, he puts Sammāra in an unpleasant position when he quotes her remarks about them, thus causing general irritation. He does not disclose, however, that those were Sammāra's views. Later he returns the diary, but not before harshly taunting her.

The Hijra Festival arrives, and a member of the group suggests that they go for a noctural drive in the fresh air. The whole group—nine in all—squeeze into Rajab's car and head for Saqqāra. When the company leaves the car for a walk, Rajab tries to make love to Sammāra, but she remains uncommitteed. On the way back, Rajab accelerates in a frightening manner, killing a pedestrian. Rajab and all the rest—with Sammāra protesting—decide to drive away and refrain from reporting the accident to the police.

Anīs, who spends a sleepless night, next morning slumbers in his office, and when his chief gives him a warning. Anīs behaves in an insulting manner, subsequently losing his job.

When the friends meet that evening—all of them having spent a terrible night—

they set about trying to persuade Sammāra that it would be senseless to report the accident, and that such an act would only result in a public scandal. But just as Sammāra shows signs of consenting, in comes the silent, unworldly Anīs to declare that justice should take its course. He threatens to step out of the boat at once and inform the police about the accident. The whole group—including Sammāra—now engage in an attempt to suppress the unanticipated eruption. Rajab offends Anīs and the two engage in a ferocious fight. The friends separate them but Rajab shouts that he is determined to kill Anīs there and then. Finally the actor himself rushes out of the boat, declaring that he is going to inform the police. Everyone runs after him, leaving Anīs and Sammāra alone in the *'awwāma*. Anīs now explains that his threat was intended only to test the ensuing reactions and that Sammāra herself did not withstand the test. Furthermore, he claims that he was also jealous of Rajab. But before Sammāra is able to find out how serious his confessions are, he takes a dose of drugs, and, in a second, is once again engulfed in his hallucinations.

BIBLIOGRAPHY

A. *The Works of Maḥfūẓ*

Abbreviation	Full Title		First Published[1]	Imprint Used[2]
	NOVELS			
ABA	*'Abath al aqdār* ('The Mockery of Fate')		1939	[1958]
RAD	*Rādūbīs*		1943	[1963]
KIF	*Kifāḥ Ṭība* ('Thebes' Struggle')		1944	[1964]
KHAN	*Khān al-Khalīlī*		1945	[1964]
QAH	*al-Qāhira al-jadīda* ('New Cairo')		1946	[1962]
ZUQ	*Zuqāq al-Midaqq*		1947(?)	[1965]
SAR	*al-Sarāb* ('Mirage')		1949(?)	[1964]
BID	*Bidāya wa-nihāya* ('A Beginning and an End')		1951(?)	[1965]
TR-I	*Bayn al-Qaṣrayn*	THE TRILOGY	1956	[1964]
TR-II	*Qaṣr al-Shawq*	THE TRILOGY	1957	[1964]
TR-III	*al-Sukkariyya*	THE TRILOGY	1957	[1964]
AWL	*Awlād Ḥāratinā* ('Children of our Quarter')		1959[3]	[1967]
LISS	*al-Liṣṣ wal-kilāb* ('The Thief and the Dogs')		1961	[1964]
SUM	*al-Summān wal-kharīf* ('Quail and Autumn')		1962	[1964]
TARIQ	*al-Ṭarīq* ('The Way', 'The Road')		1964	[1964]
SHAH	*al-Shaḥḥādh* ('The Beggar')		1965	[1965]

[1] See Appendix I.

[2] See Appendix I

[3] Serialized in *al-Ahrām*, between 21 Sept. and 25 Dec. 1959. First published as a book in Beirut (Dār al-Ādāb), 1967.

THAR	*Tharthara fawq al-Nīl* ('Chit-Chat on the Nile')	1966	[1966]
MIR	*Mīrāmār*	1967	[1967]

STORIES

HAMS	*Hams al-junūn* ('The Whispering of Madness')	1938(?)	[1963]
DUN	*Dunyā Allāh* ('The World of God')	1963	[1963]
BAYT	*Bayt sayyi' al-sum'a* ('A House of Ill-Repute')	1965	[1965]
	Khammarat al-qiṭṭ al-aswad ('The Black Cat Tavern')	1968	
	Taḥt al-miẓalla ('Under the Awning')	1969	
	Ḥikāya bilā bidāya walā nihāya ('A Story Without Beginning or End')	1971	
	Shahr al-'asal ('Honeymoon')	1971	

B. *General Bibliography*

'Abd al-Ḥayy, 'Abd al-Tawwāb. *'Aṣīr Ḥayātī.* Cairo, n.d.

'Abd al-Malik, Anwar (Abdel-Malik, Anouar). *Dirāsāt fil-thaqāfa al-waṭaniyya.* Beirut, 1967.

——, *Egypte Société Militaire.* Paris, 1962.

'Abd al-Ṣabūr, Ṣalāḥ. *Ḥattā naqhar al-mawt.* Beirut, 1966.

——, *Wa-tabqā al-Kalima.* Beirut, 1970.

Abdel-Meguid, Abdel-Aziz. *The Modern Arabic Short Story—Its Emergence, Development, and Form.* Cairo, n.d.

Abū Ḥadīd, Muḥammad Farīd. *Ibnat al-mamlūk* (a novel). 2 vols. Cairo, 1926.

al-Adab al-'Arabī al-mu'āṣir (proceedings of conference on modern Arabic literature, held in Rome, October 1961). [Paris, 1962].

Adams, Charles C. *Islam and Modernism in Egypt.* London, 1933.

Adham (Edham), Ismā'īl, and Najī (Nagi), Ibrāhīm. *Tawfīq al-Ḥakīm.* Cairo, 1945. (English title : Tewfik El-Hakim.)

Allen, Walter. *The English Novel : a Short Critical History.* London, 1963.

——, *Tradition and Dream : a Critical Survey of English and American Fiction from the 1920's to the Present Day.* Penguin, 1964.

al-'Ālim, Maḥmūd Amīn and Anīs, 'Abd al-'Aẓīm. *Fil-thaqāfa al-Miṣriyya.* Beirut, 1955.

al-'Ālim, Maḥmūd Amīn. *Ta'ammulāt fī 'ālam Najīb Maḥfūẓ.* Cairo, 1970.

Allot, Miriam. *Novelists on the Novel.* London, 1965.

Amīn, Aḥmad. *Qāmūs al-'ādāt wal-taqālīd wal-ta'ābīr al-Miṣriyya.* Cairo, 1953.

al-'Aqqad, 'Abbās Maḥmūd. *Sāra* (a novel). Cairo, 1938.

Auerbach, Erich. *Mimesis : The Representation of Reality in Western Literature.* (Trans. Willard Trask). N.Y., 1957.

ʿAwaḍ, Louis. *Dirāsāt ʿArabiyya wa-gharbiyya.* Cairo, 1965.

——, *Dirāsāt fī-adabinā al-ḥadīth : al-masraḥ, al-shiʿr, al-qiṣṣa.* Cairo, 1961.

——, *Maqālāt fil-naqd wal-adab.* Cairo, n.d. [1963]. (In the inner title page : *Dirāsāt fil-naqd wal-adab.*)

——, *al-Thawra wal-adab.* Cairo, 1967.

ʿAyyad, Shukrī Muḥammad. *Tajārib fil-adab wal-naqd.* Cairo, 1967.

Badr, ʿAbd al-Muḥsin Ṭāhā. *Taṭawwur al-riwāya al-ʿArabiyya al-ḥadītha fī Miṣr, 1870-1938.* Cairo, 1963.

Bākathīr, ʿAlī Aḥmad. *al-Thaʾir al-aḥmar* (a novel). Cairo, 1953.

Brockelmann, C. *Geschichte der arabischen Litteratur.* Dritter Supplementband. Leiden, 1942.

Booth, Wayne C. *The Rhetoric of Fiction.* Chicago and London, 1965.

Cachia, Pierre. *Ṭāhā Ḥusayn : His Place in the Egyptian Literary Renaissance.* London, 1956.

Cheikho, L. *Taʾrīkh al-ādāb al-ʿArabiyya fil-rubʿ al-awwal min al-qarn al-ʿishrīn.* Beirut, 1926.

Dāghir, Yūsuf Asʿad. *Maṣādir al-dirāsa al-adabiyya : II. al-Rāḥilūn 1800-1955.* Beirut, 1955.

Dawwāra, Fuʾād. *ʿAshrat udabāʾ yataḥaddathūn.* Cairo, 1965.

Ḍayf, Shawqī. *al-Adab al-ʿArabī al-muʿāṣir fī Miṣr.* Second revised edition. Cairo, 1961.

Forster, E.M. *Aspects of the Novel.* Penguin, 1964.

Freedman, Ralph. *The Lyrical Novel : Studies in Hermann Hesse, André Gide and Virginia Woolf.* Princeton and London, 1963.

Friedman, Norman. "Point of View in Fiction : the Development of a Critical Concept." PMLA LXX (1955), pp. 1160-84.

Fuʾād, Nīʿmāt Aḥmad. *Adab al-Māzinī.* Second revised edition. Cairo, 1961.

Gardiner, Allen. *Egypt of the Pharaohs.* London, 1964.

Gardner, Helen. *The Business of Criticism.* London, 1966.

Gibb, H.A.R. *Studies on the Civilization of Islam.* London, 1962.

——, *Arabic Literature : An Introduction.* Second revised edition. Oxford, 1963.

al-Ḥakīm, Tawfīq. *ʿAwdat al-rūḥ* (a novel). Cairo, 1933.

——, *al-Ribāṭ al-muqaddas* (a novel). Cairo, 1944.

Harvey, W.J. *Character and the Novel.* London, 1965.

Haykal, Muḥammad Ḥusayn. *Zaynab : manāẓir wa-akhlāq rīfiyya* (a novel). Second edition. Cairo, n.d. [1929].

El-Hazmi, Mansour Ibrahim. "The Modern Arabic Historical Novel." Unpublished thesis submitted for the degree of Doctor of Philosophy, The University of London, SOAS, 1966.

Ḥaqqī, Yaḥyā. *Fajr al-qiṣṣa al-Miṣriyya.* Cairo, n.d. [1960].

——, *Qindīl umm Hāshim* (a short novel). Cairo, 1944.

Hourani, Albert. *Arabic Thought in the Liberal Age, 1798-1939.* London, 1962.

Humphrey, Robert. *Stream of Conciousness in the Modern Novel.* Berkeley and Los Angeles, 1965.

Ḥusayn, Ṭāhā. *Min adabinā al-muʿāṣir.* Second edition. Cairo, 1959.

——, *Naqd wa-iṣlāḥ.* Second edition. Beirut, 1960.

——, *al-Ayyām.* Vol. I. Cairo, 1942.

——, *Du'ā' al-karawān* (a novel). Cairo, 1942.

——, *Shajarat al-bu's* (a novel). Cairo, 1944.

al-'Iryān, Muḥammad Sa'īd. *'Alā bāb Zuwayla* (a novel). Cairo, 1947.

——, *Qaṭr al-Nadā* (a novel). Cairo, 1945.

James, William. *The Varieties of Religious Experience : A Study in Human Nature.* London, N.Y., Toronto, 1928.

al-Jundī, Anwar. *al-Muḥāfaẓa wal-tajdīd fil-nathr al-'Arabī al-mu'āṣir fī mi'at 'ām, 1840-1940.* Cairo, 1961.

Kāmil, 'Ādil. *Malik min shu'ā'* (a novel). Cairo, 1945.

——, *Millīm al-akbar* (a novel). Cairo, 1944.

Kettle, Arnold. *An Introduction to the English Novel.* Second edition. London, 1967.

Khemiri, T. and Kampffmeyer, G. *Leaders in Contemporary Arabic Literature.* Part I. Leipzig, Cairo, London, 1930.

Khiḍr, 'Abbās. *al-Qiṣṣa al-qaṣīra fī Miṣr, mundh nash'atihā ḥattā sanat 1930.* Cairo, 1966.

——, *al-Wāqi'iyya fil-adab.* Baghdad, 1967.

al-Khūlī, Amīn. *Fil-adab al-Miṣrī.* Cairo, 1943.

Krieger, Murray. *The Tragic Vision.* Chicago and London, 1966.

Lane, E.W. *Manners and Customs of the Modern Egyptians.* London, 1963.

Lāshīn, Ṭāhir. *Ḥawwā' bilā Ādam* (a novel). Cairo, n.d. [1934].

Liddel, Robert. *Some Principles of Fiction.* London, 1956.

——, *A Treatise on the Novel.* London, 1965.

Lodge, David. *Language of Fiction : Essays in Criticism and Verbal Analysis.* London and N.Y., 1966.

Lubbock, Percy. *The Craft of Fiction.* London, 1965.

Lukacs, G. *The Historical Novel.* (Trans. Stanley Mitchell). London, 1965.

al-Ma'addāwī, Anwar. *Kalimāt fil-adab.* Sidon-Beirut, 1966.

Mandūr, Muḥammad. *Fil-mīzān al-jadīd.* Third Edition. Cairo, n.d.

——, *Qaḍāyā jadīda fī adabinā al-ḥadīth.* Beirut, 1958.

al-Maqdisī (Makdisi), Anīs. *al-Funūn al-adabiyya wa-a'lāmuhā fil-nahḍa al-'Arabiyya al-ḥadītha.* Beirut, 1963.

al-Māzinī, Ibrāhīm 'Abd al-Qādir. *Ibrāhīm al-Kātib* (a novel). Second edition. Cairo, 1945.

Mendilow, A.A. *Time and the Novel.* New York, 1965.

Muḥammad, Muḥammad 'Awaḍ. *Sinūhī* (a novel). Cairo, 1944.

Muir, Edwin. *The Structure of the Novel.* Penguin, 1963.

Murry, J. Middleton. *The Problem of Style.* London, 1965.

Mūsā, Salāma. *Tarbiyat Salāmā Mūsā.* Cairo, 1958. (English translation by L.O. Schuman, *The Education of Salama Musa.* Leiden, 1961.)

al-Muwayliḥī, Muḥammad. *Ḥadīth 'Īsa bin Hishām, aw fatra min al-zaman.* Cairo, 1964.

Najm, Muḥammad Yūsuf. "Fahāris al-adab al-'Arabī al-ḥadīth." *al-Abḥāth,* Beirut. An. XVI. 1. (March 1963), pp. 53-153.

——, "al-Funūn al-adabiyya" in *al-Adab al-'Arabī fi 'āthār al-dārisīn.* Beirut, 1961, pp. 311-479.

——, *al-Qiṣṣa fil-adab al-'Arabī al-ḥadīth 1870-1914.* Second edition. Beirut, 1961.

al-Naqqāsh, Rajā'. *Aṣwāṭ Ghāḍiba.* Beirut, 1970.

——, *Udabā' Mu'āṣirūn.* Cairo, 1968.

Otto, Rudolf. *The Idea of the Holy.* (Trans. John W. Harvey). O.U.P., 1925.

Pérès, Henri. "Le Roman, le Conte et la Nouvelle dans la littérature arabe moderne." *Annales de l'Institut d'Études Orientales d'Alger*, Tome III. Paris 1937, pp. 266-337.
Quṭb, Sayyid. *Kutub wa-shakhṣiyyāt*. Cairo, 1946.
Rāghib, Nabīl. *Qaḍiyyat al-shakl al-fannī ʿind Najīb Maḥfūẓ*. Cairo, 1967.
al-Rāʿī, ʿAlī. *Dirāsāt fil-riwāya al-Miṣriyya*. Cairo, 1964.
Safran, Nadav. *Egypt in Search of Political Community : an Analysis of the intellectual and Political Evolution of Egypt, 1804-1952*. Cambridge, Mass., 1961.
Saʿīd, Nafūsa Zakariyya. *Ta'rīkh al-daʿwa ilā al-ʿāmmiyya wa-āthāruhā fī Miṣr*. Alexandria, 1964.
El-Sakkout, H.S.A. "The Egyptian Novel and its Main Trends, 1914-1952." Unpublished dissertation submitted for the degree of Doctor of Philosophy, The University of Cambridge, April, 1965.
Schuman, L.O. *Een moderne Arabische vertelling : Nagīb Maḥfūẓ, Awlād Ḥaritna*. Leiden, 1965.
Sebeob, Thomas (ed.). *Style in Language*. Mass., 1964.
Shafīq, Aḥmad. *Ḥawliyyāt Miṣr al-siyāsiyya*. 4 vols. Cairo, 1926-28.
al-Shārūnī, Yūsuf. *Dirāsāt adabiyya*. Cairo, n.d. [1965].
——, *Dirāsāt fil-adab al-ʿarabī al-muʿāṣir*. Cairo, 1964.
——, *Dirāsāt fil-riwāya wal-qiṣṣa al-qaṣīra*. Cairo, 1967.
Shawkat, Maḥmūd Ḥāmid. *al-Fann al-qiṣaṣī fil-adab al-ʿArabī al-ḥadīth*. Cairo, 1963.
Shipley, Joseph T. (ed.). *Dictionary of World Literature*. New Jersey, 1966.
Shukrī, Ghālī. *Azmat al-jins fil-qiṣṣa al-ʿArabiyya*. Beirut, 1963.
——, *Kalimāt min al-jazīra al-mahjūra*. Beirut-Sidon, 1964.
——, *al-Muntamī : dirāsa fī adab Najīb Maḥfūẓ*. Cairo, 1964. (Second enlarged edition, Cairo, 1969.)
——, *Salāma Mūsā wa-azmat al-ḍamīr al-ḥadīth*. Cairo, 1963.
——, *Thawrat al-fikr fī adabinā al-ḥadīth*. Cairo, 1965.
Ṣidqī, Jādhibiyya. *Ṣuwar Ḥayya*. Cairo, 1963.
Somekh, Sasson. *Dunyā Najīb Maḥfūẓ*. Tel Aviv, 1972.
Stewart, Philip. "*Awlad Haretna* by Neguib Mahfuz." Unpublished thesis presented for the degree of B. Litt., Oxford, 1963.
Tājir, Jack. *Ḥarakat al-tarjama bi-Miṣr khilāl al-qarn al-tāsiʿ ʿashar*. Cairo, n.d. [1946].
Ṭarāzī, Phillipe de. *Ta'rīkh al-ṣiḥāfa al-ʿArabiyya*. 4 vols. Beirut, 1913-33.
Taymūr, Maḥmūd. *Muḥāḍarāt fil-qaṣaṣ fil-adab al-ʿArabī : Māḍīh wa-ḥāḍirih*. Cairo, 1958.
——, *Nidā' al-majhūl* (a novel). Cairo, n.d. [1939].
Van-Ghent, Dorothy. *The English Novel : Form and Function*. N.Y., 1961.
Watt, Ian. *The Rise of the Novel*. Penguin, 1963.
[Watt, Ian and others.] *The Novelist as Innovator*. London (BBC), 1965.
Wellek, René and Warren, Austin. *Theory of Literature*. Penguin, 1963.
West, Paul. *The Modern Novel*. Second edition. London, 1967.
Wilson, Edmund. *Axel's Castle : a Study in the Imaginative Literature of 1870-1930*. London, 1964.
Yūnus, ʿAbd al-Ḥamīd. *al-Ẓāhir Baybars fil-qaṣaṣ al-shaʿbī*. Cairo, n.d. [1960].
Zaehner, R.C. *Mysticism : Sacred and Profane*. London, 1961.

C. *Articles and Reviews on Maḥfūẓ's Novels*

This list includes only such articles as were available to me in the course of my study. They are arranged, in each group, according to the dates of their appearance.

In addition to this list, most of Maḥfūẓ's novels are discussed at considerable length in Shukrī, *al-Muntamī*, Rāghib, *Qaḍiyyat al-shakl al fannī*, and al-ʿĀlim, *Ta'ammulāt*.

The following abbreviations refer to the Arabic periodicals :

A-I	=	*al-Ādāb*, Beirut (Monthly, 1953-).
A-II	=	*al-Adab*, Cairo (Monthly, 1956-1964).
A-III	=	*al-Adīb*, Beirut (Monthly, 1942-).
A-IV	=	*Adab*, Beirut (Quarterly, 1962-1963).
FM	=	*al-Fikr al-muʿāṣir*, Cairo (Monthly, 1962-).
H	=	*Ḥiwār*, Beirut (Bi-monthly, 1962-1967).
K	=	*al-Kātib*, Cairo (Monthly, 1961-).
KA	=	*Majallat al-kitāb al-ʿArabī*, Cairo Bi-monthly, 1964).
KM	=	*al-Kātib al-Miṣri*, Cairo (Monthly, 1945-1948).
M	=	*al-Majalla*, Cairo (Monthly, 1957-).
R	=	*al-Risāla*, Cairo (Weekly, 1933-1952).

The Historical Novels

Sayyid Quṭb, *R* 2 Oct. 44; Ḥamdī al-Saʿīd, *A-II* May 58. See also Shawkat, pp. 129-37; El-Hazmi's dissertation, pt. 3., Ch. 3.

Khān al-Khalīlī

Wadīʿ Falasṭīn, *R* 15 Oct. 45; Widād al-Sakākīnī, *R* 3 Dec. 45; Sayyid Quṭb, *R* 17 Dec. 45 (= *Kutub*, pp. 171-7). See also Mandūr, *Qaḍāya*, pp. 66-74.

al-Qāhira al-jadīda

Muḥammad Saʿīd al-ʿIryān, *KM* Sept. 46; Suhayl Idrīs, *A-III* Sept. 46; Tharwat Abāẓa, *R* 7 Oct. 46; Sayyid Quṭb, *R* 30 Dec. 46.

Zuqāq al-Midaqq

Tharwat Abāẓa, *R* 26 Jan. 48; Adīb Muruwwa, *A-III* Mar. 48; Tawfīq Ḥannā, *A-II* June 58. See also Ḥusayn, *Naqd*, pp. 115-24.

al-Sarāb

Tharwat Abāẓa, *R* 23 Jan. 50; Najiyya Faraḥ, *A-II* Nov. 60. See also al-Shārūnī, *Dirāsāt fil-adab*, pp. 51-62.

Bidāya wa-nihāya

Anwar al-Maʻaddāwī, *R* 2 July 51; Tharwat Abāẓa, *R* 6 Aug. 51; Zakī al-Maḥāsinī, *A-III* Oct. 51; Maḥmūd Dhuhnī, *A-II* May 56; Maḥmūd Ḥishmat ʻAbd al-Ẓāhir, *A-I* Nov. 60.

The Trilogy

J. Jomier, *MIDEO* IV (1957); Suhayr al-Qalamāwī, *M* Feb. 57; Yūsuf al-Shārūnī, *A-I* June 57 (= *Dirāsāt fil-adab*, pp. 63-95); ʻIzzat Muḥammad Ibrāhīm, *A-II* Feb., May, and July 58; Fawzī al-ʻIntīl, *M* Mar. 58; Anwar al-Maʻaddāwī, *A-I* Apr. and May 58 (= *Kalimāt*, pp. 36-63); Jalāl al-Sayyid, *K* Jan. 63; Trevor Le Gassick, *M.E. Forum* Feb. 63; Māhir al-Baṭṭūṭī, *A-I* June 63. See also ʻAwad, *Maqālāt*, pp. 355-62; 365-73; al-Rāʻī, *Dirāsāt* pp. 245-72; Ḥusayn *Min adabinā*, pp. 80-7.

Awlād Ḥāratinā

Muḥyī al-Dīn Muḥammad, *A-I* Feb. 60; Lumʻī al-Muṭīʻī, *A-II* Feb. 60; ʻAbd al-Munʻim Ṣubḥī, *FM* May 67; Māhir al-Baṭṭūṭī, *A-I* July-Aug. 67.

al-Liṣṣ wal-kilāb

Fāṭima Mūsā, *M* Feb. 62; Māhir Shafīq Farīd, *A-II* Feb. 62; Saʻīd Muḥammad Ḥasan, *A-I* Feb. 62; Yaḥyā Ḥaqqī, *M* May 62; Yūsuf al-Shārūnī, *A-I* June 62 (= *Dirāsāt fil-adab*, pp. 161-75); Anwar al-Maʻaddāwī, *M* Aug. 62 (= *Kalimāt*, pp. 115-26); Nūr Salmān, *A-IV* No. 4, Autumn 62; Fu'ād Dawwāra, *K* Jan. 63; Ayyād Aḥmad Malḥam, *A-I* July 63; Ṣabrī Ḥāfiẓ, *A-I* Nov. 63; Laṭīfa al-Zayyāt, *K* Mar. 70. See also ʻAwaḍ, *Maqālāt*, pp. 345-52; ʻAyyad, *Tajārib*, pp. 238-44.

al-Summān wal-kharīf

Muḥammad Ghunaymī Hilāl, *K* Jan. 63; Rajā' al-Naqqāsh, *A-I* Mar. 63 (= *Udabā' muʻāṣirūn*, pp. 153-70); Fu'ād Dawwāra, *K* June 63; Ṣabrī Ḥāfiẓ, *A-I* Dec. 63. See also ʻAwaḍ, *Dirāsāt ʻArabiyya*, pp. 229-36; ʻAbd al-Ṣabūr, *Wa-tabqā*, pp. 127-37.

al-Ṭarīq

Ṣabrī Ḥāfiẓ, *A-I* June 64; Fu'ad Dawwāra, *M* July 64; ʻAntar ʻAbd al-Salām Mukhaymar, *A-II* Nov. 64.

al-Shaḥḥādh

ʻAbd al-Qādir al-Quṭṭ, *al-Ahrām*, 30 July 65; Ibrāhīm Fatḥī, *M* Aug. 65; ʻAbd al-Badīʻ ʻAbd-Allāh, *FM* Sept. 65; Ṣabrī Ḥāfiẓ, *M* Apr. and May 66; Fāḍil Tāmir, *A-I*, Apr. 66.

Tharthara fawq al-Nīl

ʻAlī Barakāt, *FM* Mar. 66; Suhayr al-Qalamāwī, *KA* May 66; Jalāl al-ʻUshrī, *FM* May 66; Ibrāhīm al-Ṣayrafī, *FM* June 66; Aḥmad Muḥammad ʻAṭiyya, *M* July 66; Ilyās Dayrī, *H* Sept.-Dec. 66; Laṭīfa al-Zayyāt, ʻAbd al-Qādir al-Quṭṭ, Shukrī ʻAyyād and Ibrāhīm al-Ṣayrafī, *A-I* Oct. 66.

INDEX

(Characters from Maḥfūẓ's novels are generally listed by their first names followed, in brackets, by the abbreviatied title of the relevant novel.)

À la recherche du temps perdu (Proust), 45

'Abath al-aqdār (= ABA), 47, 60-1, 69, 199
  Plot outline, 200-1
'Abbās al-Ḥulw (ZUQ), 84-5, 87, 92, 206-7
'Abd al-Mun'im Shawkat (TR-III), 122-3, 215-6
'Abd al-Raḥīm Pasha (TR-III), 110-1
'Abd al-Rāziq, 'Alī, 56
'Abd al-Rāziq, Muṣṭafā, 42
'Abd al-Ṣabūr, Ṣalāḥ, 33
Absurd (literature), 195
Abū Ḥadīd, Muḥammad Farīd, 25-6, 29
Adam, 138, 140
Adham (AWL), 140, 143, 148-9, 154, 216-7
'Adlī Karīm (TR-III), 110, 138
Aesop, 146
Aḥlām Shahrazād (Ṭāhā Ḥusayn), 25
Aḥmad Shawkat (TR-III), 54, 113, 122-4, 132, 138-9
Aḥmad 'Abd al-Jawād (TR), *see* al-Sayyid
Aḥmad 'Ākif (KHAN), 67-9, 76-9, 92, 162, 203-4
Aḥmad Rāshid (KHAN), 67
Aḥmad Yusrī (BID), 68, 71
al-Ahrām, 56-8
'Ā'ida Shaddād (TR-II), 39, 119, 132, 213
'Ā'isha (TR), 110, 126, 132-3, 210-6
Akhenaten, 28, 31
'Alā bāb Zuwayla (al-'Iryān), 30
'Alawiyya Ṣabrī (TR-III), 123, 132
Alexandrine Quartet (Durrell), 193
'Alī al-Junaydī, Shaykh (LISS), 165, 222-3
'Alī Ṭāhā (QAH), 40-1, 67, 75-6, 82-3, 93, 204
Allegorical novel, 57, 137, 141-2, 146, 151, 152, 173
An American Tragedy (Dreiser), 70
Amīn, Qāsim, 2, 26
Amīna (TR), 114-5, 126-8, 131-3, 210-6
'Amm 'Abduh (THAR), 179
'Āmir (MIR), 192-4
'Āmmiyya, 96-9, 134, 153; *see also* Language
"'Anbar Lūlū", 196
Animal Farm (Orwell), 141, 146, 155
Anīs (THAR), 158, 176-2, 180-2, 186, 190, 227-8
'Antara, 1
Anṭūn, Faraḥ, 8
al-'Aqqād, 'Abbās Maḥmūd, 14, 22, 25, 38, 43
Arabian Nights, 1, 61
Arabic history, 27, 49
Arabic Language Academy, 24
'Arafa (AWL), 54-5, 137, 139, 141-2, 145-7, 151, 154, 221-2
al-Arḍ (al-Sharqāwī), 66
'Awaḍ, Louis, 109
'Awāṭif (AWL), 141-2, 221-2
'Awd 'alā bad' (al-Māzinī), 30
'Awdat al-rūḥ (al-Ḥakīm), 14, 17-9, 22, 25, 46
Awlād Ḥāratinā (= AWL), 54, 56-7, 137-55, 158, 167, 174, 187, 194
  Characters: 142-6
  Structure: 146-51
  Language: 151-3
  Plot outline: 216-22
al-Ayyām (Ṭāhā Ḥusayn), 13, 37
al-Azhar, 37, 56
Bahīja (TR-I), 129, 210
Bākathīr, 'Alī Aḥmad, 25-6, 29, 49
Balzac, Honoré de, 45
Bayn al-Qaṣrayn (= TR-I), 51, 106, 110, 113-4, 117-8, 124, 127, 129-33, 141
  Plot outline: 210-2; *see also* Trilogy
Bayt sayyi' al-sum'a, 57
Bennett, Arnold, 45
Bey, the (QAH), 68, 83, 204-6

Bidāya wa-nihāya (= BID), 50, 65-73, 76, 90-1, 94, 95-6, 160, 181, 198-9
Characters: 70-3, 79-82
Structure: 89-92
Language: 95-100
Plot outline: 209-10
Book of the Dead, 18
Buddenbrooks (Mann), 107
Brazilian literature, 34
Bunyan, John, 141
Būs͟hī (ZUQ), 68, 92, 207
Bu͟thayna (SHAH), 176, 180, 226-7
Cairo novels (Maḥfūẓ), 49-50, 65-100, 109, 126, 133, 137, 156, 179
Camus, Albert, 45, 121, 141, 173
Cause novel, 3
Chekhov, Anton, 12-3, 45-6
La Chute (Camus), 173
Clemence, Jean-Baptiste, 173
Colophons, 198-9
Comte, Auguste, 40
Conrad, Joseph, 121
Dār al-ma'ārif (publishing house), 25
Darwin, Charles, 38-9
Dates (M.'s works—first editions), 198-9
Dialogue *see* Language
Dickens, Charles, 6, 45
Don Quixote (Cervantes), 10, 146, 156
Dos Passos, John, 45
Dostoyevsky, Fyodor, 12, 45, 179
Dreiser, Theodore, 70
Drinkwater, John, 44-5
Du'ā' al-karawān, (Ṭāhā Ḥusayn), 14, 20-2
Dumas, Alexandre, 6
Dunyā Allāh (= DUN), 57, 172
Durrell, Lawrence, 193
Durriyya (MIR), 192
Editions (M.'s works), 198-9
Egyptian country life, 3, 17, 66
Egyptian identity, 12
Egyptian Islamic literature, 27
Egyptian mythology, 18
Egyptian personality, 2
Egyptian revolution (1919), 106
Egyptian revolution (1952), 157, 160, 166, 223
Egyptian society *see* Social themes
Egyptian University, 11, 24-7, 40
Egyptian woman, 2, 79-89
Egyptianism *see* Pharaonic
Egyptology, 26
English literature, 12
European fiction, 11, 46
Fahmī (TR-I), 110-1, 117-8, 124-5, 127-8, 131, 210-2
Faraj Ibrāhīm (ZUQ), 84-7, 93
al-Faraj ba'd al-S͟hidda, 1
Farouk, King, 62
Fate (in M.'s works), 61, 69, 71, 111, 160
Faulkner, William, 45
Fawzī, Dr. Ḥusayn, 12
Fil-s͟hi'r al-jāhilī (Ṭāhā Ḥusayn), 37
Flaubert, Gustave, 45, 127
Forster, E.M., 78, 126
France, Anatole, 45
French literature, 2, 12
Freud, Sigmund, 38, 101
Fu'ād I Academy, 48-9
Folklore, 107 fn.
Fuṣḥā, 17, 96, 98-100, 134, 190; *see also* Language
Futuwwa, Futuwwāt (AWL), 142-3, 146, 148-9, 216-22
Galsworthy, John, 45, 108
Gibb, Sir Hamilton, 4
Goethe, J.W. von, 45
Gulliver's Travels (Swift), 142
Ḥaddād, Nīqūlā, 8
Ḥadī͟th 'Īsā bin His͟hām (al-Muwayliḥī), 9, 10
Ḥāfiẓ Ibrāhīm, Muḥammad, 10
Haggard, Sir Henry Rider, 60 fn.
al-Ḥakīm, Tawfīq, 14, 17-8, 25, 30, 38, 46, 50, 106
al-Hamad͟hānī, 9; *see also* Maqāma
Ḥamdīs (QAH), 74
Ḥamīda (ZUQ), 67, 69-70, 83-8, 92-4, 179, 206-7
Hammām (AWL), 149, 217
Hams al-junūn (= HAMS), 46, 199
Ḥanas͟h (AWL), 154, 221-2
Ḥaqqī, Yaḥyā, 12, 18, 25, 31-2, 38, 46
Ḥasan (BID), 73, 89-91, 209-10
Ḥasan (SUM), 169, 224
Ḥasanayn (BID), 70-5, 82-3, 89, 91, 95-6, 209-10

Hawwā' bilā Ādam (Lāshīn), 14, 19-20
Haykal, Muḥammad Ḥusayn, 1-2, 5, 27
Hegel, G.W.F., 40, 114
Hemingway, Ernest, 45
Ḥikāya bilā bidāya walā nihāya, 196
Historical novels, 26-9, 31, 47, 49, 60-64, 94, 137
Hourani, Albert, 3
Hugo, Victor, 6
Ḥusayn (BID), 65, 67, 89-91, 209-10
Ḥusayn (ZUQ), 92
Ḥusayn, Ṭāhā, 13-4, 20, 22, 25, 30, 37-8, 50, 56
Ḥusnī (MIR), 192-4
Huxley, Aldous, 45
Hyksos King (KIF), 62, 202-3
Ibn al-Fāriḍ, 'Umar, 27
Ibn al-Rūmī, 38
Ibnat al-Mamlūk (Abū Ḥadīd), 25
Ibrāhīm al-Kātib (al-Māzinī), 14-7, 22, 25, 30
Ibsen, Henrik, 38, 45
Idrīs (AWL), 140, 149, 216-7
Iḥsān (QAH), 75, 82-3, 93, 179, 204-6
al-Ikhshīdī (QAH), 76, 204-6
Ilhām (TARIQ), 160, 170, 179, 185, 225-6
'Ilīsh (LISS), 163, 165, 222-3
'Ināyāt (SAR), 104, 208-9
Iqra' (series), 25
al-'Iryān, Muḥammad Sa'īd, 26, 30
'Īsā (SUM), 157, 160, 166-9, 182, 223-5
Islamic history, 7, 26-7, 49
Jabal (AWL), 139-40, 145-6, 151, 217-8
Jabalāwī (AWL) 54-7, 140-1, 143-4, 146-8, 151, 174, 216-22
Jalāl, Ibrāhīm, 30
James, Henry, 127-8
James, William, 175
Japanese literature, 34, 193
al-Jārim, 'Alī, 25-6, 30
Jesus, 138-9, 144, 150-1
Joyce, James, 45-6
Juvenilia (Maḥfūẓ's), 37
Kafka, Franz, 45, 121, 185
Kamāl (TR), 36, 39, 53-4, 107, 111-3, 118-24, 128, 130-2, 138-9, 210-6
Kāmil (SAR), 101-5, 207-9
Kāmil, 'Ādil, 25-6, 28, 31, 48-9, 68
Kant, Immanuel, 38
Karīma (TARIQ), 160, 170-1, 181, 185, 225-6
Khadīja (TR), 122, 126, 210-6
Khammārat al-qiṭṭ al-aswad, 195
Khān al-Khalīlī (= KHAN), 37, 49, 67-9, 76-9, 91-2, 94, 162, 198-9
  Characters: 76-9
  Structure: 89, 91-2
  Language: 94-100
  Plot outline: 203-4
al-Khūlī, Amīn, 27
Khunfus (AWL), 149
Kifāḥ Ṭība (= KIF), 48, 50, 60-2, 150. 198-9
  Plot outline: 202-3
Kitāb al-bukhalā', 1
Lajnat al-nashr lil-jāmi'iyyīn (publishing house), 48
Language, 33, 94-100, 133-6, 151-3, 187-90, 196; *see also* 'Āmmiyya, Fuṣḥā
Lāshīn, Ṭāhir, 12, 14, 19, 68
Lawrence, D.H., 45
Layālī Saṭīḥ (Ḥāfiẓ Ibrāhīm), 10
Leblanc, Maurice, 6
al-Liṣṣ wal-kilāb (= LISS), 58, 157, 158, 160-6, 169, 179, 181, 182, 183-4, 185, 187, 190
  Characters: 162-6
  Structure: 183-4
  Language: 187-90
  Plot outline: 222-3
Lughz see Sirr
Lyricals novels, 141, 165-6, 181, 184, 187
al-Ma'arrī, Abū al-'Alā', 38, 40
Mach, Ernst, 40
al-Ma'addāwī, Anwar, 50
Maḥfūẓ, Najīb
  attitude towards art: 42, 136
  attitude towards Fabian and Utopian Socialism: 41
  attitude towards literature: 43-4
  attitude towards philosophy: 42, 44, 55-6, 139, 159
  attitude towards poetry: 43
  attitude towards politics: 39-40, 48, 51, 53-4, 106, 110-2, 192-6
  attitude towards religion: 39, 55-7, 105, 137-40

attitude towards Socialism: 41, 52, 55-6, 65, 105, 107 fn.
biography: 35-59, 107
career as civil servant: 47, 51, 59
childhood: 35-7
critics on his works: 50-1, 56, 58, 102, 108-9, 112, 118 124, 176, 192, 194, 198-9
early works: 37-8, 42-3, 198-9
education: 37, 40-3
family life: 51
health: 51, 135
pessimism: 48, 65, 66fn., 156, 192
prizes: 48-9, 51
writers who influenced M.: 38-9, 44-5
Maḥjūb (QAH), 70, 74-6, 83, 93, 95, 204-6
al-Majalla al-jadīda; 38, 41, 47
Makhlūf, Aḥmad Zakī, 48
Malik min shu'ā' ('Ādil Kāmil), 28
Malraux, André, 45
Ma'mūn (QAH), 75, 93, 204-5
Man of Property (Galsworthy), 108
al-Manfalūṭī, Muṣṭafā Luṭfī, 37
Mann, Thomas, 45-6, 107, 141
Manṣūr (MIR), 192-4
Maqāma, 1, 9, 33, 187
Marianna (MIR), 192-4
al-Marāyā, 191 fn.
al-Ma'rifa, 41
Marx, Karl, 38
Marxism, 41
Maryam (TR), 118, 124, 127, 131-2, 211-4
Maupassant, Guy de, 13, 46
Mauriac, François, 45
Maẓhar, Ismā'īl, 38
al-Māzinī, Ibrāhīm, 14-5, 25, 30, 38
Miller, Arthur, 45
Millīm al-akbar ('Ādil Kāmil), 31, 49
Mīrāmār (= MIR), 191-5, 197
"The Modern School", 12, 19, 24-5
Moses, 138-9, 144
Muḥammad (The Prophet of Islam), 138-9, 143-5
Muḥammad 'Iffat (TR), 129
Muḥammad 'Alī Pasha, 26
Muḥammad, Muḥammad 'Awaḍ, 28
Mūsā, Salāma, 38, 41, 47, 49, 110
Music, 42, 136, 189
Muslim Brothers, 29, 53, 122
Muṣṭafā (SHAH), 175, 226
al-Mutanabbī, 38
Mutawallī, Shaykh (TR), 132
al-Muwayliḥī, Muḥammad, 9-10
Mystic themes (in M.'s works), 156-8, 162, 165, 168, 174-7 195; *see also* Ṣūfī(sm)
Nabawiyya (LISS), 163, 164, 222
Nafīsa (BID), 70-1, 80-3, 89-91, 179, 209-10
Najīb, Ḥāfiẓ, 37
Naturalism, 68, 108-10
Nawāl (KHAN), 77, 79, 92, 204
Nāẓir (AWL), 142, 145, 148, 155, 216-22
Nefertiti, 28
Nitōcris (RAD), 63, 201-2
Nidā' al-Majhūl (Taymūr), 14, 23
Nūnū (KHAN), 68
Nūr (LISS), 159, 163-5, 179, 181, 183-4, 190, 223
O'Neill, Eugene, 45
Orwell, George, 146, 155
The Origin of Species (Darwin), 39
Ostwald, Wilhelm, 40
The Outline of Literature (Drinkwater), 44
La Peste (Camus), 141
Pharaoh Merenre'(RAD), 62-3, 113, 201-2
Pharaonic (themes, novels), 3, 26-8, 38, 46, 48-9, 52, 60-1, 88, 150
Pilgrim's Progress (Bunyan), 141
Plays (by M.), 196
Plot outlines of M.'s novels, 200-28
Political novels, 159
Proust, Marcel, 45-6, 168
Psychology (in M.'s works), 100-5, 114, 116-7, 124, 129, 157, 161-2, 164-6, 168-71, 174-5
Qadrī (AWL), 149, 217
al-Qāhira al-jadīda (= QAH), 40, 50, 66-9, 94, 122, 198-9
Characters: 70, 74-6, 80, 82-3
Structure: 89, 93-4
Language: 95-100
Plot ouline: 204-6
Qamar (AWL), 143, 219-20
Qaṣīda, 9
Qāsim (AWL), 139-40, 143-6, 148-9, 219-21

Qaṣr al-Shawq (= TR-III), 39, 51, 53, 106, 110, 113, 119-20, 124, 128, 130-3
  Plot outline: 212-4; *see also* Trilogy
Qaṭr al-Nadā (al-ʿIryan), 30
Qindīl umm Hāshim (Ḥaqqī), 25, 32
Quṭb, Sayyid, 50, 198
Rabāb (SAR), 102-4, 207-9
Rādūbīs (= RAD), 48, 60, 198-9
  Characters: 62-4, 113
  Structure: 62-4
  Language: 64
  Plot outline: 201-2
Rādūbīs (RAD), 63, 201-2
Rajab (THAR), 190, 182, 227-8
Rashomon (Kurosawa), 193
Ra'ūf (LISS), 163-4, 223
Realistic novels, 12, 45, 137, 141-2, 145, 154
Revolution *see* Egyptian Revolution
al-Ribāṭ al-muqaddas (al-Ḥakīm), 25, 30
Rifāʿa (AWL), 139-40, 142-3, 145-6, 148-50, 218-9
Rīrī (SUM), 166-7, 179, 182, 224
al-Risāla, 24
al-Riwāya, 24
Le Rouge et le Noir (Stendhal), 70
Ruḍwān (TR-III), 110, 122, 124, 215
Ruḍwān al-Ḥusaynī (ZUQ), 86, 92, 207
Rushdī (KHAN), 67, 69, 79, 91-2, 203-4
Russian literature, 12
Ṣābir (TARIQ), 157, 159-60, 169-73, 180, 182, 185, 225-6
al-Saḥḥār, ʿAbd al-Ḥamīd Jūda, 24, 26, 48-9
Saʿīd (LISS), 157, 160, 162-6, 179, 181-5, 187, 222-3
Salāma Mūsā *see* Mūsā
Salīm ʿIlwān (ZUQ), 68-9, 84, 92-3, 113, 206
Salmān (BID), 80-2, 90, 209
Salwā (SUM), 160, 166, 168, 223-4
Samīr (SUM), 168
Sammāra (THAR) 178, 180, 186, 227-8
Sanā' (LISS), 184, 222
Saniyya ʿAfīfī (ZUQ), 92, 207
Sāra (al-ʿAqqād), 14, 22
al-Sarāb (= SAR), 49-50, 52, 66, 94, 100-5, 160-1, 170-1, 193, 198-9
  Plot outline: 207-9
Sarḥān (MIR), 192-4
Ṣarrūf, Yaʿqūb, 8, 38
Sartre, Jean-Paul, 45, 108 fn.
Satan, 140
al-Sāwī (TARIQ), 171, 185, 225
Sawsan (TR-III), 123, 179-81, 216
al-Sayyid, Aḥmad Luṭfī, 2-3, 26
al-Sayyid (= Aḥmad ʿAbd al-Jawād) (TR), 109-11, 113-8, 120, 123-4, 126-9, 131, 133, 162, 210-4
Sayyid Sayyid al-Raḥīmī (TARIQ), 171-2, 225
Scott, Sir Walter, 6, 59, 60 fn.
Sex (in M.'s works), 47, 101, 103-4, 109, 122, 125-6, 158, 170, 173, 177
al-Shaḥḥādh (= SHAH), 58, 158, 159, 162, 173-6, 180, 182, 190, 194
  Characters: 173-6
  Structure: 182
  Language: 187-90
  Plot outline: 226-7
Shahr al- ʿasal, 196
Shāʿir, 1, 147-8
Shajarat al-bu's (Ṭāhā Ḥusayn), 30
al-Sharqāwī, ʿAbd al-Raḥmān, 33 fn. 65
Shaw, Bernard, 38, 45
Shawkat, Mrs. (TR), 126, 212, 214
Short novels (by M.), 46, 146-90
  Characters: 160-81
  Structure: 181-7
  Language: 187-90
Short stories (by M.), 46-7, 57, 195-7
Sinūḥī (Muḥ. Awaḍ Muḥammad), 28
Sīrat Banī Hilāl, 1
Sīrat al-Ẓāhir Baybars, 1
Sirr, lughz, 54, 105, 120, 151, 165, 173
Six Day War, 191
al-Siyāsa al-usbūʿiyya, 13, 27
Social themes (in M.'s works), 47, 52, 55-6, 65-100, 106, 158-9, 193
Stendhal, 45, 70
Strindberg, August, 45
Style *see* Language
Ṣūfī(sm), 5, 31, 55, 57, 105, 120-1, 160, 165, 168, 179; *see also* Mystic themes
al-Sukkariyya (= TR-III), 38, 51, 53, 106, 110, 113, 119-22, 124, 128-33, 138, 179
  Plot outline: 214-6; *see also* Trilogy

al-Summān wal-kharīf (= SUM), 58, 157, 159-60, 162, 166-9, 179, 182, 188, 194
Characters: 166-9
Structure: 182
Language: 187-90
Plot outline: 223-5
Swift, Jonathan, 142
Symbolism, 141, 149, 152, 168, 172-3, 175, 183-4
Ṭāhā Ḥusayn *see* Ḥusayn
Taḥiyya (QAH), 74, 76, 205
Taḥt al-miẓalla, 196
al-Ṭahṭāwī, Rifā'a Rāfi', 26
Ṭahū (RAD), 63, 202
al-Ṭarīq (= TARIQ), 58, 157, 159-60, 162, 169-73, 179-80, 181-3, 184-5, 186, 190, 194
Characters: 169-73
Structure: 184-5
Language: 187-90
Plot outline: 225-6
Taṣawwuf *see* Ṣūfī(sm)
Taymūr, Maḥmūd, 12, 14, 23, 38, 43, 46-7, 68
Telemachus, 171
Terrail, Ponson du, 6
al-Thā'ir al-aḥmar (Bākathīr), 29
al-Thaqāfa, 24
Tharthara fawq al-Nīl (= THAR), 58, 158-62, 176-8, 179-83, 185-7, 194
Characters: 176-8
Structure: 185-7
Language: 187-90
Plot outline: 227-8
Time-Change-Death theme (in M.'s works), 47, 112, 131
Tītī (ZUQ) *see* Ḥamīda
Tolstoy, Leo. 6, 12, 38, 45, 128
Translation, 1, 5-6, 42, 58-9
Trilogy (= TR-I, TR-II, TR-III), 35-6, 39, 47, 50-4, 58, 68, 106-38, 144, 149, 151, 159, 162, 181, 187
Characters: 113-27
Structure: 127-33
Language: 133-6
Plot outline: 210-6
Ṭulba (MIR), 192, 194
Turgenev, Ivan, 12, 45
Ulysses (Joyce), 45
'Umar (SHAH), 158-9, 173-6, 180, 182, 190, 226-7
Umayma (AWL), 143, 216-7
'Uthmān (SHAH), 175, 226-7
Violence (in M.'s works), 196-7
al-Wafd, 40, 166
War and Peace (Tolstoy), 128
Warda (SHAH), 174, 226
Wells, H.G., 38, 45
Williams, Tennessee, 45
Woolf, Virginia, 182
World War I, 51
World War II, 33, 48, 51, 67, 92, 118, 132
Yaḥyā (AWL), 143, 219-20
"Yaqẓat al-mūmiyā", 46
Yāsimīna (AWL), 142, 218-9
Yāsīn (TR), 109-10, 113, 117, 122, 125-8, 131-3, 210-6
Yūnus, 'Abd al-Ḥamīd, 34
"Za'balāwī", 57, 172
Zaghlūl, Sa'd, 40, 110-1, 129, 224
Zahra (MIR), 192, 194
Zannūba (TR), 109, 117-8, 126, 213-5
Zaydān, Jurjī, 7-8, 26
Zaynab (Haykal), 1-5, 12-3
Zauberberg, Der (Mann), 141
Zévaco, Michel, 6, 60 fn.
Zīṭa (ZUQ), 68, 92, 94, 207
Zola, Émile, 45, 109
Zubayda (TR), 116, 210
Zuqāq al-Midaqq (= ZUQ), 36, 50, 58, 67-9, 79-80, 83-8, 89, 92-4, 198-9
Characters: 79-80, 83-8, 113
Structure: 89, 92-4
Language: 94-100
Plot outline: 206-7